Global Voices

Global Voices

Picture Books from Around the World

SUSAN STAN

AN IMPRINT OF THE AMERICAN LIBRARY ASSOCIATION

CHICAGO 2014

Susan Stan is a professor of English at Central Michigan University, where among the courses she teaches are those in international and multicultural literature for children and young adults. Her experience in the field of children's books includes a decade working for the Lerner Publishing Group in both the marketing and editorial departments and eleven years as editor of *The Five Owls*, a now-defunct journal about children's books. Stan's interest in international children's literature began with trips to the Frankfurt and Bologna Book Fairs while she was at Lerner and led her to write a dissertation on international picture books.

Since 1986, when she attended her first IBBY World Congress in Japan, Stan has been an active member of the United States Board on Books for Young People (USBBY). She has served as USBBY's president and is the author of *The World through Children's Books* (Scarecrow, 2002), one of the books in the Bridges to Understanding series sponsored by USBBY. A longtime member of the American Library Association, Stan has served on several committees, including selection committees for the Caldecott and Batchelder awards.

Printed in the United States of America

18 17 16 15 14   5 4 3 2 1

Extensive effort has gone into ensuring the reliability of the information in this book; however, the publisher makes no warranty, express or implied, with respect to the material contained herein.

ISBN: 978-0-8389-1183-9 (paper).

Library of Congress Cataloging-in-Publication Data
Stan, Susan.
  Global voices : picture books from around the world / Susan Stan.
    pages cm
  Includes bibliographical references and indexes.
  ISBN 978-0-8389-1183-9 (alk. paper)
  1. Picture books for children—Bibliography. 2. Children's literature—
Translations into English—Bibliography. 3. Picture books for children—
Educational aspects. I. Title.
  Z1033.P52S73 2014
  011.62—dc23
                              2013011519

Cover design by Kimberly Thornton. Images © Shutterstock, Inc.
Text design by Mayfly Design in the Whitman, Myriad Pro, and Minya Nouvelle typefaces.

♾ This paper meets the requirements of ANSI/NISO Z39.48-1992 (Permanence of Paper).

Contents

Acknowledgments

My heartfelt thanks to the following people to whom I am greatly indebted.

For permission to reproduce illustrations and cover art, I thank Mitsumasa Anno, Niki and Jude Daly, Emily Gravett, Suzy Lee, Binette Schroeder, Olivier Tallec, Shaun Tan, Gita Wolf, Abrams Books, Candlewick Press, Frances Lincoln Books, Groundwood Books, Kane Miller Books, and Kids Can Press.

For permission to reprint her blog, I thank Tara Books founder Gita Wolf.

For help in acquiring permissions, I thank Claudia Zoe Bedrick, Melanie Blais, Anita Eerdmans, David Gale, Monika Giuliani, Fred Horler, Satoko Inoue, Jennifer Abel Kovitz, Barbara Lehman, Kira Lynn, John Mason, Liz Page, Eva Svec, and Yurika Yoshida.

For answering questions and providing valuable feedback, I thank Patsy Aldana, Kenneth and Sylvia Marantz, Chieko Miyoshi, and Anne Pellowski.

For support in the form of a sabbatical grant I thank Central Michigan University (CMU), the English Department, the College of Humanities and Social Behavioral Sciences, and my children's literature colleagues who picked up the slack.

For help in borrowing books I thank Margaret Dodd and her staff at CMU Park Library's Documents on Demand.

For extreme technological support I thank Brian Roberts of FaCIT.

And finally, for the invitation to write this book and shepherding it along the way, I thank Stephanie Zvirin.

Part I

Chapter 1

Why Read Books from Other Countries?

The legendary children's book editor Margaret McElderry once tried to explain the appeal of reading a book from another country by citing her own childhood experiences: "Their very 'awayness'—and the fact that children in those other countries were reading and enjoying them—made them seem extra special to me."[1] McElderry was very aware that her books were from another country because they came in a package mailed from Ireland by close family. There is a quality to books manufactured in other countries that differentiates them, even if the differences are subtle. Trim sizes may be slightly larger or smaller than the conventional ones in the United States due to the type of machinery used for printing and binding; the jacket may have wider flaps, the text paper may be thicker, the margins wider or narrower. These slight differences can create a feeling of unfamiliarity, perhaps that feeling of "awayness" that McElderry mentions. Stephen Roxburgh, an editor and champion of translated literature, likens this feeling to the exhilaration of being in a place for the first time and "seeing things, even familiar things, in a new light."[2]

For a variety of reasons, few children today have that experience. The international books collected for this book first appeared in other countries but have been reprinted and bound according to American standards, so that they look and feel the same as books by American authors and illustrators. Readers—adult or child—are probably not concerned with where their books were first published. This was certainly the case for me and my favorite books from childhood, the Swedish series by Maj Lindman featuring triplet girls Flicka, Ricka, and Dicka, and its companion series featuring the boys Snipp, Snapp, and Snurr. I knew they were about Swedish children because it said so in the very first line, but I didn't know Swedish children were reading them too. I'm not sure I could have loved them any more than I did, even if I had known that.

While the provenance of a book—where it originated—may be important to educators, librarians, and those who confer book prizes, it matters little to young readers. What they care about is the story, told through words and pictures. What children get from an international picture book that they don't get from an American picture book is something that they can't see and probably can't articulate: a shift in perspective that can range from unnoticeable to stimulating to disorienting. Because the perspective of the writer is rooted in the cultural values and beliefs of his own society, it may not coincide with the American way of looking at the same subject.

Consider this example: Two books, one from Japan and one from the US, both narrated by young girls of about the same age, each declaring her accomplishments. In *My Friends* by the Japanese author-illustrator Taro Gomi (Chronicle, 1990), a small girl states how her friends have all been important to her learning. "I learned to study from my friends the teachers." Compare this to the American book *I'm Gonna Like Me* by writer Jamie Lee Curtis (HarperCollins 2002), in which the main character also explains everything that she knows how to do but never acknowledges that she may have had help along the way. "I'm gonna like me when I'm called to stand. / I know all my letters like the back of my hand." Curtis's young protagonist exudes the self-reliance and individualism that Americans prize, while Gomi's narrator displays the Japanese value of placing the interests of the group over those of the individual. In Japan, children are raised to be interdependent and blend into society; "the nail that sticks up gets pounded down" is a familiar Japanese proverb. This pairing illustrates a difference in cultural perspectives on a universal topic—steps in a child's development—and demonstrates how the simplest children's book also carries the values of a society and helps shape children's attitudes and behaviors.

A more pronounced alternate perspective is found in Shaun Tan's wordless book *The Arrival*, which deals with immigration. Through pictures, Tan represents what it might be like to come to a new country where you know no one and don't understand the language. While "reading" this book, I found that the lack of words, or silence, replicated the uncertain, unpleasant feeling in my head when I've been traveling in countries and had no one I could talk with. The artist represents what he encounters in a combination of realistic and fantastical forms, conveying how one might view objects never before seen. The result is confusing at times, pleasurable at others—just like the immigrant experience. Descended from an immigrant family, Tan is Australian, but he renders his book universal by using alien creatures as well as recognizable artifacts that could relate to multiple countries.

Some books that come to us from other countries are indistinguishable from our own books. They tell us nothing about how people act, think, or feel elsewhere in the world. Others have strongly depicted, realistic settings and characters that evoke a particular time and place. Still others introduce Americans to characters such as Astérix and Tintin, who have become beloved by generations of Europeans over the years and are Europe's equivalent of Mickey Mouse. That all of Europe knows Mickey, but few Americans know Astérix and Tintin, speaks to the one-way street on which we export American culture.

A relatively small percentage of the picture books published in the US each year come from other countries. Of those that do, books from Great Britain and Australia predominate. Although these texts do not have to be translated, they are often Americanized, a process that can range from minor spelling changes (*centre* to *center,* for example) to more invasive changes, such as renaming characters or adding new text. For example, *I Love Vacations* by Anna Walker (Simon and Schuster, 2011) was originally published in Australia as *I Love Holidays.* In a *Horn Book* article some years ago the writer recounts a friend's experience in which a British writer inscribed on the flyleaf of a US edition of her book, "This is NOT what I wrote!"[3]

Picture books that require translation are frequently subject to editorial changes to bring them into line with American cultural expectations. The German writer and illustrator Birte Müller was dismayed when she saw a copy of *Finn Cooks,* the English-language edition of her picture book about a little boy who takes over the family cooking for a day. Predictably, his menu consists of candy and salty snacks that leave him with an upset stomach. In the original version, his mother holds him to the bargain and does not cook that day, giving him toast for dinner. The American editors imposed an overt message concerning healthful eating habits onto the text and also made sure that the mother, while technically sticking to the bargain, arranged for Finn to eat a more substantial dinner. Thus the book, intended to be playful, turned into a lesson in nutrition and a prescription for model parenting, American-style.

The over-Americanization of picture book texts often erases all trace of a book's foreign origins. Add to these books the many picture books that have only generic settings to begin with, and you can see why it is so difficult to find books that offer specific, detailed representations of life in other countries. To add insult to injury, books go out of print so quickly these days, sometimes within a year of publication. It takes time for a book to find its market, especially international books that fill an important niche but are not by recognizable names or attached to licensed characters. Finding these books becomes something akin to a scavenger hunt, one clue leading to the next until a book is ultimately discovered. So often by then, it cannot be ordered directly from the publisher but must be found in the used book market. Publishers who are committed to acquiring international books for publication in the US often feel they are fighting an uphill battle in a country that cares little about the rest of the world. Even idealistic editors must ultimately bow to the bottom line; if a book loses money, it closes the door for similar future projects.

Two areas that have seen growth in the past decade are the publication of wordless books (both American and international) and French translations. In a study of translated books in print in 1990, Maureen White found just thirteen books from France that she deemed successful translations, based on having received positive reviews (note that this figure includes both picture books and books for older children and young adults).[4] Somewhat more than two decades later, that number has grown exponentially, thanks in part to the rising popularity of graphic novels, which are a longtime French specialty (known there as *bandes dessinées*). Several publishers have created new lines in which to publish French imports. Toon Books, an imprint of Candlewick, publishes translated books in graphic form for the easy-to-read set; Graphic Universe, an imprint of Lerner Publications, aims its translations at the middle-grade reader. Since their debut list in 2003, Enchanted Lion Books has also been responsible for the rise of translations from France. In fact, the list of French picture books published by Enchanted Lion in just a few years single-handedly surpasses the number of successful French translations Maureen White found in the entire Books in Print catalog in 1990.

The growth in the availability of French *albums,* as picture books are known in France, coincides with the recent proliferation of wordless books. Japanese artist Mitsumasa Anno was a master at the wordless book. In some books, such as his "journey" series (e.g., *Anno's USA, Anno's Britain, Anno's Italy*), the pictures contain several simultaneous narratives, while in others, they pose visual problems to be solved. Martin Handford's *Where's Waldo?* (*Where's Wally?* in Britain) was another early precursor of the wordless book-as-game. Today's wordless books fall into the same categories: visual narratives that tell a story, usually with multiple subtexts; and books that offer pages of similar items that young viewers must sort through to find one designated item. Books in the latter category hone a child's concentration skills and ability to distinguish small differences. The uptick in the number of wordless books altogether may suggest a new emphasis on the importance of developing visual literacy or may simply reflect the growing place of visual communication in today's society.

The rationale for introducing young children to international books has never been stronger. The readership for these books is growing up in a global society for which the old paradigm no longer suffices. It's no longer feasible to expect the rest of the world to think like Americans, to conform to American expectations, to follow American rules of etiquette and behavior. Instead, twenty-first-century American citizens must get used to meeting the rest of the world halfway by being exposed to other cultures and developing a tolerance for multiple points of view. There is no better group to start with than the very young, and no better time to start than the present.

Notes

1. Stan, "Conversations: Margaret McElderry," 73.
2. Roxburgh, "The Myopic American," 50.
3. Whitehead, "'This Is Not What I Wrote!'" 687–693.
4. White, "Children's Books from Other Languages," 261–275.

Children's Book
Illustration and Culture

Illustrators of quality picture books are, above all, artists, and picture books are a child's first introduction to art. Whether a baby is focusing her eyes on the bold color and clean design of Dick Bruna's Miffy board books or a 7-year-old is reading Anthony Browne's Willy the Chimp books, each is assimilating artistic principles and styles at work on the printed page.

During most of the twentieth century, the illustration styles found in American, Canadian, British, and Australian picture books were similar enough that most readers wouldn't think to draw national distinctions. This makes perfect sense, since the picture books in all these countries share the same British ancestry—that of Randolph Caldecott, Kate Greenaway, Arthur Rackham, and others at work during the nineteenth century in what has come to be known as the golden age of children's book illustration. Although each of these illustrators had an individual style, all were representational; that is, the pictures looked like their subjects. The illustrations also pictured childhood as a distinct phase, a protected time, a time of innocence. The children reflected in these books wear clothes made especially for them and play in nurseries well equipped with toys, games, and books. These are children of the aristocracy.

Representational art, along with some folk art, continues to dominate the American picture book scene, whether the story is realistic, fantastic, or set in a historical period. The award-winning illustrations of Trina Schart Hyman, Maurice Sendak, Paul Zelinsky, Barbara McClintock and so many others stand as examples. Of course, exceptions immediately come to mind as well: Lane Smith's unconventional illustrations with characters that are completely disproportionate, and the surrealistic illustrations of Chris Van Allsburg and David Weisner. These illustrators challenged the status quo, some not without struggle. Lane Smith recalls that *The True Story of the 3 Little Pigs* (Viking, 1989) was rejected by most publishers; the paintings were "dark and weird" and "the story had a bit of an edge." When Viking took it, they put out a limited run that surprised them by selling out quickly, and over a decade later, the book is still a winner.[1]

These and other artists who challenged the conventions of children's book illustration in the 1980s were by no means the first to do so. In the 1930s and 1940s, many artists trained in Europe immigrated to the United States and brought with them their particular ways of seeing the world. Feodor Rojankovsky was trained in Russia; Leo Lionni received his informal art education in the museums of Holland and Italy; Roger Duvoisin's art background began in Switzerland. In 1936, Roger Duvoisin's illustrations for *Mother Goose,* rhymes collected by William Rose Benét, evoked mixed responses. Barbara Bader writes that "buyers for big chains spoke darkly of 'sophistication'; reviewers divided, some regarding the break from tradition as a sacrilege; librarians were cautious—were Duvoisin's 'hectic tempo' and brilliant color 'suitable fare for the nursery?'"[2]

Such examples suggest that it is adults who have consistently resisted changes in children's book illustration—adult editors, adult reviewers, adult buyers. By the time most people reach adulthood, their aesthetic preferences have been solidified based on their exposure to art in all its variations—book art, magazine art, advertising art, comic strips, museum art. The narrower that exposure, the more conventional the taste. Add to that an underestimation of what young children are capable of decoding or responding to, and you have a recipe for maintaining the status quo. Somewhere along the line the assumption that other artistic traditions are not "good art" may also take root. Given that funding for art education in public schools has been steadily declining, children's book illustration may be the only form of art that children see while they are young and still open to all forms of aesthetic expression.

"Impenetrable" Illustrations

Some people have declared that continental European illustrations are impenetrable to American children. Roaring Brook's publisher Neal

An illustration from Kvĕta Pacovská's *Little Flower King*. Some adults believe that abstract-expressionist styles such as this one do not appeal to American children.

Porter told an interviewer that "much European illustration, which tends to be more design-driven and less character-based than its American equivalents, is simply not to most Americans' taste."[3] By "design-driven and less character-based," Porter is referring to illustrations with distorted representations or unappealing appearance, so that the characters may not engender identification or empathy. Kvĕta Pacovská's Little King is one such example.

European artists on the continent have experimented with the picture book to a much greater degree than American or British artists. While European artists view the picture book as an art form available to children, American and British artists—or perhaps their editors—put the child reader front and center when creating books. Most British and American books are illustrated in a representational style, whether drawn as a cartoon or painted more realistically. In addition, American and British artists rely on a strong narrative to pull the reader through the book, and the illustrations will portray enough aspects of the story so that the reader will not have questions about what is happening. Continental European books

Both Lauren Child's *I Am Too Absolutely Small* from the UK (left) and Stian Hole's *Garmann's Summer* from Sweden portray a child's fears of attending school for the first time. Child's art, with its graph paper background, suggests a rational approach in keeping with the text. In contrast, Hole's surrealistic picture suggests his heightened senses and reflects the child's inner turmoil.

that are, in Porter's words, "design-driven" may use illustrations that are metaphorical rather than literal to create a mood or feeling. Some books may even end with enigmas that leave the reader having to puzzle out what happened on his own. Few of these books will ever reach American shores.

Compare these two books about the fear of starting kindergarten: Lauren Child's *I Am Too Absolutely Small for School* (Candlewick, 2004) from Britain and Stian Hole's *Garmann's Summer* from Sweden. Child's book features Charlie and his younger sister, Lola, who is "nearly almost big enough to go to school." On each spread, the cartoon illustrations show Lola in the situations described by the text. Although Charlie explains to Lola all that she will learn in school, Lola finds many reasons she is not ready for school, including missing her imaginary friend, Soren Lorensen, with whom she eats lunch every day. Thus she is convinced to go when she learns that Soren Lorensen will also be going to kindergarten and will need to sit next to her at lunch; on the walk there with Charlie, Lola projects all her nervousness onto Soren Lorensen. Child's approach to Lola's fear is rational, and the story has a conflict that is resolved in the end when Lola brings home a new flesh-and-blood friend.

An illustration from *Laura* by Binette Schroeder. This German artist's books have been lauded in France, Japan, and elsewhere, though they receive little attention in the UK and the US.

Children will recognize Lola's fear, but they will not feel it, as they do in *Garmann's Summer*. Garmann is dreading the end of summer because it means the start of kindergarten, and throughout the book he questions family members as to what makes them scared. His three aging aunts have answers that create odd pictures in Garmann's mind. At the book's end, the conflict is not resolved; the following day Garmann will be going to school, and he is still scared. Hole's illustrations, collages of digitally manipulated photos and prints, stimulate the senses. In one close-up of Garmann's face, a ladybug rests on his nose, and the reader's own nose almost itches. The compositions are often unbalanced, with large heads pasted onto small bodies, and items included in the collages appear almost random. The artwork is designed to evoke a sense of instability and tension that enhances the text but doesn't necessarily advance the story, which is short on plot and long on contemplation. In a starred review for *Booklist,* Thom Barthelmess observed that "Hole has crafted an elegant, fanciful, wholly poetic exploration of the nature of fear and the strength and hope required to conquer it."[4] *Garmann's Summer* was recognized as a 2009 Batchelder Honor Book.

Binette Schroeder, an internationally known German illustrator, is one of those artists whose work has never gained a large audience in the UK or the US. Her stylized illustrations offer a personal, otherworldly, often surrealistic vision of reality. Puzzled as to why her work didn't fit in with "the Anglo-American way of seeing," she was finally told by a well-known British critic that she didn't know how to draw. As her art education in Basel, Switzerland, was rigorous, this claim was of course not true, but she finally understood that "for the English market, my books lacked that very specific element of witty draftsmanship that distinguishes English picture books."[5] Her critic, who could have been speaking for American critics as well, had one norm by which he evaluated all picture book art.

Schroeder notes that "illustrators react—and they absolutely must do so—to social, political, economic and cultural conditions."[6] Her influences were fairly straightforward—the art movements she experienced during her years of study in Basel—but she tells the story of how the choice of artistic style or media may also be influenced by what is at hand. German artist Klaus Ensikat began his career in East Germany during the 1950s and 1960s, when the country was cut off from the West. Because the only printing presses available were antiquated, he adopted and honed the techniques used in the past to develop an intricate pen-and-ink style that earned him the 1996 Hans Christian Andersen Illustrator Medal.

Visual References to Place

In the UK, where cultural mores and aesthetic tastes are similar to those in the US, economic issues come into play to curtail a sense of place in picture book illustration. Because sales in the UK alone will not be sufficient to cover the cost of producing a picture book, editors must be able to sell coeditions to other countries. Therefore British editors keep one eye on America, the largest market, when working on picture books. Martin Salisbury, a British illustrator and educator, discusses the effect this has had on illustrators. "All manner of... 'dos and don'ts' for illustrators have sprung up in picture book editors' offices," he explains.[7] Illustrators are warned not to include any "local" visual references, such as the red double-decker buses so long associated with London or the position of the steering wheel in British vehicles. Thus landscapes, buildings, parks, and skylines become generic, representative of everywhere and nowhere. Salisbury also mentions animals: "Badgers and hedgehogs are frequently sent crawling back to the drawing board as being unrecognizable to an American audience."[8]

While most of us find it ludicrous that hedgehogs, a staple of animal fantasies, are getting the heave-ho in picture books, the erasure of place in picture books is no laughing matter. Americans' knowledge of geography is sorely lacking, as shown in a 2006 study commissioned by the National Geographic Educational Foundation.[9] It confirmed the findings of an earlier study in 2002 in which young Americans between the ages of 18 and 24 placed next to last in a survey when compared with the same demographic groups from seven other countries. Picture books won't help answer those survey questions, but they do stimulate a curiosity about other people and places that can result in greater attention to world events as children grow up. Further, the mere exposure to unfamiliar and alternative perspectives at a young age can result in greater open-mindedness and tolerance.

Hidden Cultural Codes

Not all cultural information contained in illustrations is obvious, nor need it be recognized for an illustration to be appreciated. One often hears that art is a universal language, but Jeffrey Garrett offers an intriguing example of how hidden cultural codes can be embedded in illustration. Drawing on the research of a Japanese social psychologist, Garrett relates the findings that Japanese and Americans read faces differently: Japanese look to the eyes first as carriers of emotion, while Americans look to the mouth.[10] This difference might explain why characters in Japanese illustrations, especially manga, often have disproportionately large eyes. American children asked to read the emotions of the father and son on the cover of Taro Gomi's *I Lost My Dad* might reply that they both look mad or sad, based on the downturned mouths. Yet based on the eyes, a Japanese child might state that they look happy.

In a fascinating study of Caldecott Award and Honor books acquired for Japanese publication—contrasted with those *not* acquired—Japanese translator Miki Kobayashi isolates characteristics that each group of books has in common.[11] First, picture books chosen for translation have illustrations that leave room for the viewer's imagination to participate, as opposed to being so detailed that one can only observe. For example, Ed Young's spare style in *Seven Blind Mice* contrasts with Paul Zelinsky's Renaissance-style portraiture in *Rapunzel*, a book not published in Japan.

American children asked to read the emotions of the father and son on the cover of Taro Gomi's *I Lost My Dad* might reply that they both look mad or sad, based on the downturned mouths. Yet based on the eyes, a Japanese child might state that they look happy.

As a corollary, the relationship between the text and the illustrations is inconsistent in the books chosen for publication in Japan. Again, using *Seven Blind Mice* and *Rapunzel* as examples, in the former, the text tells what each blind mouse "sees," while the illustrations show the reader what is really there. In *Rapunzel*, even as the illustrations add details not found in the text, they never contradict the text. Finally, each of the translated titles features an active protagonist rather than someone who is acted upon. Using the same examples, the seven mice must work together to solve the puzzle of what it is they are facing, while Rapunzel is at the mercy of the sorceress and does not even leave the tower of her own volition. Kobayashi's analysis suggests that Japanese prefer books that make children work a bit by using their imaginations to fill in gaps or resolve contradictions, as well as books that show respect for children by reinforcing their agency.

Non-Western Art

Art from non-Western cultures, which includes indigenous art, is all but missing in the picture books on American bookstore and library shelves. One explanation for the lack of picture books from Asian and African countries, as explained in the introductions to the bibliographies of those chapters, is that strong publishing industries do not always exist in some of these regions, and many of the publishing programs to be found cater to the educational needs of the country. Added to that are poor market conditions: the multiple indigenous languages that prohibit publishing from being economically feasible; low literacy rates; the lack of a ready market in the form of library systems or distribution outlets; and the number of families without disposable income for books.

But that does not explain the lack of art from indigenous cultures in countries that do have strong publishing industries, such as the United States and Australia. For that we turn to the nature of the art itself, which does not conform to the lessons taught in Drawing 101 or Art History 101—the Western norm for visual representation. Much non-Western art is symbolic rather than representative. In the Gond tribal community of central India, for instance, objects are depicted as flat rather than three-dimensional, and their relative size indicates their importance and not their relationship to one another in real life. Australian Aboriginal artists often use symbols and images that Westerners don't have the background to read. In an illustrator's afterword to *Pheasant and Kingfisher* by Catherine Berndt, artist Arone Raymond Meeks explains that "in some Aboriginal art, animals are drawn with lines that show how they are cut up for eating."

Effects of Globalization

Naturally, all these factors—which boil down to adults' codified ideas of what constitutes good art as well as our stunted notion of what children are capable of responding to or interpreting—diminish the opportunities for broadening American children's aesthetic perceptions as they get older. And yet other factors are at work in our rapidly changing world that may someday make these points moot. Globalization has been said to be shaking up the hierarchy and evening out the playing field—Thomas Friedman's

An illustration from *The London Jungle Book* by Bhajju Shyam. On his first visit to London, Gond artist Bhajju Shyam observed that Big Ben is the symbol of time for Londoners just as the rooster is the symbol of time in Gond art. Both are equally important in the lives of their respective communities, and thus of equal size.

very point in *The World Is Flat* (Farrar, Straus, Giroux, 2005). The Internet has erased national borders for editors, artists, and writers, so that editors are now able to work directly with illustrators around the world.

This practice has been going on for some time outside of the United States, most noticeably with NordSüd Verlag in Switzerland, which has long worked with illustrators and writers from throughout Europe. Many of NordSüd's books are published by the American sister firm NorthSouth Books, so we have, for instance, *Loopy*, written by Aurore Jesset (France) and illustrated by Barbara Korthues (Germany). This same practice is apparent in Latin America, where, to give one example, the Argentinian illustrator Isol has worked directly with an Argentinian publisher, a Mexican publisher, a Venezuelan publisher, and a Canadian publisher. Many illustrators today have their own websites that act as portfolios of their work for potential clients.

American editors are beginning to do this as well, working with illustrators they have met at the Bologna Book Fair or another international venue or whose work they first published via an acquisition from a foreign publisher. This was the case for *Oh, No! Where Are My Pants*, a poetry collection edited by Lee Bennett Hopkins and illustrated by the German artist Wolf Erlbruch (HarperCollins, 2005). While Erlbruch's characters look similar to those in some of his other books, one suspects that Erlbruch had some editorial direction for these pictures, as they are literal interpretations of the poems, a bit more tame than his usual approach to illustration.

At the same time, illustrators are not staying put in the country where they were born. When Peter Sís came to the United States in 1982, he brought with him his Czech art training, along with his outsider's eye. His hallmark style of intricate pen-and-ink drawings as found in *The Three Golden Keys* (Doubleday, 1994) and *The Wall* (Farrar, Straus, Giroux, 2007), to name two examples, is decidedly not in the Anglo-American tradition, yet these books have been embraced by adults and children alike and have garnered many awards, including Caldecott Honors. His artwork is incredibly sophisticated, layered with hidden images, cultural allusions, and symbolism.

Other examples include Suzy Lee, born and raised in South Korea, who trained in Seoul and London and now lives and works in Singapore. She works directly with publishers in France, Italy, Korea, and Switzerland. Michèle Lemieux, from Quebec, has lived and worked in both Germany and France, which may account for her strong reputation in Europe. Her award-winning book *Stormy Night* (Kids Can Press, 1999) was first published in Germany. More recently, Jon Klassen moved from Ontario to California to work in the animation industry and since then has ventured into children's books. Even though he is Canadian, he works directly with American editors on his book projects. His American publishers distribute the books in Canada, where his illustrations for *Cats' Night Out* by Caroline Stutson (Simon and Schuster, 2010) won the 2010 Governor General's Award for Illustration, Canada's closest counterpart to the Caldecott Award. More recently, *House Held Up by Trees* (Candlewick, 2012) and *The Dark* (HarperCollins, 2013) were named 2012 and 2013 Governor General's Award finalists, respectively. In 2013, Klassen took both a Caldecott Honor for his illustrations in *Extra Yarn* by Mac Barnett (Candlewick, 2012) and the Caldecott Medal for *This Is Not My Hat* (Candlewick, 2012), which he also wrote. And then there is Oliver Jeffers, born in Australia, educated in Ireland, and now living in the US, whose books consistently make Best Book lists in the both UK and the US.

As a result of our more mobile society and the increasing exposure to images, artists, and art forms far and wide, illustrators are no longer confined by their national borders or by traditional principles of book illustration. Today the social, political, economic, and cultural conditions that Binette Schroeder referenced as factors in book illustration have shifted from national to international, giving illustrators the freedom to realize their unique visions through all kinds of media, from age-old paint on canvas to digitization and manipulation of images on screen. It is truly a stimulating time for the creation of picture books.

Notes

1. "Cover Story—Lane Smith and Molly Leach," YouTube video, 5:08 (quote at 3:45), posted by BN Studio, June 23, 2008, www.youtube.com/watch?v=_NO3x6dOFCQ.
2. Bader, *American Picturebooks from Noah's Ark to The Beast Within,* 129.
3. Marcus, "Outside over Where?" 49.
4. Barthelmess, review of *Garmann's Summer,* 64.
5. Schroeder, "Illustration beyond the Ordinary," 10.
6. Ibid.
7. Salisbury, "No Red Buses Please," 7.
8. Ibid., 9–10.
9. National Geographic Education Foundation and Roper Public Affairs, "2006 Geographic Literacy Study."
10. Garrett, "Screams and Smiles," 21.
11. Kobayashi, "Which US Picturebooks Get Translated into Japanese?" 5–12.

Reading across Cultures

Anyone who studies multicultural or international literature for a time eventually discovers that the more culturally specific a story is, the more universal it becomes. Conversely, the more a story tries to be universal, omitting specific cultural details so that it will appeal to everyone, the fewer points of connection exist for readers. One doesn't have to be a Nicaraguan refugee like José in *The Long Road* (by Luis Garay; Groundwood, 1997) to understand what it is like to leave one place for another. The same feelings apply whether a child moves across the state or the continent, and the same questions arise: Will I fit in? Will I make new friends? A well-written story enables readers to connect with the main character at the core and bring their own experiences into the mix.

Some experiences are so endemic to human life that almost all children have them in common no matter where they live: family life, sibling relationships, even occasionally, the loss of a loved one. Frequently, picture books from other countries chosen for publication in the United States feature animal characters living in generic situations, such as a cartoonish forest, so that the setting doesn't signal nationality or culture. Others feature animals living in human ways—in an apartment or a house, say—but with a tight focus on the characters. Komako Sakai's *Mad at Mommy*, for instance, recounts the exchange between a toddler rabbit and his mother one Saturday morning when she wants to sleep in and he wants her to get out of bed. The setting is generic as is the situation, but readers' interpretations are not. Japanese readers find the story humorous in the way it captures the emotions of a child, while some American reviewers have seen it as a testament to a mother's unconditional love—and one has even speculated that the mother may be depressed.

What follows in this chapter are some topics that recur across national lines. The first two categories, Family Life and Depression and Loss, represent books that speak to children's experiences. The two remaining categories, Urban and Rural Ecosystems and War and Conflict, speak more to the concerns of authors who want to make children aware that the destruction or preservation of the world and its resources lie in human hands. Finally, a section on folk and fairy tales uses the Grimms' tale "Hansel and Gretel" to show how by situating a story in his own country, an illustrator can turn an existing text into contemporary social commentary. In most cases, annotations for these books, other than the American books mentioned, can be found in the relevant country sections of the bibliographies in part II.

Family Life

New Baby

Many children will experience the arrival of a new baby in the family, so the number of books that reflect this situation, using human or animal characters (or a mix), is not surprising. Interestingly, all these books come out of an Anglo or European tradition, and none (with the exception of *Elizabeti's Doll*, written by an American) is set in Africa, Asia, Latin America, or the Middle East. Could this suggest that feelings of jealousy at the addition of a sibling are a particularly Anglo concept tied to the notion of individuality?

In both *Julius the Baby of the World* by American Kevin Henkes, starring the irrepressible Lilly, and *Tommy's New Sister* by Germans Gerda Marie Scheidl and Christa Unzner, older siblings are not pleased with the time and attention new babies require. Even though both sets of parents bend over backward to include their firstborn children in special moments with the babies, their efforts fail. Lilly pronounces baby brother Julius disgusting, tries to scare him, and asks if she will get her room back when he goes away. Likewise, Tommy is inspired by the story of Peter Pan to sprinkle fairy dust on baby sister Wendy so that she will fly away like the Wendy of the story. His fairy dust is actually a mixture of flour, cocoa powder, and sugar that makes the baby cry. Both Lilly and Tommy have an about-face, but for different reasons. All it takes for Lilly is a cousin to call him disgusting, and suddenly Lilly is praising Julius's wet pink nose, small black eyes, and sweet white fur. Tommy, after trying all means to get rid of Wendy, hears her crying and wonders why neither of his parents has gone to see what is wrong. He finally goes into her room himself, and when he comforts her, she stops crying. In both cases, the children own the moment; they have accepted their siblings on their own terms.

Yelena Romanova's *The Perfect Friend* tells this same story from a dog's point of view. Archie wishes he had "someone to throw a ball for him to catch." When Archie's human family leaves home in the morning, they promise him a surprise. Upon their return, he examines all the items they have unloaded and finally notices the squiggly bundle they call Max. Suddenly everyone is busy with Max, and Archie is feeling left out (and shows it in particularly doggy ways). Time passes before the family finally notices his feelings and makes amends, but still something is missing until the day that a ball bounces his way, thrown by Max. Romanova and the book's illustrator, Boris Kulikov, were born and raised in Russia and now live in the US; Kulilov's quirky illustrations have a timeless, Old World feel, due both to the absence of modern conveniences and the presence of a 1930s-era auto.

Anthony Browne's *Changes,* too, begins with a parent leaving and the prognosis that "things were going to change." This cryptic statement prompts Joseph to imagine all sorts of changes around the house, captured in Browne's surrealistic paintings. Joseph sees everyday objects developing wings or tails or turning into whole animals. Finally, sick of it all, he retreats to his room to await his parents. When his father returns home with his mother, she is carrying a baby. The book ends with "Hello, love, . . . this is your sister." Published in 1990, this book foreshadows Browne's later work in its introduction of trademark images, such as the gorilla and the banana, and use of artistic allusions, such as in Joseph's bedroom, which is patterned after Van Gogh's "Bedroom at Arles" and even contains a picture of "Starry Night" on the wall. Appropriately, a Renaissance-style Madonna and Child painting hangs on the living room wall as a clue to the outcome of the story, and the television is tuned to a channel showing a mother bird feeding her baby. Browne, former Children's Laureate of Britain and a Hans Christian Andersen medalist, is successful in creating the uneasy feeling one can have when facing the unknown. An interesting tidbit: when Browne's book first came out in the US, the editor must have felt that American readers were either not clever enough or too lazy to put two and two together and therefore added two lines: "Joseph smiled. This is what his father had meant."

My Sister Gracie, written and illustrated by Gillian Johnson, a native Canadian now living in England, tells the same story but removes it one step by focusing on dogs within a human family. Fabio is a poodle with everything, including a family, who wants just one more thing: a baby brother to sniff the neighborhood with. Instead, he gets a sister, Gracie, who is twice his size and lacking in energy, but worst of all, *a girl*. When he takes her out on a walk intending to send her back to the pound, however, his neighborhood friends make fun of her, and just like Kevin Henkes's Lilly, Fabio has an immediate change of heart. Gracie may not be what he had expected, but she's his sister.

Elizabeti's Doll is the only book that doesn't draw on feelings of jealousy, displacement, or uncertainty. Written by Stephanie Stuve-Bodeen and illustrated by Christy Hale, the story comes out of Stuve-Bodeen's time as a Peace Corps volunteer in Tanzania, where this story is set. Elizabeti's mother has just had another baby, and Elizabeti decides she wants a baby to care for too; her instinct is the same one that makes little girls everywhere play with dolls, but she has no doll. She chooses just the right rock and names it Eva; whatever care Mama gives baby Obedi, Elizabeti gives to Eva. When it's time for Elizabeti to fetch water from the village well, she lays Eva down next to other rocks so she won't feel lonely, but Eva is missing when she gets home. Fortunately Eva is rescued from the pit where she has been used to build a fire, and all is well. Elizabeti's mother and her older sister both take her play seriously, and for Elizabeti, having a baby brother becomes a step in training for the day she becomes a mother herself.

Adoption

There is no shortage of books about adoption in the United States. Most are straightforward stories designed to reassure adopted children that they are loved, often verging on the didactic or sentimental. The approaches differ. Some tell the story of international adoptions and the child's journey across the ocean; others begin with the parents' process of applying for a baby and preparing space in their home and in their hearts. Still others are told from the perspective of an older sibling in the family. Although cross-cultural adoptions are common these days, many children wonder why they look different from their parents or siblings, and some books address this question. The handful of books on this topic from other countries shows us that adoption is not unique to North America, but these writers and artists focus on story rather than message.

The Little Green Goose, a collaboration between writer Adele Sansone of Austria and artist Anke Faust of Germany, recognizes that sometimes single males want to be parents. With no wife to lay an egg for him, Mr. Goose asks the hens in the barnyard to give him an egg, but they refuse. Then the farm dog finds a big egg as he is digging a hole, and Mr. Goose happily takes it. He dreams of a son all the while he is roosting on his egg, and when his little green goose hatches, he takes wonderful care of it. As he grows and ventures out into the barnyard, the little green goose hears the barnyard chatter. The rooster tells him that Mr. Goose could not possibly be his daddy: "Take a look at yourself. You don't have feathers. You don't have a beak. And you're green!" This sends him on a search for his real daddy, but in the end, he realizes that he already has what he wants: a daddy who loves him.

In a similar vein, three other picture books—from Germany, Taiwan, and India respectively—use animals to raise issues that adopted children may have. Birte Müller's *Giant Jack* stresses the importance of self-identity. Jack, so much larger than his mouse siblings, is unhappy until his mother explains that he is a rat she found as an infant; knowing his roots helps Jack cope with his difference. Chi-Yuan Chen's *Guji Guji* suggests that nurture outweighs nature in the case of the crocodile hatched in a duck's nest. He may look like a crocodile, but he feels like a duck, and he outwits the crocodiles who want him to betray his siblings. Anushka Ravishankar's *Elephants Never Forget!* also reinforces the notion that what is important is who raises a child rather than who bears it. A small elephant separated from his mother is taken in and acculturated by a herd of water buffalo; some years later he encounters some elephants at a watering hole who toot to him, and although the sound resonates deeply, he chooses to stay with his adopted family. Using animals in place of humans enables these writers and artists to approach the topic sideways rather than head on and broadens the audience to all children, adopted or not.

Orphanages have all but disappeared from the American landscape, replaced by foster care programs and other social services, but not so everywhere. *Madeline* and its sequels by Ludwig Bemelman ensure that the beloved Paris orphanage run by Miss Clavel will always be present in picture books. Although those books date back to the mid-twentieth century, contemporary orphanages are still the setting for picture books. From Spain comes *The Best Family in the World* by Susana López, in which young Carlota has been told that a family is coming to get her the following day. She imagines parents with exotic jobs such as animal trainer or astronaut, but instead they are a postal worker and an insurance agent, along with a big brother, and are better than anything she could have dreamed. The orphanage is pictured as a happy place with active children, a kind director, and bedrooms. A somewhat darker view of orphanages can be seen in *Andrei's Search* by Barbro Lindgren, illustrated by Eva Erikson. Published in Sweden, the book is set in Saint Petersburg, Russia, where Andrei has been abandoned by his mother. Two aunts come to get him and take him to the orphanage, and he is shown occupying one bed out of nine in a dormitory room. He misses his mother and what he remembers of their life together; at this point in the story Andrei's imagination takes over and replaces the reality of everyday life with a fantasy life at home with his mother, his motherless friend, Vova, and a stray dog they have encountered along the way. Children are resilient, yet some situations are so bleak that fantasy becomes their only coping mechanism. Not all orphans are as fortunate as Carlota to be adopted by the "best family."

Depression and Loss

Americans are generally known for being optimistic and liking happy endings. For the most part, we avoid introducing subjects like depression and death in picture books unless they are intended as straight bibliotherapy. When American writers do choose to write about death or depression, they find ways to soften the topic. Take for example the two books *Everybody Gets the Blues,* by Americans Leslie Staub and R. G. Roth (Harcourt, 2012), and *The Red Tree,* by Australian author-illustrator Shaun Tan (Simply Read, 2002). Both picture books are narrated by children, a boy and a girl respectively, and both address feelings of despair.

As a native of New Orleans, Leslie Staub was living there when Hurricane Katrina hit; she wrote *Everybody Gets the Blues* in response to that disaster. Although her inspiration was the pervasive depression caused by overwhelming loss and change such as that wrought by Katrina, the emotion has been recast less as indicative of situational depression and more like ordinary feelings of sadness. These feelings are embodied as "Blues

Guy," who often appears when something bad happens. Although Katrina is not mentioned in this book, New Orleans's spirit is very much present in the structure of the text, which is in the form of a blues song. The city also makes a cameo appearance in the text: "Everybody gets the blues sometimes: ... scary bullies, beauty queens, little old ladies from New Orleans." When Blues Guy visits the narrator, sometimes he just sits there keeping the narrator company, and other times they sing so loudly that they fly off to where others are crying. Offsetting the somber topic, the rhyming, rhythmic text keeps the tone light, and illustrator Roth's collage pictures, with their pastel-colored backgrounds, follow suit. This tone, too, echoes a common attitude of New Orleanians, who have a tradition of rising to meet challenges and minimizing their emotional suffering. When things start looking up for the narrator, Blues Guy takes off. "Good-bye, blues. Good-bye Blues Guy." Hello, unambiguous happy ending.

In contrast, *The Red Tree* presents a starker and more complex picture of what it is to be depressed. Narrated by a young red-haired girl, the text begins with her musing that "sometimes the day begins with nothing to look forward to." While Staub created Blues Guy as a metaphor for general unhappiness, Shaun Tan uses visual metaphors to accompany the narrator's plain words describing various aspects of depression. "Darkness overcomes you," says the girl, and the illustration shows an enormous weeping fish over the girl's head casting her in shadow. A feeling of helplessness is illustrated with a picture of the girl lost in a chaotic landscape of ladders and windows, and to illustrate her feeling of isolation Tan shows her encapsulated in a bottle, head covered by a diving helmet. The "happy" ending consists of a glimmer of hope in the form of another metaphor, a blaze-red maple sapling that brings a small smile to the girl's face. Two books about depression, although neither uses that term: the American book skims the surface and assures readers that all will be better soon, and the Australian book takes them into its depths while providing a hint that the depression is lifting.

Michael Rosen's Sad Book also uses first-person narrative to describe what it feels like when he is sad: "It's everywhere. All over me." Rosen ascribes part of the reason to the death of his son Eddie, but also acknowledges that sometimes sadness "comes along and finds you" for no apparent reason. Master illustrator Quentin Blake manages to portray the stark reality of depression, and yet his cartoon style keeps the mood from being oppressive. Together, the British team of Rosen and Blake show that all kinds of people suffer from depression (although Rosen never uses that term) and can still have happy moments. Michael Rosen chose to give his book an honest rather than a happily-ever-after ending.

In *The Scar* from France, a young boy relates his feelings after his mother dies from a terminal illness. He pretends he doesn't understand what his father means by "it's over," even though he knows very well, and his feelings vacillate between anger and sadness; he feels responsible for his father's welfare but lost as to how to make things better. When his grandmother comes to visit, he worries that he will have two sad grown-ups to take care of. The scar of the title is really the lifelong wound of losing his mother, manifested in a scraped knee that he continually scratches, since when his knee hurts he hears the comforting voice of his mother. The child's point of view remains constant, and when the scab turns into a scar without the boy noticing, readers know that he has moved to the stage of acceptance.

Wolf Erlbruch's picture books do not take into account the age of his readers—the books are for anyone who can connect to them. *Death, Duck and the Tulip* gives death a persona, a fairly congenial fellow with a skull for a head. When Duck finally notices that Death is following her, they begin to form a relationship, uneasy for Duck at first but then quite comfortable. One night Duck literally embraces death but does not die. They spend the rest of the summer together, and then Duck feels chilly and, as the first snowflakes fall, stops breathing. Death very tenderly picks her up, smoothes her feathers, and places the purple tulip on her as he sets her in the great river to float downstream. It's hard to think of a lovelier image of death, or a more matter-of-fact one. Erlbruch's allegory lacks sentimentality and neither espouses a religious belief nor conflicts with one; instead, it is a reassuring statement of the inevitability of death.

Urban and Rural Ecosystems

One of the best picture books to address urban sprawl is also an American classic: Virginia Lee Burton's *The Little House*. Published by Houghton Mifflin in 1942, this paean to the pastoral life points out the drawbacks to what others view as progress—poor air quality, constant noise, shrinking space for flora and fauna. Burton anticipates books published decades later, including three sets of companion works: portfolios by Swiss artist Jörg Müller, *The Changing Countryside* and *The Changing City*, published by Margaret McElderry in 1977; Australian artist Jeannie Baker's *Window* and

Home, published by Greenwillow in 1991 and 2004 respectively; and the two pop-up books *Popville* and *Wake-Up, Sloth!* by Anouck Boisrobert and Louis Rigaud from France, published by Roaring Brook in 2010 and 2011.

Müller's two portfolios each contain foldout panoramas depicting the same scene at three-year intervals. *The Changing City* has eight panels that begin in 1953 and end in 1972; observers see the traditional neighborhood, with its small shops, canal, corner park, and three-story brick buildings, turn into a collection of modern generic multistory buildings that will soon be completely bypassed by the highway that is in the process of being built. The final panel shows protesters demonstrating against the highway construction and includes an inordinate number of signs advertising American companies or borrowing English words: Ford, Kodak, Firestone, Coca Cola, Snack Bar, City Parking, ITT. The *Changing Countryside* also begins in 1953 and ends in 1972. Here we see a very small village built along a railroad track, surrounded by meadows and farms. But for the mountain range in the background, it would be totally unrecognizable by 1972, as the country road leading to the mountains has now become a four-lane highway lined with factories, a discount store, and office buildings. Ironically, a sign posted by the builders proclaims that life in Güllen is becoming even more pleasant, as one driver is flashing his lights at another to get her to change lanes. These two portfolios are quite rare; a few libraries still lend them, but most are in noncirculating collections.

In *Window*, Jeannie Baker traces a similar trajectory as Müller did in *The Changing Countryside*. Through the same window frame, we see the evolution both of a red-haired baby boy and the neighborhood outside his rural home. Details in the illustrations mark the passing of time in this wordless book, as the boy grows to manhood and the city encroaches on the house. In the last scene, the man has married, and, holding his own baby, he gazes out the window of a new house once again on the outskirts of the same city, just farther out. With *Home*, however, Baker shows the opposite trend as she traces the life of the baby girl who grows up to marry the red-headed boy of *Window*. While he has grown up in the suburbs, she has grown up in the inner city. Her parents have moved into a decayed neighborhood and taken part in restoring it. By the time this young woman is ready to marry, the neighborhood has become a community, and the wedding is held in the street in front of her house with all the neighbors in attendance.

Popville makes clever use of paper engineering to show how an isolated country church surrounded by farmland and trees develops over time into a full-fledged city, complete with school, apartment buildings, power plant, roads, and factories. The only words are at the book's end, when the creators challenge readers to consider what they might add if they were building a city. By the same team, *Wake Up, Sloth!* begins in a forest and relies on text throughout to point readers to various forest creatures, including the sloth. As the first machine arrives to clear part of the land, some creatures flee, but only when all trees are gone does the sloth disappear. Happily, the book does not end here. A man plants seeds that grow over time, and by pulling on a tab, the reader can see the young seedlings that mark the beginning of a new forest and the return of the sloth.

War and Conflict

Why is it that most American picture books written to address the concerns of war are littered with well-meaning platitudes and earnest adult voices? The exception, of course, is Dr. Seuss's *The Butter Battle Book*, published by Random House in 1984, which pits the Zooks against the Yooks in an absurd arms race (the opposing groups differ only in how they eat their bread—butter side up or down). Perhaps the controversy it inspired upon publication answers the question—Americans prefer to address difficult topics in a manner designed to reassure children rather than through allegory that invites interpretation and allows for questions.

A lack of homegrown literary picture books with themes of conflict may be the reason that the books most often available on this theme come from Europe. Perhaps the most startling example is *Why?* a wordless fable by Russian artist and illustrator Nikolai Popov. Popov has a personal connection with war, having been a child during World War II when Nazi planes were bombing his Russian city. *Why?* which has been republished in several countries, begins on a beautiful summer day as a mouse with a parasol eyes the flower a frog is holding. Never mind that many flowers of the same kind are growing all around—the mouse wants *that* flower and grabs it. Bigger frogs appear on the scene to chase him, but the mouse returns in a makeshift tank with a weapon, and thus begins an arms race similar to that in Dr. Seuss's book. *Why*'s ending is not ambiguous, however; when all is finished, the mouse and frog sit alone amidst the wreckage and scorched earth. The story told through these illustrations epitomizes the

1966 poster created by the American anti-Vietnam group Another Mother for Peace: "War is not healthy for children and other living things."

David McKee, best known in the US as the creator of the loveable patchwork elephant Elmer, has twice addressed the topic of war. He first tackled this subject in 1972 in *Six Men* (reissued in 2011 by NorthSouth). In this book, his rough pen-and-ink drawings accompany an elaborate story of how six men who set out to find a place to live and work in peace are corrupted by greed and fear. They end up creating a situation that pits two armies against one another with catastrophic results. In the end only six men remain on each side, and the story reaches full circle as each group sets out in a different direction in search of somewhere to live and work in peace. The reader, knowing what has happened in the past, does not hold out much hope for their future.

McKee revisits this theme again in *The Conquerors* (Roaring Brook, 2004), created much later in his career and illustrated in the same style, this time in a larger format and with color added to the drawings. Here the bleak, ironic conclusion of *Six Men* has given way to a more imaginative and optimistic ending. In *The Conquerors,* the army of a large, rich country has succeeded in conquering every country but one—a small insignificant country that didn't seem worthwhile until it was the last remaining country not under the General's rule. When the army invades, the soldiers find no resistance—all, including the General, are welcomed into the country, fed, and housed. The soldiers of the occupying army enjoy their time getting to know their hosts, trading stories and songs, and even helping with chores. As soon as the General realizes what is happening, he sends his troops home and brings in fresh ones with the same results. Finally, the General decides to leave a small force in the conquered country and returns home with his troops proclaiming victory. What readers see, however, is that what matters is not what is proclaimed but what actually happens: the occupying soldiers remove their uniforms and integrate into the life of the small country, while the soldiers who have returned to the big country have integrated the ways of the small country into their daily lives. When the General's son asks for a bedtime song, what springs to the General's mind first is one he learned while away.

While McKee's first book was a cautionary tale of war, this one is almost Zen-like in contrast, finding a path to peace that substitutes kindness and generosity for hatred and death. Some Americans may feel that

McKee is pointing a finger at the United States, which in the first decade of this century was seen in some regions as an invader rather than an ally for freedom. McKee could, however, just as easily be writing about his own country of Britain, which in the height of its power had colonies throughout the world. As in *The Conquerors*, the British who served in these colonies brought home a taste for the food, arts, and entertainment of these faraway places.

In *I Am I* (Roaring Brook, 2006), Marie-Louise Fitzpatrick brings the concept of escalating conflict down to a child's level when she shows two young boys facing one another on competing mountaintops, each proclaiming himself to be more important, his mountain bigger, his flower more beautiful, until their words take flight and destroy what they have, leaving parched earth. Full of remorse, their words then acknowledge their new understanding, and the earth begins to come alive once more. The boastful "I am I" of each boy changes to an expression of individualism that acknowledges the worth of the other, while the fable-like setting of the desert cedes to the front yard of two attached houses. Two families, two peoples: throughout, Fitzpatrick draws on a symbol she attributes to the Choctaw people, a river that separates two cultures but can also bring them close enough to touch. Fitzpatrick is from Ireland, and in an earlier book, *The Long March* (1998), she describes an affiliation between the Choctaw and the Irish that began when the Choctaw donated money from their meager resources to send to Ireland during the Great Famine of the mid-1800s.

Another book with child protagonists, *The War* by French writer and illustrator Anaïs Vaugelade (Carolrhoda, 2001), shows how a common enemy often turns enemies into allies. The illustrations lend a medieval setting to this story of the Reds and the Blues, who no longer remember why they are at war. Prince Julius, the son of the Red King, has challenged Prince Fabian, the son of the Blue King, to a duel to end the war. Prince Julius rides up on a large warhorse, while Prince Fabian, a reluctant fighter, arrives on a sheep. The sheep bleats at the horse, the horse rears up, and Julius falls to his death. Fabian is immediately banished from both kingdoms, but he tricks both the Red and Blue kings into meeting at the battlefield to fight the Yellows, pretending to have joined up with them. Over time as the Yellows fail to arrive, the Reds and the Blues begin to talk and their wives come with food, followed by the children and old people; as they mingle, thoughts of enmity disappear. Having ended the war singlehandedly, Fabian does indeed decide to live with the Yellows, whose kindness and compassion he finds much more to his liking.

Olivier Tallec's wordless book *Waterloo and Trafalgar* (Enchanted Lion, 2012) presents yet another twist on this theme, with the two eponymous characters, named after major battles in French history, in a standoff behind walls on either side of a no-man's land. The two characters are differentiated by the colors of their uniforms—one is blue and the other orange—but they have much the same in the way of supplies and weaponry as they persist through the months and the seasons. The point of view changes frequently, preventing readers from identifying with either Waterloo or Trafalgar and pointing up the absurdity of their situation. In such a stalemate, negotiation is needed, and here it is provided by a blue and orange bird that has hatched from a speckled egg. It maneuvers a face-to-face meeting and aligns itself with both sides, leading to not only a détente but a friendship. In Europe—as well as other parts of the globe—those who were once enemies are now allies, and vice versa.

Folk and Fairy Tales

Historically, so many of the picture books acquired for publication from other countries have been illustrated editions of familiar folktales from the collections of Wilhelm and Jacob Grimm or Hans Christian Andersen. Each illustrator brings his or her own interpretation to the tale, keeping the text intact but reenvisioning the story by choosing which aspects to emphasize and where to set it. Some illustrators stick with an indeterminate middle-European setting, but others choose a particular time and place as demonstrated in the following example of three versions of "Hansel and Gretel." Similar examples can be found for most other familiar tales.

Both the British illustrator Anthony Browne and the Canadian illustrator Ian Wallace have offered fresh interpretations of "Hansel and Gretel" by situating the story in modern times, each placing the story in his own country. In the Grimms' tale, the father's occupation as a woodcutter was not arbitrary. As one of the lowest-paying, most undervalued jobs, it signaled the family's poverty to listeners of the time. In setting out to reinterpret this tale, both Browne and Wallace artfully incorporate this element of the story without compromising the story's contemporary setting.

Anthony Browne's poor woodcutter and his family live in a brick two-story house in sore need of repair. The house sits at the edge of a large forest and in the shadow of smokestacks, perhaps indicating a factory that may once have employed the father. The first illustration shows the family gathered around a table, the father reading the paper—perhaps scanning the want ads or simply taking in the grim news. This book was published in 1981, as England was in the final throes of a recession, and Browne's book brings home the dire situation that many of England's working-class families found themselves in.

So too did Ian Wallace, working in the early 1990s, consider which occupation might convey the same desperation in modern Canada; he found the woodcutter's parallel in the tenuous existence of the Newfoundland fisherman whose livelihood has disappeared with all the fish. Wallace portrays the father as an out-of-work fisherman whose only option is to cut wood from his forests and sell it. He and his family live in a modest white clapboard house with inexpensive, out-of-date furnishings; to judge from the way the children are sitting on the couch under blankets, the heat has been turned off as well.

Both Browne and Wallace infuse their illustrations with symbols and visual allusions. In Browne's book the images of the stepmother and the witch suggest that they are one in the same. Wallace's illustrations strongly associate the witch with the forest, suggesting her pervasiveness; a bird's-eye view of the forest reveals the witch's profile in the very landscape the family crosses. "Hansel and Gretel" has always been a story that begins and ends in a realistic world. Through their illustrations, Browne and Wallace give the story added resonance without changing it.

Although the examples noted above are particularly obvious, comparing editions of the same folktale from artists in several countries can be counted on to yield surprises. The illustrations for "Little Red Riding Hood" run the gamut from picturing the grandmother hiding in the closet to the woodsman slitting open the wolf's stomach to save Red Riding Hood and her grandmother (the latter picture is found in Lisbeth Zwerger's *Little Red Cap*). The scenes that an illustrator chooses to picture are a function of cultural mores as much as artistic vision. Of course, that is true of all children's book art.

Part II

A Note about the Bibliographies

The picture books included in the following annotated lists have been selected to represent the countries under which they are listed in a variety of ways. Where possible, the bibliographies include books by authors and illustrators well-known in their own countries, prize-winning picture books, and national classics, including folktales. Books by nonnatives, set in a country where the author or illustrator has lived or worked for a time, are also included; for some countries these are the only books accessible to American readers. The basis for each selection has been its authentic perspective as well as its literary and artistic merit.

To be useful, bibliographies such as these should be restricted to books that are available for purchase or circulation. The lists in this volume introduce books that are either currently in print or available as new copies from resellers at a reasonable price. More and more books are going out of print in record time. When only the paperbound edition is still in print, that is the ISBN listed and noted as such (ppb). In a few cases, an out-of-print book no longer available on the resale market has been included because it is exceptional and deserves attention. These out-of-print books are held in hundreds of library collections across the country and can be readily accessed.

Occasionally, quality books that larger publishers have let go out of print will be picked up by smaller, independent publishers. When this is the case, the citation lists bibliographic information for the newest, in-print edition. Frequently libraries will already hold the original edition of this book.

Africa and the Middle East

Few of the books annotated in this section were originally written and published in the country under which they are listed, with the exception of the books from South Africa and Israel. Instead, the books listed come from indigenous writers and/or illustrators who have emigrated to Australia, Europe, or North America from Africa or the Middle East, or from people who have spent time in an African or Middle Eastern country working with an aid organization or in a private sector job. Thus, while the portrayals in these books may be authentic, they are also written and published within a European or North American context with those readers in mind.

The exceptions, South Africa and Israel, are home to established publishing industries with firms that publish a range of academic, literary, and informational books. Few children's books published in Israel make it to the United States; those that do usually come by way of Europe, in particular Germany and France. South African books are generally more available, due to ties between publishers in South Africa and the UK, where the books are often published either before or simultaneously with US publication. South Africa's publishing industry has historically published authors writing in Afrikaans or English only, offering perspectives that represent only a minority of the South African experience. Since the end of apartheid, efforts have been under way to broaden the cultural and linguistic variety of books published for South African children.

The commercial publication of children's books in other African countries is inconsistent from country to country and even sometimes within a country. Since 1983, the Zimbabwe International Book Fair in Harare has brought together writers, publishers, and booksellers from across the continent and even the world, along with local readers and buyers. Once described as "the continent's literary shop-window on the world, attracting international publishers hunting for African talent," the fair suffered from Zimbabwe's political and economic unrest and was on hiatus from 2006 through 2008.[1] While the fair has once again become an annual event, the book market in Zimbabwe has not been so quick to recover, and the number of international publishers in attendance has not rebounded. The likelihood that books originating in African countries will make their way to North America is thus greatly diminished.

Sometimes a difference in cultural or aesthetic norms prevents books from being marketable in the United States, as they would have no appeal to American children. "Quite a number of attractive books are produced in Egypt and other Arab countries," explains Anne Pellowski, "but many have few or no illustrations because of the Muslim cultural preference for not showing pictures. They put all of their aesthetic emphasis on the beauty of the script" (pers. comm.). Pellowski, who founded and directed the Information Center on Children's Cultures of the US Committee for UNICEF, now travels frequently to communities in Asia, Africa, and Latin America to conduct cloth bookmaking workshops.

In Iran, the Institute for the Intellectual Development of Children and Young Adults has long published outstanding illustrated books in Farsi. In a rare example of translations from Farsi, Carolrhoda Books published three books from this institute in 1972: *Uncle New Year, The Crystal Flower and the Sun*, and *Bastoor*. These books bring American readers beautifully illustrated Persian folktales and legends; although now out of print, each is still held in approximately one hundred public library collections across the country. The International Children's Digital Library contains other books in Farsi that offer stunning examples of the art and design in contemporary Iranian books.

Book awards are one way of encouraging the publication of more and better books. For the past thirty years, the Israel Museum Ben-Yitzhak Award for the Illustration of a Children's Book has been given biennially. Catalogs of the 2008 and 2010 winners are available online and are well worth viewing for a glimpse of the range and sophistication of illustration styles in Israeli picture books. In South Africa, the Vivian Wilkes Award, given to the best illustrated children's book of the year, was funded for a period of ten years; following that, a new sponsor emerged, and the award is now called the Exclusive Books IBBY SA Award and given every other year. To encourage the growth of the children's book industry in the Arab countries, the Arab Children's Book Publishers Forum recently established the Etisalat Award for Arabic Children's Literature. Given to the best book written and published in Arabic, the award is supported by the telecommunications provider Etisalat UAE and carries a large monetary prize to be split between the book's publisher, author, and illustrator.

In areas lacking homegrown books, organizations like UNESCO are working with local and international nongovernmental organizations and agencies to develop and publish books specifically for local readers in local languages. In 1997 representatives of fifty-one out of the fifty-four African nations met to establish a set of general guidelines to help each country in establishing their own language policies, recognizing that one set of policies cannot address the varied linguistic situations of all countries. In Namibia, for instance, children are taught in their mother tongue through grade 3, and then taught in English through high school, continuing to study their mother tongue as a subject. Where reading materials in a language don't exist, they must be developed.

The Association for the Development of Education in Africa (ADEA) teamed up with UNESCO's regional office in Dakar, Senegal, to produce a series of books in French and English that address serious issues in a contemporary setting, with Portuguese and Kiswahili editions planned. Sample titles, all published in 2011, include *Bouba and Zaza Accept People's Differences, Bouba and Zaza Find out the Truth about AIDS,* and *Bouba and Zaza Protect the Planet.* The series, Childhood Cultures, is designed to develop both literacy skills and a sense of social justice and environmental awareness. Educators hope that the Bouba and Zaza stories reach beyond school to family and community where these issues are not always freely discussed. These books can be purchased directly from the UNESCO website.

In 2011, ADEA held an international conference on book development in Kenya at which representatives of various organizations shared their initiatives and successes. One presentation described a project, supported by corporate funding, to establish printing businesses in five countries and train local residents to run the presses; other presentations addressed the need for workshops to cultivate local authors and illustrators and for library programs to promote reading among people of all ages.

In keeping with its mission to see that all children have access to books they can read, the International Board on Books for Young People (IBBY) set up a Children in Crisis Fund to supply books to children traumatized by political conflict or natural disaster. From 2007 on, they have supported local sections in Lebanon, Afghanistan, and the occupied Palestinian territories (as well as elsewhere in the world) with projects to reach these children. In 2010, they funded the publication of *Gardens of Hope*, a collaboration between the national sections of Palestine and the United Arab Emirates. This bilingual book in English and Arabic contains selections written by children living in Gaza and illustrated by children from the Emirates. IBBY works through its national sections, which exist in approximately seventy countries; those in Africa and the Middle East include Egypt, Iran, Israel, Kuwait, Lebanon, Palestine, South Africa, Turkey, Uganda, United Arab Emirates, Zambia, and Zimbabwe.

Finally, several of the books listed in this section have been published in conjunction with nongovernmental organizations or charities, with part of the proceeds going to the groups whose work is described in the books. These are clearly books written for North American or European children, both to acquaint them with the lives of their contemporaries elsewhere and to instill in them a desire to be part of the larger effort to alleviate hunger and suffering wherever it may exist.

Note

1. Smith, "Harare Book Fair Returns."

Botswana

Nelson, Marilyn. *Ostrich and Lark*. Illustrated by San Artists of the Kuru Art Project of Botswana. 978-1-59078-702-1. Honesdale, PA: Boyds Mills, 2012. All ages.

Marilyn Nelson is a celebrated American poet who has also translated Danish poetry into English. Here she has written an original folktale to accompany paintings by artists indigenous to the Kalahari Desert. As Nelson explains in a foreword, the San people are hunter-gatherers whose traditional way of life is disappearing; they have turned to creating art as a means of earning a living and have revived motifs and images important to their culture. The brightly colored paintings in this book feature characteristic elements of San life, including ostriches, rivers, trees, and insects. Although the illustrations in this book are not of the same quality as those being added to museum collections today, they do provide the reader with an introduction to one of the few non-Western artistic styles found in picture books and to the culture from which it arises.

Cameroon

Bognomo, Joël Eboueme. *Madoulina: A Girl Who Wanted to Go to School.* 978-1-56397-769-5. Honesdale, PA: Boyds Mills, 1999. Ages 5–8.

Eight-year-old Madoulina lives in a poor section of Yaoundé, and when her father abandons the family, her mother must sell fresh produce and fritters in the marketplace. Each day Madoulina and her younger brother Babo help make the fritters, after which only Babo goes to school; Madoulina is resigned to walking through the neighborhoods selling fritters. One afternoon the teacher buys fritters and wonders why Madoulina doesn't attend school. He strikes a bargain with her mother that he will buy the fritters for school lunches if she sends Madoulina to school. Simple line drawings filled in with watercolor offer an unadorned view of life in Madoulina's neighborhood.

Chad

Rumford, James. *Rain School.* 978-0-547-24307-8. Boston: Houghton Mifflin, 2010. Ages 3–8.

At the start of each school year, the teacher guides the students in building their own open-air school made of mud bricks, rush mat walls, and a grass roof. The previous year's building gets ruined during the rainy season, just as this one will be. By the time the students are ready for their academic lessons, they have learned practical and collaborative skills and developed a stake in their own education. Rumford's dialogue conveys the teacher's open approach: "Perfect, my learning friends!" and "Well done, my hard-working friends!" During a geography lesson, the illustrations show a map of Africa with Chad colored in, and again on the final page is a wall map that names all the countries on the African continent. Rumsford uses line illustrations that look to be colored in with crayon, with expressive faces and gestures. The cultural diversity of Chad is shown subtly through, for example, Western, Islamic, and African clothing styles and signage in both French and Arabic.

Democratic Republic of the Congo

Stanley, Sanna. *Monkey for Sale.* 978-0-374-35017-8. New York: Farrar, Straus, Giroux, 2002. Age 5 and up.

This warm story of two girls who save a monkey through judicious bargaining and trading is a lesson in both marketplace economics and the humane treatment of animals. It's market day in the village, and Luzulo's father coaches her in the art of spending: "Look around, choose what you really want, and then bargain for a fair price." After Luzulo and her friend Kiese have bought their items, they hear that Mama Lusufu is selling a wild monkey she caught in her yard, and they must bargain with a string of vendors to obtain what Mama Lusufu requires in trade for the monkey. Ultimately they succeed and free the monkey in the jungle, warning it to "stay away from Mama Lusufu!" Stanley's vibrant illustrations—copper etchings overlaid with color—are especially adept at capturing the feel and look of the marketplace; her experience growing up in this place as a child of missionaries is evident in all the tiny and realistic details.

Egypt

Ellabbad, Mohieddin. *The Illustrator's Notebook.* 978-0-88899-700-5. Toronto: Groundwood Books, 2006. Age 7 and up.

True to its title, this book offers a peek into the world of an artist—his early drawings, what his artist's eye sees, how he creates an image that is his own rather than an imitation. Because this artist is Egyptian, readers also learn how reading and writing from right to left (as is done in Egypt and elsewhere) affects illustration, and they get firsthand experience: this book opens in the way it was created, with the spine on the right. The publisher has reproduced the original pages exactly, and the calligraphic writing is translated in a narrow side column. So much fascinating information about Egypt and art and culture is packed into this slim volume that, although it may not have general appeal, the right reader will find this book infinitely engaging.

Farmer, Nancy. *Clever Ali.* Illustrated by Gail de Marcken. 978-0-439-37014-0. New York: Orchard, 2006. Ages 5–9.

Two events mark Ali's seventh birthday—he moves into the men's part of the house, and he begins accompanying his father to his job as keeper of pigeons at the sultan's palace. Farmer sets the story in Egypt in the "long ago" past, when pigeons were the fastest form of communication in the desert. When Ali disobeys the warning not to overfeed the pigeons, the results are disastrous. Ali must find a way to bring the sultan six hundred cherries from Syria within three days or his father will die, and since it takes two weeks for the cherries to arrive by boat, the task is impossible. But clever Ali uses pigeons to save his father and then accomplishes the impossible again after the guilty pigeon eats one of the cherries. This time it's Ali who is punished; he is thrown down a hole to die and rises again on the arm of a beast, who then takes the sultan back down with him. This substantive original tale, spun around a cherry anecdote that Farmer came across while reading a history of the Islamic empires, is spellbindingly told, and de Marcken's beautiful paintings capture both the realistic and fantastic elements of the story.

Ethiopia

Gudeta, Ashenafi. *E Is for Ethiopia.* Photographs by Ashenafi Gudeta, Atakiti Mulu, Betelhem Abate and Dama Boru. 978-1-84507-825-6. London: Frances Lincoln, 2010. Distributed by Publishers Group West. Age 4 and up.

Using the alphabet as a device to structure information is tricky when another language is involved. Here letters sometimes represent an English word related to the photograph on the page and other times represent words in Amharic or other traditional languages spoken in East Africa, which are then translated into English. Sharp, well-reproduced color photographs show Ethiopia as a country inhabited by both Muslims and Christians, a country where goods are transported by both donkeys and trucks, and a country rich in traditions and arts. Ethiopians are proud of their country and the fact that it is the birthplace of coffee, which is also its largest export.

Kessler, Cristina. *The Best Beekeeper of Lalibela.* Illustrated by Leonard Jenkins. 978-0-8234-1858-9. New York: Holiday House, 2006. Age 5 and up.

Almaz lives in the Ethiopian mountains, where beekeeping is a male occupation and bees hive in long baskets hanging from tall trees. Although Almaz wants to make honey, she has a fear of heights and must find another way to raise bees. She succeeds with a mud hive on the ground until the ants discover it; in an aha moment, she realizes that ants can't swim, and she constructs a table on which to put her hive, then puts the legs of the table into pails of water. Jenkins's illustrations emphasize the human figures in their environment with few other details. Kessler's text was republished in Ethiopia in Amharic and English with different illustrations by the nonprofit EBCEF (Ethiopian Books for Children and Educational Foundation).

Ghana

Asare, Meshack. *Sosu's Call.* 978-1-929132-21-2. La Jolla, CA: Kane Miller, 2001. Ages 4–8.

Sosu's family lives on a sandbar on the coast of Ghana, an ideal location for fishing and also farming. Although his legs don't work, his family has always treated Sosu normally; others in his village, however, think he brings bad luck, so he is forced to stay home alone while his siblings go to school and his parents work in the fields. On one such day a huge storm hits, sending crashing waves into the village and threatening those who can't move out of the water's path. Sosu saves the day by dragging himself to the chief's shed where the drums are kept and sends out a call to bring the able-bodied running in from the fields. Originally published in Accra, Ghana, by Sub-Saharan Publishers, *Sosu's Call* won the 1999 UNESCO Award for Children and Youth Literature in the Service of Tolerance.

Milway, Katie Smith. *One Hen.* Illustrated by Eugenie Fernandes. 978-1-55453-028-1. Toronto: Kids Can Press, 2008. Age 6 and up.

While microfinance seems like a topic too sophisticated for young children, the story of how a young boy built a large poultry farm from just one hen is twice told, both as a cumulative tale and simultaneously in page-length text. "This is Kojo. This is the loan that Kojo gets. This is the hen that Kojo buys with the loan he got," begins the tale, while the text is more elaborate, fleshing out the story. Fernandes's marvelous, oversized paintings are composed with elements of the past, present, and future all rolled together, conveying multiple pieces of information from the paragraph rather than a single scene. Kojo's story never really ends, as readers learn in an afterword. The man on whom the story is based now provides microloans to other Ghanaians, helping improve their lives and also, by extension, his entire country.

Iraq

Rumsford, James. *Silent Music: A Story of Baghdad.* 978-1-59643-276-5. New York: Roaring Brook, 2008. Age 7 and up.

Writing in the voice of a young Iraqi boy who loves soccer, loud music, dancing, and calligraphy, Rumsford draws a parallel between Ali's life in 2003 during wartime and the life of a famous thirteenth-century calligrapher who also wrote as Baghdad was under attack. Ali's explanation of the beauty and value of Arabic script is a testament to "the power of literacy as a creative force in the midst of war, then, as a metaphor, [a] reflection on the difficulty of practicing peace," as noted by the committee that selected *Silent Music* as a Jane Addams Honor Book.

Israel

Bergman, Tamar. *Where Is?* Illustrated by Rutu Modan. Translated by Noah Stollman. 978-0-618-09539-1. Boston: Houghton Mifflin, 2002. Ages 4–8.

After Mommy drops Noni off at his grandparents (all portrayed as cats), he is still thinking about her, wondering if she is working, exercising, buying flowers, or drinking lemonade with Uncle Yirmi. When she returns, it's her turn to wonder where Noni is as he hides in place after place. Readers will love being able to spot him when Mommy can't. Modan's simple illustrations—line drawings filled in with flat colors or patterns—reveal that Mommy is a doctor and Daddy plays the string bass. Modan won the Best Illustrated Children's Book Award from the Israel Museum in Jerusalem for this book.

Harel, Nina. *The Key to My Heart.* Illustrated by Yossi Abulafia. 978-1-929132-40-9. La Jolla, CA: Kane Miller, 2003. Ages 4–7.

Jonathan's dad picks him up from school on foot, they play a bit of soccer in the school yard, and at the door of their apartment they discover that Dad's keys are missing. They retrace his steps before arriving at the school: the post office, the barber, the pizza parlor, the news kiosk. No keys, but a good chance for Jonathan to get a slice of pizza, a haircut, and his hands stamped. This time when they arrive home, Mom is there with the keys that the teacher has found. Abulafia's illustrations are rife with details of city life and small narratives. We see a police officer who has just ticketed a parked car containing an oblivious kissing couple; cats everywhere, including one chasing a mouse and catching it a few pages later; people making a variety of fashion statements; signage in Hebrew. Abulafia's pictures will look familiar, as he is also the illustrator of Barbara Ann Porte's Harry books.

Tepper, Yona. *Passing By.* Illustrated by Gil-Ly Alon Curiel. Translated by Deborah Guthman. Tulsa, OK: Kane Miller, 2010. Ages 2–4.

Yael, a toddler, stands on her balcony looking between the bars of the railing at the activity on her street. Second-story views of the street alternate with close-ups of the passersby, which include a dog and a cat, a red car and a bicyclist, a tractor, a bird, and, finally, Daddy, each signaled by a recognizable sound. Signage—posters, store names, newspaper scraps—is all in Hebrew script, which young lapsitters who are beginning to learn the alphabet may wonder at, providing a good entrée for conversation. In style and approach, this book has much in common with Kevin Henkes's *A Good Day* (Greenwillow, 2007).

Kenya

Conway, David. *Lila and the Secret of Rain.* Illustrated by Jude Daly. 978-1-84507-407-4. London: Frances Lincoln, 2008. Distributed by Publishers Group West. Ages 4–7.

Conway's tale with its folkloric feel emphasizes the importance of rain for the Maasai people of rural Kenya. In the midst of a long drought, the burning sun has dried up everything, including the well, and is threatening the welfare of Lila's village. One evening Lila's grandfather recounts a story about the secret of rain: "You must climb the highest mountain and tell the sky the saddest thing you know." The next day Lila follows that advice, but it is only when she begins crying about the end of life in her village that the skies open up and weep along with her. Daly's folk-art, full-page spreads are sparely composed, dominated by an enormous gold sun shining down on the already parched landscape until the very moment that the thunderstorm appears.

Cunnane, Kelly. *Chirchir Is Singing.* Illustrated by Jude Daly. 978-0-375-86198-7. New York: Schwartz and Wade, 2011. Ages 4–7.

Chirchir wants to help, but she is shuttled from one family member to another, each saying, "This work is not for you." She is concentrating more on making up wonderful songs than on her own work, however; she drops the bucket down the well, builds the fire too high, sprays her sister with mud, and spills the sack of potatoes down the hill. But then she hears her baby brother crying, finds her older brother asleep, and takes over his job. For the rest of the day, she sings to the baby about all the activities his family members are engaged in. Cunnane's poetic text includes Swahili and Kalenjin words that are defined in a glossary as well as an endnote that places the story in contemporary rural Kenya. Daly's uncluttered illustrations show the family living in a traditional compound lacking plumbing and electricity yet in touch with the world through their transistor radio.

Doner, Kim. *On a Road in Africa.* 978-1-58246-230-1. Berkeley, CA: Tricycle Press, 2008. Age 5 and up.

"Where you gonna go, Mama O, Mama O?" Rhymed verse takes readers on the road collecting various items from individuals, stores, open-air markets, and schools, but the destination as well as Mama O's identity is revealed only when she arrives at the Nairobi Animal Orphanage; then we find out that she is a longtime volunteer at the orphanage (hence the O) and has brought food for the animals. The Land Rover is always at the center of the action, although its driver is never fully seen. Doner uses a variety of perspectives for dramatic effect: we see the vehicle from above, from alongside (where we catch reflections in the side mirror), and from within (as if we are in the passenger seat). How many children will notice that the driver's seat is on the right and that the car is in the left lane? The trip takes travelers on busy roads past bus stops, into the midst of a caravan of safari buses, past jungle habitats. An afterword by the author describes the real Mama O, Chryssee Perry Martin, who then offers her own afterword describing the work of the animal orphanage, including photos of volunteers and rescued animals. Endpapers contain glossaries, Swahili-English in the front and English-Swahili in the back.

Nivola, Claire. *Planting the Trees of Kenya: The Story of Wangari Maathai.* 978-0-374-39918-4. New York: Farrar, Straus, Giroux, 2008. Age 5 and up.

Wangari Maathai realized that those who are part of the problem can also be part of the solution. When she returned home to Kenya from attending college abroad, she saw the damage her fellow villagers were inflicting on the very land they needed for survival. Armed with a biology degree, she showed them how to collect seeds, nurse them, and plant trees to replace those cut down for firewood, and how to grow their own food, as they had before the big farms moved in and replaced the small family farms. Nivola's two spreads comparing the landscape of Maathai's childhood with that two decades later provide a visual explanation of the changes. Although the text is long for a picture book, it is also simply told, and the detailed colorful illustrations offer their own information about how to live sustainably.

Williams, Karen Lynn. *Beatrice's Dream: A Story of Kibera Slum.* Photographs by Wendy Stone. 978-1-84780-019-0. London: Frances Lincoln, 2011. Age 9 and up. Distributed by Publishers Group West.

Thirteen-year-old Beatrice's dream is to become a nurse so she can help people, and her love of learning will aid in making that dream a reality. Her father died in a car accident and her mother of tuberculosis, and she now lives with her older brother and helps with the cooking and housework after school. On weekends she helps in his shop at the market. Through Beatrice's story and the photographs that accompany it, the reader learns about everyday life in the very poorest part of Kenya's capital city, Nairobi, which stretches as far as the eye can see.

Malawi

Williams, Karen Lynn. *Galimoto.* Illustrated by Catherine Stock. 978-0-688-10991-2. New York: HarperCollins, 1991. Age 4 and up.

Although his older brother doubts his ability, young Kondi makes a toy car—*galimoto*—out of scraps of wire that he scavenges from shopkeepers and junkyards around his village. A note on the copyright page explains that *galimoto* means "car" in Chichewa, the common language of Malawi. Author Williams lived in Malawi as a Peace Corps volunteer; illustrator Stock spent part of her childhood in South Africa and spent time in Malawi while researching this book. Although the book is over twenty years old, the way of life it reflects remains true in rural regions of the country. This book is read aloud in classrooms to prompt discussions of recycling, materialism, creativity, and persistence; art teachers use it to introduce a lesson in building push toys or sculptures out of pipe cleaners.

Mali

Bynum, Eboni, and Roland Jackson. *Jamari's Drum.* Illustrated by Baba Wague Diakité. 978-0-88899-531-5. Toronto: Groundwood, 2004. Ages 5–10.

As a young boy, Jamari liked to sit at the feet of Baba Mdogo, the village drummer, who explained to him that playing *Kubwa Chapa*, the drum, protected the village from mighty Chafa, the volcano. As time goes on, the elders of the village die and Jamari grows into a young man. Baba Mdogo, the last of the elders, gives Jamari the drum and tells him he must play it every day. At first he does, but then as he marries and becomes busy providing for his family, he forgets. When the mountain erupts and lava begins flowing toward the village, Jamari rushes to find *Kubwa Chapa* and begins beating out the familiar rhythm, *bede bada boom kabede*, as the villagers around him run for safety. The sky clears, the village is saved, and Jamari never again forgets to beat the drum. Diakité's illustrations, prepared on ceramic tiles, offer a portrait of village life.

Diakité, Penda. *I Lost My Tooth in Africa.* Illustrated by Baba Wague Diakité. 978-0-439-66226-0. New York: Scholastic, 2006. Ages 4–8.

The author, daughter of the Mali-born illustrator, narrates this story in the voice of her younger sister, Amina, who really did lose a tooth in Africa. Each summer the family travels from their home in Oregon to Diakité's family compound in Bamako, Mali, and Amina has been told that if she puts her tooth under a gourd, the African tooth fairy will bring her a chicken. She gets not one but two chickens—a rooster and a hen, who is soon laying eggs. By the end of the family's visit, Amina has a brood of chickens. Woven throughout this story line are scenes of day-to-day life in the family compound: evenings spent sitting outside telling stories; Amina's morning visit to her N'na (grandmother) to receive her daily blessing; meal preparation as a communal event. The ceramic-tile illustrations, presented as scenes framed by object-filled borders, show the lush foliage of fruit-bearing trees and the presence of animals inside and outside the compound, from turtles and geckos to cattle and goats. Spot art includes details such as Amina sleeping under a mosquito net and a luggage tag written in French, one of Mali's official languages. Baba Wague Diakité has also retold and illustrated several tales from Mali, including *The Magic Gourd* (2003) and *The Hatseller and the Monkeys* (1999).

Skinner, Ryan. *Sidikiba's Kora Lesson.* 978-1-59298-242-4. Edina, MN: Beaver's Pond Press, 2008. Age 7 and up.

Ten-year-old Sidikiba was born into a family of *kora* players. Both his father and his grandfather play this stringed harp, and the time has come for him to learn to play it too. He must first bring his grandfather a ritual gift of kola nuts and receive his blessing; then his grandfather plays for him an initiation song that was composed by a long-ago ancestor. Sidikiba's early attempts at playing will feel familiar to anyone who has ever tried to learn an instrument—at first the sounds are nothing like those of his father, grandfather, and uncle. But as he practices, Sidikiba becomes more adept. Becoming a *kora* player involves both practice and traditional rituals, and finally Sidikiba is able to play the same initiation song that his grandfather first played for him, proving that he is truly a *kora* player. Skinner's text and realistic illustrations offer many details of everyday life in this West African household, and best of all, the book includes an audio CD of *kora* music played by the real Sidikiba, Sidiki Diabaté.

Morocco

Alalou, Elizabeth, and Ali Alalou. *The Butter Man.* Illustrated by Julie Klear Essakalli. 978-0-58089-127-1. Watertown, MA: Charlesbridge, 2008. Ages 5–8.

This book addresses what it really means to be starving by telling a story within a story. An American child complains to her Moroccan-born father that she is "starving," which prompts him to tell her about his childhood in the Moroccan mountains when the crops failed and his father had to leave home to look for work. Young Ali was never full and longed for a smidgen of butter to put on his bread, so his mother suggested he go outside and wait for the butter man to ask for just a little bit. Day after day as he waited he learned to make the ever-smaller piece of bread last longer in case the butter man, whose itinerary was unpredictable, should pass by. He never arrived, but Ali's father, having found work across the mountains, did return bearing flour, vegetables, and meat. An illustration pictures their celebratory meal of couscous with meat and vegetables, which is the exact same meal the grown-up Ali has prepared for his wife and daughter. Textile designer Essakalli uses a palette of earth tones in her paintings to convey the hot, dry climate of the Moroccan hills during drought, and her folk-art style shows just enough detail for readers to imagine the rest.

Ichikawa, Satomi. *My Father's Shop.* 978-1-929132-99-7. Kane Miller, 2006. Ages 4–9.

Young Mustafa helps in his father's carpet shop in a bustling market frequented by tourists. His father wants him to learn some foreign phrases so he can help solicit customers, but Mustafa is more interested in playing with the small rug with a hole in it that his father has let him have. When he puts it on his head, he resembles a rooster so much that a live rooster in the market begins to follow him around. Mustafa crows to the rooster in Moroccan ("Kho-kho-hou-hoûûû!") The pair attracts a French family, followed by Spanish, English, and Japanese tourists, all groups demonstrating how roosters crow in their languages. Mustafa is so excited that he rushes home to tell his father that he can speak rooster in five languages, not realizing that the crowd of tourists has followed him right into his father's shop. The portrayal of each group of tourists rests on gentle stereotypes not far from the truth.

Nigeria

Atinuke. *Anna Hibiscus*. Illustrated by Lauren Tobia. 978-1935279730
Tulsa, OK: Kane Miller, 2010. Ages 6–9.

Anna Hibiscus lives in Africa in an old white house with an African father,
a Canadian mother, and a raft of extended family, including grandparents,
aunties, uncles, and cousins. This early chapter book contains four stories
that impart her engaging personality as well as cultural aspects of her middle-class life. How the members of the extended family are organized to
take care of each other bears out the adage "It takes a village"; when Anna
unknowingly takes business away from the children selling oranges near
the gate, her grandfather shows great wisdom in devising a way to both
make up for the orange sellers' losses and help Anna understand a bit more
about economic inequity. Atinuke's skilled use of language makes these stories especially wonderful to read aloud. *Anna Hibiscus* has several sequels.

Atinuke. *No. 1 Car Spotter*. Illustrated by Warwick Johnson Cadwell. 978-
1-61067-051-7 (ppb). Tulsa, OK: Kane Miller, 2011. Ages 7–11.

Building on the success of her Anna Hibiscus series, Atinuke has created
a second series, this time featuring the resourceful, inventive Oluwalase
Babatunde Benson, self-appointed No. 1 Car Spotter. Unlike Anna, who
lives in a city, Oluwalase lives in a rural village near the main road where
the occasional car rushes past. His farming village has neither electricity
nor running water and offers little in the way of income, so most of the men
work far away to send money home to wives, parents, and children. The epi-
sodic plot structure is built around everyday situations that showcase village
life, including Oluwalase's ingenious conversion of the abandoned Toyota
Corolla into a wagon, dubbed the Cow-rolla, to replace the broken-down
one used for carting vegetables to market. Oluwalase's voice as narrator is
lively, descriptive, and humorous, and the book's black-and-white spot illustrations are just right for this early chapter book and its sequels.

Onyefulu, Ifeoma. *Ikenna Goes to Nigeria*. 978-1-84507-585-9. London:
Frances Lincoln, 2007. Age 6 and up. Distributed by Publishers Group West.

Author-photographer Onyefulu documents her son's visit to Nigeria to visit
his grandparents and numerous aunts, uncles, and cousins. Not all live in

the same town anymore, and so Ikenna's visit includes large cities, including Nigeria's capital, Abuja, and smaller towns, all with something special to offer. As this is an import, independent readers may notice British spellings and usage throughout, such as *kilometres*. Back matter includes a glossary, a recipe for a rice dish, and an index, and both front and back endpapers are covered with photos of the trip. Also by Onyefulu, available from the same publisher, is *Here Comes Our Bride!* which relates the customs surrounding a traditional Nigerian wedding in Onyefulu's home city.

Saint-lot, Katia Novet. *Amadi's Snowman*. Illustrated by Dimitrea Takunbo. 978-0-88448-298-7. Gardiner, ME: Tilbury House, 2008. Ages 4–7.

Despite his mother's efforts to the contrary, young Amadi thinks he doesn't need to learn to read; as an Igbo man, he will be a trader. But then he chances upon a slightly older boy at the market reading a book about children making a snowman. What is a snowman? What is snow? Amadi discovers that reading can open whole new worlds, making this book perfectly pitched for the child who is just learning to read. Takunbo's beautifully composed paintings show everyday activities in Amadi's village and do much to convey meaning through the gestures, body language, and facial expressions of the characters.

Somalia

Moriarty, Kathleen, reteller. *Wiil Waal*. Illustrated by Amin Amir. Somali translation by Jamal Adam. 978-1-931016-17-9 (ppb). St. Paul, MN: Minnesota Humanities Center, 2007. Age 6 and up.

In this traditional Somali folktale with bilingual text, the nickname given to the sultan is Wiil Waal, which indicates that he is both brave and clever. Hoping to find someone who is his match, he calls together the men of the area and poses a riddle: each is to bring him the most important part of a sheep. While the others bring legs, shoulders, or organs, one man brings a gullet, the part of the sheep that people throw away. When asked why, he can only say that his daughter told him to. Wiil Waal questions the daughter, who explains that the gullet delivers food to the stomach and is the symbol of either greed or generosity; it reminds those who have much to share with those who have little so they will be united rather than divided. This book

Illustrating South Africa

Niki and Jude Daly

Niki (Nicholas) Daly was born and educated in Cape Town, South Africa. At the age of 24, he moved to London intending to work as a singer and songwriter but became involved in the world of children's books instead. Judith (Jude) Daly was born in London but grew up in South Africa. They married in 1973 in London, and the family moved to Cape Town in 1980 when the movement against apartheid was gaining ground. As Niki Daly told one interviewer, "Originally we returned to Cape Town with our son Joe when he was a baby because we wanted to surround him with my large, unruly family. However, during the process of staying and seeing the changes taking place in the country, I felt that, as a South African, I didn't want to miss the experience of transformation" (*Something about the Author*, "Niki Daly (1946–)," 28).

During that period, Niki Daly strove to create books that included all South Africans and would enable white readers to see black South Africans from a new and more personal perspective. He also established a publishing imprint, Songololo Books, dedicated to publishing books by other writers and artists that bridged the divide between black and white. *Charlie's House,* written by Reviva Schermbrucker and illustrated by Niki Daly, was published by Songololo in 1989. Set in Guguletu, a township near Cape Town, it features Charlie Mogotsi, who lives with his mother and granny in a one-room tin shack and imagines a better life for his family. For the children in families who employed people like Charlie's mother, this book may have been the first inkling that their household worker not only had children, but that those children were very much like them on the inside. *Somewhere in*

Africa, cowritten by Niki Daly with Ingrid Mennen and illustrated by Nicolaas Maritz, challenged Western stereotypes of Africa by showing Ashraf, who "lives in a big city at the very tip of the great continent of Africa," learning about Africa's wild animals the same way most American students would— through a book from the library.

Jude Daly's debut as illustrator came at Songololo Books with *The Dove,* written by Diane Stewart. Since then, she has illustrated texts set in a range of countries and works with both South African and British publishers. Her paintings are most often described by reviewers as delicate and lush, and her style is distinctive enough to be recognizable even as it suggests elements of a particular culture or setting, as with David Conway's *Lila and the Secret of Rain,* a story set among the Masaai (see Kenya, p. 64–65). Both Niki and Jude Daly work directly with US publishers and write and illustrate all kinds of books, not just those set in their homeland. The selections annotated here are set in South Africa. Several of these books came out in hardcover from American publishers in the 1980s and 1990s, but rights have reverted and they are now available from the British publisher Frances Lincoln via the American distributor Publishers Group West.

Daly, Niki. *Not So Fast, Songololo.* 978-0-71121-765-2 (ppb). London: Frances Lincoln, 2007. Age 4 and up.

Malusi accompanies Gogo, his grandmother, on the bus into the city to do her shopping. When she has bought all the items on her list, she still has enough money to buy Malusi a pair of new shoes that he has admired in the store window, red *tackies* (sneakers) to replace the worn hand-me-downs that he has been wearing. The warmth between granny and son is evident in both the dialog and the realistic watercolor illustrations. Published in South Africa in 1985, the illustrations subtly picture an apartheid nation where only whites drive vehicles and blacks ride buses.

Daly, Niki. *Happy Birthday, Jamela!* 978-1-84507-422-7 (ppb). London: Frances Lincoln, 2007. Age 4 and up.

Jamela is turning 7 and having a birthday party. Gogo and Mama take her shopping for a party dress and then decide she needs new shoes too. Jamela wants the princess shoes, but Mama buys the practical black shoes Jamela can wear to school. At home, Jamela decorates them with sequins and beads and proudly shows her mother, who is not pleased. Sitting outside on the curb feeling bad, Jamela looks up when a stylish woman from the market gushes over her shoes and suggests they make more like them. They do, the shoes are a big hit, and they divide the profits, with Jamela repaying her mother for her ruined shoes. At her birthday party, Jamela receives both a new pair of school shoes *and* princess shoes. Daly's loose, colorful watercolor illustrations capture the vitality of everyday life in

An illustration from *Happy Birthday, Jamela!* by Niki Daly

Jamela's neighborhood. Readers who know previous Jamela books will recognize Christmas, the chicken from *What's Cooking, Jamela?* (2001). Other books in the series include *Jamela's Dress* (1999), *Where's Jamela?* (2004), and *A Song for Jamela* (2009).

Stewart, Dianne. *The Dove.* Illustrated by Jude Daly. 978-1-84507-022-9 (ppb). London: Frances Lincoln, 2005. Age 4 and up.

When rain continues to fall during planting season, Grandmother Maloko realizes that their crops will be late, and so she spends the rainy days making beaded jewelry to sell, hoping to earn enough money to tide herself and granddaughter Lindi over. When they get to town to sell her work, however, Grandmother and Lindi find a surplus of beaded work and no buyers. Lindi, inspired by the bird that lit in their yard after the rain, convinces her grandmother to make a beaded dove. Taken with its originality, the store owner asks for more, proving Lindi's belief that "the dove was special for us." Daly's meticulous folk-art illustrations contain tantalizing details, such as the picture of Mama that hangs on the wall.

When Thulani sold the sheep and proudly brought
home a cow, Dora was delighted.
"Oh, Thulani! It will be good to have milk again."

An illustration by Jude Daly from *A Gift of the Sun* by Dianne Stewart

Stewart, Dianne. *A Gift of the Sun.* Illustrated by Jude Daly. 978-184507-787-7 (ppb). London: Frances Lincoln, 2007. Age 4 and up.

This original noodlehead tale set in rural South Africa has the structure and feel of a folktale, but Daly's illustrations, with their electric wires and TV antennas, place it firmly in the modern era. Thulani and Dora split the chores around their small farm; that is, Thulani naps in the sun all day and milks the cow at dusk, while Dora does everything else. Sick of milking, Thulani takes the cow to market and trades it for a goat, which eats all the seeds, so he sells the goat and buys a sheep, and so on, until finally he comes home with a bag of seeds that turn out to be sunflowers, no good for eating. Can't he do anything right? But wait—the hens love the sunflower seeds and start laying extra eggs, the eggs are sold for a sheep, who has two lambs, the ewe is sold for a cow, and soon Thulani and Dora have sheep, a cow and a calf, hens, and many other animals on their farm, making Thulani so busy that milking the cow is a welcome break. So much information about their home, the landscape, and local life is told through Daly's sophisticated folk-art pictures.

is part of the Somali Bilingual Book Project, which also includes *The Lion's Share* retold by Said Salah Ahmed, *The Trials of Igal Shidad* retold by Kelly Dupre, and *Dhegheer: A Scary Somali Folktale* retold by Marian A. Hassan.

South Africa

Daly, Niki. *The Herd Boy*. 978-0-8028-5417-9. Grand Rapids, MI: Eerdmans, 2012. Ages 7–10.

Up with the sun, Malusi breakfasts and takes his grandfather's sheep and goats out to graze. "It's a big job for a small boy," and on this particular day it includes fending off a baboon that has attacked one of the lambs. Fortunately, Lungisa, also a herd boy, and his dog hear Malusi's shout and come running, and dog Koko's fierce growl discourages the baboon. But herding is not all work, and often Malusi has the time to watch nature in action—in this case termites and dung beetles—and to play soccer and stick-fight with Lungisa. On their way home, they meet a car with a distinguished-looking passenger who rolls down the window and greets them in their language. Seeing Malusi carrying the wounded lamb, the old man comments that "a boy who looks after his herd will make a very fine leader." Some children may recognize the face of Nelson Mandela, South Africa's first president, who indeed came from the same part of South Africa and once wore the trademark red blanket of the herd boy. Daly's illustrations are lush with color and texture and spill off the page, inviting readers to be part of the arid landscape that Malusi's family and others call home.

Javaherbin, Mina. *Goal!* Illustrated by A. G. Ford. 978-0-7636-4571-7. Cambridge, MA: Candlewick, 2010. Age 5 and up.

Soccer, or football as it is known in South Africa, is made even better with a federation-size soccer ball, which Ajani has earned for being the best reader in school. A pickup game with his neighborhood friends, however, means they must always be on guard for the arrival of older boys who push them around. This time the bullies catch the players by surprise, and Ajani acts quickly to hide his ball; when the bullies make off with the old plastic ball, the younger boys resume their game. The setting is a township, but the elements of the story—boys dreaming of being in the World Cup and older boys bullying younger ones—can and do happen everywhere. Ford's realistic paintings place the reader at eye level to create tension and experience the action.

Tanzania

Kilaka, John. *Fresh Fish.* 0-88899-656-X. Toronto: Groundwood, 2005.

Animals play the role of humans in this original story set in a Tanzanian village. Sokwe Chimpanzee has a boatful of fish to take to market and generously gives one to Dog when he offers to help carry "that nice big fat one." But Dog is not satisfied, and next day at the market he runs off with a basket of the fish. Meanwhile Lion, who has tried to stop him, has broken his leg tripping on Mrs. Hippopotomus's basket of oranges. When Dog is eventually caught, his punishment is that he and his family must plant double the number of trees on Tree Planting Day. The importance of working together is evidenced in multiple ways, and touches of sly humor abound in both text and illustrations. Kilaka's illustrations recall *tingatinga* paintings in their emphasis on animals, full-surface coverage, and prolific patterning, yet Kilaka's animals are dressed anthropomorphically and imbued with human expressions. Also available by this author-artist are *True Friends* (Groundwood, 2006) and *The Amazing Tree* (North South, 2009).

Mollel, Tololwa M. *My Rows and Piles of Coins.* Illustrated by E. B. Lewis. 978-0-395-75186-1. New York: Clarion, 1999. Ages 5–8.

Every Saturday, Saruni saves the coins he gets for helping his mother carry goods to the market. He has been practicing carrying big loads on his father's bicycle and is dreaming of buying his own bike to help transport the heavy loads they take to market. He gazes longingly at bikes for sale, but they are priced far out of his reach. Then his father comes home with a motorbike and sells his bicycle to Saruni for exactly the amount Saruni has saved but returns the money to Saruni. Readers may be surprised that instead of using the money to buy something for himself, he decides to save up for a cart for his bicycle so that they can carry even more to market. Set in the Tanzania of Mollel's childhood, this story portrays a typical rural family, perhaps better off than many since they can afford both a motorbike and a bicycle.

Turkey

Weulersse, Odile. *Nasreddine*. Illustrated by Rébecca Dautremer. 978-0-8028-5416-2. Grand Rapids, MI: Eerdmans, 2013. Ages 4–8.

One day, Nasreddine's father, Mustafa, asks him to bring the donkey and accompany him to the market that week. Mustafa sits atop the donkey with the load of dates, while Nasreddine walks behind. When they get to the city, they overhear a group of men commenting about the lazy man who lets his son walk in the mud. Mustafa responds calmly to the men that their words "are hurting my ears." Nasreddine's reaction is embarrassment. The following week he pleads a twisted ankle so that he rides with the market goods and his father walks, but they encounter a new set of critics. Each weekly trip to the market is a variation on this theme, until Nasreddine finally proposes that they carry the donkey *and* the goods. This is the point at which Mustafa turns Nasreddine's foolishness into a lesson: one must not let the fear of what others think get in the way of common sense. With its repetitive structure, this noodlehead tale lends itself well to reading aloud. The full-spread illustrations are distinctive with their saturated colors, varied perspectives, and elements of Turkish culture. An endnote tells readers that Nasreddine is a familiar character in stories told throughout the Middle East.

Uganda

McBrier, Page. *Beatrice's Goat*. Illustrated by Lori Lohstoeter. 978-0-689-82460-9. New York: Atheneum, 2001. Ages 5–8.

When Beatrice is 9, her family receives a goat through the Heifer International Project. That goat produces milk to provide nutrition for Beatrice and her siblings, and the family is also able to sell the extra milk. The goat has twins, which increases the family's good fortune. Little by little, Beatrice's mother, who was eking out a living by selling cassava flour in the market, is able to save enough money to enroll Beatrice in the local school. The book ends there, but Beatrice's true story continues. She won a scholarship to high school in Kampala, and then scholarships to study in the United States. She earned a master's degree in Public Service from the University of Arkansas and now works for an organization that is finding ways to help African communities lift themselves out of poverty and hunger.

Asia

Why are relatively few children's books from Asian countries published in the United States? Asia encompasses countries that differ vastly in landmass, population, and economic resources as well as in aspects such as political stability and literacy levels. Some countries—such as India and Indonesia, for example—were once colonies of European nations, a situation that significantly influenced the kind of children's literature that was available in their countries during the past century. Other countries, such as China and Myanmar, have political systems in place that have discouraged relationships with the West and preclude much cultural exchange. Still others, such as Bangladesh, have been subject to devastating natural disasters that render their people in constant survival mode, with neither the resources nor the opportunities to consume and produce children's books. As a result of these and other situations, the children's books that come to the United States from Asian countries are few and far between, with most books coming from only a few nations.

Japan is the largest producer of children's trade books in Asia and one of the largest publishing markets in the world. Japan has everything needed for a robust children's book industry: well-funded schools and public libraries, bookstores, a 99 percent literacy rate, and a cultural emphasis on childhood education. Although many of the classic children's books from North America and Europe are familiar to Japanese children, the opposite is not true. Aside from the Hello Kitty franchise, probably the most recognizable name in Japanese children's books is Mitsumasa Anno, the 1984 Hans Christian Andersen winner, with *Everybody Poops* author Taro Gomi a close second. By and large, Japanese picture books have a sensibility that resonates with Americans: a focus on childhood as a time of innocence and illustrations that convey a feeling of comfort and security. Japan developed a strong antiwar stance after World War II, and many of the acquisitions from Japan pursue peace education by reflecting the horrors of war. Recent years have seen an influx of Japanese books in the form of Manga, a hugely popular genre in Japan that has become an international sensation.

After Japan, India is likely to be the source of most Asian children's books taken for US publication. "Although children's literature as a genre is relatively new in the Indian subcontinent," notes Meena Khorana, "the concept of entertaining and instructing children through literature, both oral and written, is ancient."[1] The largest Asian country in both population and size, India has sixteen major languages and thousands of dialects, which makes it economically difficult to publish books in local languages, although Tara Books and Tulika Publishers are both succeeding in publishing indigenous voices. Most of the children's books that come to us from India, however, were first published in English, an official language that is the legacy of colonization.

It is rare to find children's books from other Asian countries republished in the US in English; in the past it was because most children's books were published as part of an educational curriculum. These days, however, South Korea, China, Taiwan, and their neighbors have all started to publish high-quality picture books, but they usually buy and sell rights regionally instead of trading with Europe or the US.[2] Sometimes the artistic styles and book design are simply not polished enough to compete on the American market, but often the reason is that these books have been published as part of a country's educational curriculum and are not suited to American children. Therefore much of the cultural information available to young children about these other countries comes from books written by European, North American, or Australian writers who have lived in those countries or have written the book from research. Those writers are often journalists or aid workers who have been posted to Asian countries and who hope to bridge cultural divides with their stories. The other main source of authentic Asian literature is from Asian emigrants who want to share their culture or experience with their new compatriots. This was the case with two of six books annotated in the section about China—one by Chen Jiang Hong, an émigré to France, and another by Ed Young, an émigré to the United States. Two others in that section originated in France and were written by French authors, and the remaining two books have Chinese authors and illustrators and originated in China.

Notes

1. Khorana, *Indian Subcontinent in Literature for Children and Young Adults*, xi.
2. Tan, "Children's Books: Publishing in Asia," 35

China

Chen, Jiang Hong . *Little Eagle.* 978-1-59270-071-4. Translated by Claudia Zoe Bedrick. New York: Enchanted Lion, 2007. Age 7 and up.

Set in the fifteenth century when the Great Wall was being built, this book by a Chinese emigré to France tells of an orphan boy raised by a master of eagle boxing, which is a form of kung fu. The training is long and rigorous, and many years pass before the orphan, Little Eagle, is proficient. In a fight with the tyrannical General Zhao, who wants to steal the master's book of secrets, the master is killed, but his secrets live on in Little Eagle. Chen's ink-and-watercolor illustrations often foreground the natural world—the master's eagle, the rocky landscape. Readers will be impressed with Little Eagle's training regimen: he does exercises to hone his powers of observation and listening, and in one spread Little Eagle is shown performing a series of demanding physical tasks.

Ji, Zhaohua, and Cui Xu. *No! That's Wrong!* 978-1-933605-66-1. La Jolla, CA: Kane Miller, 2008. Ages 3–7. Out of print, but available from resellers and libraries.

Could it be that underwear is just as funny to Chinese children as it is to American ones? It seems so, judging from this tale of what happens when a red pair of ladies' panties is blown off a clothesline and picked up by a rabbit, who thinks he has found a hat. Familiar animal characters try the panties on their heads with humorous results. The text reads on two levels: within the illustration, the animal characters discuss whether the "hat" fits (using opposites such as small/large, along with several superlative adjectives), while outside the illustration's border, an unseen narrator continually insists, "No, that's wrong. It's not a hat." Eventually, the rabbit tries the panties out on the other end but finds them ill suited to his tail, whereupon his friends comment, "That's silly" and "It's a hat." Cultural details in the illustrations suggest a Chinese setting, and playful front and back endpapers combine to create a story of their own.

LeBlanc, André. *The Red Piano.* Illustrated by Barroux. 978-0-9806070-1-7. Victoria, Australia: Wilkins Farago, 2009. Age 6 and up. Distributed by Independent Publishers Group.

During China's Cultural Revolution, all who were part of China's wealthy or educated classes—including artists, writers, and musicians—were forced into work camps to be reeducated. The young piano prodigy in this story was a member of an artistic family whose seven members were each sent to a different camp. Having played concerts on Beijing radio, she is now relegated to planting rice and picking vegetables from dawn to dusk, but at night, when everyone is asleep, she performs a criminal act: she plays the piano. Eventually she is caught and the piano destroyed, and she is further punished by being the last to be freed when the Cultural Revolution ends. Barroux's large, bold illustrations painted in brown with red accents reflect the bleakness of life in this outpost near the Mongolian border. LeBlanc was inspired by the experience of concert pianist Zhu Xiao Mei, who lives in France, where the book originated.

Louis, Catherine. *My Little Book of Chinese Words.* Calligraphy by Shi Bo. Translated by MaryChris Bradley. 978-0735821743 (ppb). New York: NorthSouth, 2008. Age 6 and up.

Louis is a French illustrator who became intrigued with kanji, the characters used in China and Japan to form written texts. Here she has selected over a hundred Chinese characters, presenting each opposite a picture of the word it represents. She has arranged the words to demonstrate how the characters build on one another; for instance, the characters for *woman, good,* and *child* are presented in that order, and readers can see that to write *good* one uses the characters for *woman* and *child* next to one another. Louis's color-saturated illustrations combine silk screen and collage in simple designs with appeal for all ages.

Young, Ed, and Libby Koponen. *The House Baba Built: An Artist's Childhood in China.* Illustrated by Ed Young. 978-0-316-07628-9. Boston: Little Brown, 2011. All ages.

In 1931, the year Ed Young was born, Japan invades Manchuria, and Young's father foresees that war will spread throughout China. He moves the family to the safest part of Shanghai and builds a fortress of a house that becomes a safe zone as well the site of much pleasure for the next twenty years. Eddy and his siblings and cousins ride bikes and scooters on the concrete roof, swim in the pool, and have endless adventures in the huge labyrinthian house. Young's illustrations combine drawings, photos, collages, and detailed scaled replicas to convey both the grandeur of the house and the lives that were lived within it; abundant use of foldout pages add both a feeling of space and an element of surprise.

Yu, Li-Qiong. *A New Year's Reunion.* Illustrated by Zhu Cheng-Laing. 978-0-7636-5881-6. Somerville, MA: Candlewick, 2011. Ages 4–7.

According to the afterword, the situation narrated by this young Chinese girl is one experienced by millions of families in China. Maomao's father works so far from home that she and her mother see him only once a year, over the New Year holiday. He is home for mere days, bringing New Year's gifts and participating in the rituals of the holiday, doing necessary household maintenance, and renewing his relationship with his young daughter. The colorful paintings present scenes of city life, with its closely packed buildings and tight living quarters. Some scenes are familiar, such as the barbershop where her Papa goes to get his New Year's haircut, and others less so, for example, the canal facing their building where merchants ply their wares from boats. Together illustrations and text enumerate the many traditions of the festival, including paper decorations on the door, sticky rice balls (one containing a lucky coin), new clothes, the dragon dance, fireworks, and red money envelopes. First published in Taiwan, this informative and pleasing glimpse into Chinese culture won the Feng Zikai Chinese Children's Picture Book Award in 2009.

Cambodia

Gaillard, Jason. *Running Shoes*. 978-1-58089-176-9 (ppb). Watertown, MA: Charlesbridge, 2008. Ages 5–7.

This fictional story set in contemporary rural Cambodia sheds light on the importance of education and the practice of educating boys only. Sophy lives eight kilometers from the nearest school, but with the running shoes given to her from an annual visitor and permission from her mother, she runs the distance to school and back every day. Although she is the only girl, she wins the respect of the other students, and the following year she rewards the visitor by showing what she has learned.

Lord, Michelle. *Little Sap and Monsieur Rodin*. Illustrated by Felicia Hoshino. 978-1-58430-248-3. New York: Lee and Low, 2006. Ages 6–9.

In the early 1900s, Cambodia is invited to participate in an exhibition of overseas colonies in Paris. The king travels there with a company of dancers and musicians, including Sap, a rice farmer's daughter, who had been chosen to train as a dancer when she was 6. In the audience is the French sculptor Auguste Rodin, who is so captivated by the art form that he sketches a series of the dancers, focusing especially on Sap and two others. Through following Little Sap's training, readers learn some of the meanings behind the delicate hand gestures and poses and come to appreciate an important aspect of Cambodian culture.

Lord, Michelle. *A Song for Cambodia*. 978-1-60060-139-2. Illustrated by Shino Arihara. New York: Lee and Low, 2008. Ages 6–9.

The healing power of music drives this true story of Arn, one of eleven children in a Cambodian family torn apart during the reign of communist dictator Pol Pot. Arn is sent to a work camp where he works alongside other children in the rice fields until he is chosen to learn the *khim*, a traditional string instrument. When South Vietnam invades Cambodia, Arn escapes and eventually lands at a refugee camp in Thailand, where he is adopted by an American aid worker. Playing the *khim* and the *khloy*, a flute, helps Arn adjust to his new life, and as an adult he uses this traditional music to help others both in North America and in Cambodia.

Laos

Landowne, Youme. *Mali Under the Night Sky: A Lao Story of Home.*
978-1-933693-68-2. El Paso: Cinco Puntes, 2010. Ages 4–8.

Laos is situated between Vietnam and Thailand, with Cambodia to the south. During the Vietnam conflict, the country was a conduit for supplies for North Vietnam and consequently a frequent target for bombs. Mali spent her first five years in Laos, and her memories of that time are lovingly recreated by Youme, who uses her first name only. Her descriptive text is sprinkled with Laotian words, readily understood through context, and her pictures include speech bubbles with handwritten Laotian text. Readers see the warmth of everyday family interactions, the natural world that is young Mali's playground, and the social nature of life in her community, all of which changes when the bombing starts. Mali's family slips away one night and crosses the border into Thailand, the beginning of a long journey without a defined destination. Only the strings around her wrist, put there by friends and family members who stayed behind to show that "their hearts would always be together," give her hope by tying together her past, present, and future.

Xiong, Blia. *Nine in One, Grr! Grr!* Adapted by Cathy Spagnoli. Illustrated by Nancy Hom. 978-0-89239-110-3 (ppb). San Francisco: Children's Book Press, 1997. Ages 4–8.

This folktale comes from the Hmong people, a minority ethnic group in Laos, and is illustrated in the style of the Hmong story cloth, a distinctive narrative art form using traditional Hmong embroidery. A tiger is eager to know how many cubs she will have, so she journeys up the mountain to see the great Shao, who tells her she will have nine cubs each year. He warns her, however, that she must remember these words. All the way downhill she repeats to herself "nine in one, grr! grr!" so that she will not forget, but a clever bird, not wanting the world to become overpopulated with tigers, confuses her so that she ends up repeating "one in nine, grr! grr!" The stylized illustrations portray Hmong ethnic clothing and are filled with animals found in the Laotian countryside.

India

Ananth, Anuradha. *Rangoli: Discovering the Art of Indian Decoration.* Illustrated by Shailja Jain. 978-1-84780-179-1. London: Frances Lincoln, 2011. Ages 4–7.

A city boy visiting his grandmother's village notices all the decorations on the ground and walls—these are *rangolis*. He considers how he can create a *rangoli* when he returns to his family's city apartment, but his grandmother shows him a simple pattern that he can put outside his apartment door. First published in India by Tulika Books.

Atkins, Jeannine. *Aani and the Tree Huggers.* Illustrated by Venantius J. Pinto. 978-1-880000-24-3. New York: Lee and Low, 1995.

Aani finds refuge from her large family under her favorite tree, where she can dream in peace. When government contractors come to cut the trees for lumber, they ignore the villagers' protests that they need the trees for the fruit and nuts they provide, the roots that keep the land from mudslides, the branches that become their houses and hoes. Aani reacts by hugging her tree, and before long all the trees are being hugged by women, making it impossible for the loggers to proceed. Based on a true story that took place in the 1970s in northern India, this book immortalizes the movement known as *Chipko Andolan* that resulted in the right of local councils to determine how to thin their forests and at the same time keep them healthy.

Balachandran, Anitha. *The Dog Who Loved Red.* 978-1-935279-83-9. Tulsa, OK: Kane Miller, 2011. Out of print. Ages 4–8.

This humorous story about a naughty dog who loves to chew anything red is accompanied by illustrations that show life in a modern city neighborhood. Tanvi is always scolding Raja—he chews on her shoes, her mother's shawl, and her father's socks. She finally takes him to the park to play with his ball, but it is nowhere to be found. As he searches, Raja takes readers through the colors—the green bushes, the orange cat, the gray pigeons, the blue hose. Finally Raja spies the ball in the yard of Mr. Mehta, well-known dog hater, and takes readers through another set of colored objects as he attempts to retrieve the ball and creates chaos as he narrowly escapes. Mr. Mehta's chase of Raja is reminiscent of Mr. MacGregor's equally unsuccessful effort to catch that other naughty animal of children's books, Peter Rabbit.

Bond, Ruskin. *Cherry Tree.* Illustrated by Allan Eitzen. 978-156397-621-6. Honesdale, PA: Boyds Mills, 1991. Out of print. Subsequently reissued by Puffin in paperback. Now available as Kindle edition only.

Rakhi lives with her grandfather in the Himalayan foothills of northern India. One day when she is 6, she eats some cherries and plants one of the seeds, and the next year she notices that it has sprouted. Four years later the tree is taller than Rakhi, and a couple of years later she is able to lie under it and gaze up at the sky through cherry-laden branches. Celebrating one of nature's miracles, this quiet story portrays the loving relationship between Rakhi and her grandfather in the context of the remote and beautiful Himalayan landscape, reinforced by Eitzen's illustrations that always show the pair outdoors. Ruskin was an author finalist for the Hans Christian Andersen Award in 1998.

Claire, Elizabeth. *The Little Brown Jay.* Illustrated by Miriam Katin. 978-1-879531-23-9. Boston: Houghton Mifflin, 1994. Age 5 and up.

This pourquoi tale from India explains the origin of the bluejay's striking color and sharp voice. A beautiful princess, kind but with a sharp voice, dreamed of being noticed by the blind prince who passed her way daily. One day when she heard a brown jay singing beautifully she wished aloud that she could sound like that, and the jay volunteered to exchange voices with her. Grateful, she wrapped the bird in her blue shawl, and he took on its color. Illustrations are executed in the style of Indian painting, and additional information in the back comments both on the pourquoi tale and on life in India today. This book is part of the series Folktales from Around the World.

Heydlauff, Lisa. *Going to School in India.* Illustrated by B. M. Kamath and Nitin Upadhye. 978-1-57091-666-3. Watertown, MA: Charlesbridge, 2005. Age 7 and up.

India's diverse locales and populations are reflected in the scrapbook-style design of this look at the children of India. Some ride the school bus to school; others walk across rickety bridges or are taken on their parents' bicycles or scooters. Whether in a building in the middle of a teeming city or a one-room schoolhouse high in the mountains or a tent in the desert, children study government, science, geography, and literature. In crowded Mumbai where space is at a minimum, one school is even held in a bus; elsewhere school is taught at night for girls who must work during the day. The combination of illustrations and photographs evokes the sights, smells, and sounds of India, while the text often features the words of the children themselves.

Krishnaswami, Uma. *Monsoon.* Illustrated by Jamel Akib. 978-0-374-35015-4. New York: Farrar, Straus, Giroux, 2003. Ages 5–8.

So many Americans have never experienced the long wait for rain, the dusty, hot air, the growing tension, the worry that the rain might not come. Through recounting everyday details of a family living in a northern Indian city, Krishnaswami builds that tension so that readers feel the relief when the rains finally come. Akib's full spreads convey the crowdedness of city life, with cars, taxis, scooters, bicycles, and the occasional cow jockeying for space in the street, and people, kiosks, tea stalls, and open markets jockeying for sidewalk space. Billboards advertise films, goods, and services, while laundry blows in the wind atop a building. An afterword explains the meteorology of the monsoon and also its importance in Indian culture.

Krishnaswami, Uma. *Out of the Way! Out of the Way!* 978-1-55498-130-4. Illustrated by Uma Krishnaswamy. Toronto: Groundwood, 2012. Ages 4–8.

Over the course of seventy-plus years, a dusty path becomes a busy highway, and the small volunteer tree that a boy tends grows into a large shade tree under which he sits as an old man. The title comes from the shouts of those who use the thoroughfare: a mango seller on foot, a bullock-cart man, bicyclists—all of which eventually give way to trucks, cars, motorbikes, and buses. As the surrounding area grows correspondingly from rural village to modern city, both the tree and the old man stand as witnesses to the past. A natural pairing for this book is Donna Rawlings's *My Place*, set in Australia; thematically, both books fit into the "Rural and Urban Ecosystems" section in chapter 3.

Rao, Sandhya. *My Mother's Sari.* Illustrated by Nina Sabnani. 978-0-73582-101-9. New York: North-South, 2006. Ages 3–6.

While the sari is an article of clothing for women, here it provides fodder for imaginative children to entertain themselves: the sari can be long like a train; it can be a river, a rope, or a good hiding place. Combining photographs of lush fabrics with hand-drawn children, the illustrations show a variety of saris, some sequined, some woven with metallic thread, some with printed or woven designs. The close connection between mother and child is felt on every page through the tactile element of the cloth. A source of both play and comfort, the sari is a symbol of the mother who, although never shown in the pictures, is nonetheless very present. Front and back endpapers provide clear instructions on how to wear a sari. First published in India by Tulika Publishers.

Ravishankar, Anushka. *Elephants Never Forget!* Illustrated by Christiane Pieper. 978-0-618-99784-8. Boston: Houghton Mifflin, 2008. Ages 3–7.

Separated from its mother during a thunderstorm, a small elephant finds company in a herd of water buffalo. They take him in, and as he grows, he helps them by clearing trees, giving them showers, and keeping tigers at bay. Then comes the day that elephants appear at the watering hole where he and the water buffalo are frolicking. The elephants toot, the water buffalo bellow, and the elephant looks back and forth. In a surprise ending, he opts to stay with the water buffalo, and the meaning behind the title of the book shifts accordingly. What he has not forgotten, readers realize, are the many experiences shared with the water buffalo, who have become his true family. Ravishankar, a poet living in New Delhi, writes in the cadences of Indian English, and her rhyming verse cries to be read aloud, often emphasized by typography that swirls or shouts. The woodcut-style illustrations in black with patches of color are clean and spare, suiting the open spaces of the animals' habitat. First published in India by Tara Books.

Ravishankar, Anushka. *Tiger on a Tree.* Illustrated by Pulak Biswas. 978-0-374-37555-3. New York: Farrar, Straus, Giroux, 2004. Ages 3–7.

Biswas's striking orange-and-black illustrations are full of movement that matches the rhythmic, rhyming text in this story of a tiger running from his captors. The whimsical text begs to be read aloud, and the surprise ending will please conservationists, as once the tiger is captured, his captors vote to free him again. First published in India by Tara Books.

Ravishankar, Anushka. *To Market! To Market!* Illustrated by Emanuele Scanziani. 978-81-86211-99-1. Chennai, India: Tara Publishing, 2007. Ages 4–8. Distributed by Consortium Books.

This oversized book with the text running parallel to the spine invites the reader into a typical Indian marketplace, with stalls selling jewelry, cloth, food, live animals, flowers, and anything else one could think of. The narrator is a small girl who is accompanying her mother and has been given some loose change to spend. In the delight of reimagining herself in every stall ("Jangle, Jangle, Jangle, I'm a bangle-holding stand") the girl exits the market and only then realizes that she didn't buy a thing. Much cultural information is contained in the pictures, beginning with the front cover, where we see five boys riding on a single bicycle!

Ruddra, Anshumani. *Dorje's Stripes.* Illustrated by Gwangjo and Jung-a Park. 978-1-935279-98-3. Tulsa, OK: Kane Miller, 2011. Ages 5–9.

This fable-like story, set in a Buddhist monastery in Tibet, speaks to the plight of the Royal Bengal tiger, India's national animal. When Dorje, a Bengal tiger, arrives at the monastery, he is weak and has only a few stripes, and each time he leaves the monastery for the jungle he returns with one less stripe, until he has only a couple of short ones over his eyes. Finally Master Wu enters Dorje's dreams as the tiger is sleeping and experiences the tiger's life in the wild, as one by one Bengal tigers are being killed for their skins. Each time a tiger dies, Dorje loses a stripe. But this is a tale of hope, and Dorje regains a stripe when he encounters a female Bengal. Just as the monks protected Dorje, so too does the reader understand that only human intervention can save this wondrous species.

Shyam, Bhajju, Durga Bai, and R. S. Urveti. *The Night Life of Trees.* 978-81-86211-92-2. Chennai, India: Tara Books, 2006. All ages. Distributed by Publishers Group West.

Trees play a central role in the belief system and daily life of the Gond people. The peepul tree is worshipped by Hindus as the home of the Creator, and numerous varieties supply food, wood, and other necessities. Each page of this handmade book features a piece of Gond art silkscreened in two colors on heavy black paper opposite a piece of text that inspired it, which ranges from creation tale to legend to poetic description. As noted by *Publishers Weekly,* the book provides "an alluring glimpse into an integrative worldview that's in poignant contrast to the fragmented postmodern world" (253.21 [May 22, 2006]: 47). Each book is truly a work of art, bound by hand and numbered.

Whitaker, Zai. *Kali and the Rat Snake.* Illustrated by Srividya Natarajan. 978-1-933605-10-4. Out of print. La Jolla, CA: Kane Miller, 2006. Ages 5–8.

Kali goes to school with children from many villages, and when they introduce themselves on the first day of class, they giggle at his father's occupation as a snake catcher. As a member of the Irula tribe, Kali feels like an outsider and becomes more and more withdrawn as the months go by. Then comes the day that a rat snake appears in the classroom. Amid the shrieking and shouting of the other students and the teacher, Kali knows just how to capture the snake and becomes an instant hero. Watercolor illustrations depict a classroom of uniformed students with slates and capture the chaos from several perspectives. First published in India by Tulika Publishers.

Wolf, Gita. *The Churki-Burki Book of Rhyme.* Illustrated by Durga Bai. 978-93-80340-06-7. Chennai, India: Tara Books, 2010. Ages 3–7. Distributed by Publishers Group West.

Churki and Burki are two young girls whose love of language extends to chanting and creating rhymes about whatever is going on around them. Wolf has written a lively text based on the artist Durga Bai's recollections of growing up in a village in eastern India. Through the girls' activities,

Tara Books

This small press in India draws on folk and tribal artists to create a new tradition of children's books.

by Gita Wolf, Publisher of Tara Books

When we started publishing in 1995, there were very few picture books for children in India. Ours has been a largely oral tradition, and the notion of children's literature came from abroad. So Indian children's books tended to be derivative. To create something that was original, we looked around for Indian illustrators, and what excited us most was the potential we saw in traditional artists.

These were folk and tribal artists, from rural and remote communities, who painted according to certain traditional styles of rendering. Although there were many very different traditions, most of this art arose from common everyday sources: the decorating of homes, community spaces, or places of worship. Much of it was, and still is, painted on walls and floors. Many artists now also paint on paper and sell their work. But before we began working with them, hardly anyone had made a book. Illiterate and poor, many of them were, by definition, outside the conversation of mainstream bookmaking. And yet they had a wealth of talent, imagination, and intelligence that we found humbling.

Traditional artists, as the name suggests, work within an inherited tradition, but many of them are eager to explore new ways of taking their work forward. Tradition is something that changes constantly. How to bring these art styles into the form of a contemporary children's book without losing the original essence has been an ongoing concern with us. Whatever direction a particular project takes, there is one basic premise upon which our collaborations are based. We would like each artist to be an "author," the active creator of a book. So when we work with an artist from a particular tradition, the book is not "about" this tradition—it

Collating handmade sheets at Tara Books.

The intricate patterned illustrations on this page of Wolf's *The Churki-Burki Book of Rhyme* are by Durga Bai, an artist from the Gond community in central India. All Gond artists have their own identifying patterns; Durga Bai's can be seen on the bodies of the women.

is not a documentary. It is the physical location from which the art form speaks and tells its story.

To do this successfully, the book should communicate in the way it is intended. When it does that, the child reader actually identifies with the protagonist. If this protagonist happens to be an individual who is normally "invisible," then the book becomes transformative, and publishing turns into a truly political act. If power is all about whose voice speaks and defines reality, by giving agency to those who are not normally heard, we imply that their skills and experiences are valuable, worth preserving and passing on. The challenge here is not to set them up as exotic outsiders, in a niche. They are our equals, creating norms that are just as universal as mainstream ones.

What do such voices bring to children's literature? Exposing children to a real variety of perspectives sounds simple, but is in fact one of the hardest things to achieve, particularly now. Today, it feels like we have more choice than ever before in our history, but much of it is really homogenous—popular books are marketed worldwide, television programs are beamed across the globe, Internet content is available everywhere. All of them give us an illusion of unlimited choice, yet they all originate from very similar—and limited—sources. These sources have the power to be heard, so they are loud. Seen another way, it is the market and the media that largely decide what is distributed and what is worth taking notice of. This is also the power of the publishing mainstream.

But you could also see this as timidity, finding safety in repeating formulas that sell. There is a place for something new in this scheme of things, but it always has to be within the acceptable and the familiar. Variety is welcome, but only as long as it can be accommodated by the known. Genuine difference, on the other hand, is radical, acknowledging a multiplicity of experience that is by definition outside the normative and the habitual. This difference is a quality to be celebrated, not feared. So universality need not be a global sameness, but a recognition of common humanity that comes out of an empathy with those who are not like us.

Tara Books (www.tarabooks.com) are published in India and distributed in the US and Canada by Publishers Group West.

This page from Wolf's *Do!* is illustrated in the traditional Warli style of painting done by people belonging to a tribal community that lives in Maharashtra, in western India. Every copy of *Do!* is handmade. Illustration by Ramesh Hengadi and Shatarau Dhadpe.

readers are offered a glimpse of the culture and daily activities of village life in eastern India. Whether helping their parents collect food for dinner, scaring away the jackals who come to eat the corn, or playing with their friends, the girls' find fun everywhere. Bai's colorful patterned illustrations in the traditional Gond style portray a lifestyle where villagers work cooperatively and share in the bounty.

Wolf, Gita. *Do!* Illustrated by Ramesh Hengadi, Shantaram Dhadpe, Rasika Hengadi, and Kusum Dhadpe. 978-81-907546-1-3. Chennai, India: Tara Books, 2009. Ages 3–7. Distributed by Publishers Group West.

Each spread of this book of words contains myriad small pictograms that illustrate one or two action verbs. An attentive reader can spend hours viewing the activities of these simple figures, which after a while take on lives of their own. Illustrated in the traditional Warli style of painting, the figures are rendered in white paint on sturdy taupe-colored paper, replicating the designs and colors that Warli women have long used to decorate their homes (washing the walls with brown cow dung and special mud, and using paint made of lime and a type of chalk). Like the designs on their homes, the pictures here celebrate important events and are both narrative and descriptive. This book has been silkscreened, sewn, and bound by hand. "Making of *Do!*" a video on the Tara Books website, demonstrates this process (www.tarabooks.com/2009/10/29/making-of-do/).

Japan

Chiba, Minako. *The Somebody for Me.* 978-0-7358-2323-5. New York: North-South, 2010. Ages 2–4.

Eleven identical stuffed toys with long ears and striped legs sit in the toy shop waiting to be chosen, each wanting to be loved by someone. One by one they leave, until the last, named Sumiko, is shunted into the corner of the shop with the other toys that no one wants. Fans of Don Freeman's *Corduroy* will recognize the story line, right down to the child who falls in love with the stuffed toy, whose parent says no, and who reappears the following day to take it home. As with *Corduroy*, the satisfying ending is bound to please. While Corduroy is unique on the toy shelf but missing a button, Sumiko looks just the same as the others. Happily, both find their own "somebodies."

Gomi, Taro. *I Lost My Dad!* 978-1-929132-04-1. La Jolla, CA: Kane Miller, 2001. Ages 3–6.

A boy and his father are in a large Japanese department store when suddenly the boy loses sight of his dad. A clever system of die-cut pages creates suspense as the boy spies parts that may belong to his dad—a hat, legs and shoes, his suit from the back—only to find that each part belongs to someone or something else. A worried father and frantic son eventually spy each other going different ways on the escalator and are reunited. This story subtly promotes a father-son relationship in a culture where fathers have often been absent due to demands of the workplace.

Gomi, Taro. *Spring Is Here.* 978-0-8118-2331-9 (board book). San Francisco: Chronicle Books, 1999. Ages 0-3.

Many books take the reader through the seasons, but none so directly and simply as this one. Gomi has a knack for paring everything down to the essentials—each spread contains a single idea stated in a short sentence with a focused illustration. This book, along with *My Friends* and *Bus Stop,* was first issued in hardcover and paperback, but all three are perfectly suited to the board book format.

Kajima, Naomi. *Singing Shijimi Clams.* 978-1-933605-12-8. La Jolla, CA: Kane Miller, 2006. Ages 4–8.

Spare pen-and-ink illustrations and a deceptively simple story line follow an impoverished and unhappy old witch who lives in the city with her grumpy cat. She buys a batch of shijimi clams for supper, but when she sees them snoring contentedly, she cannot bring herself to put them in the broth. When they finally wake up and discover their plight, the clams begin crying, and the hearts of both the witch and the cat soften completely. They decide to take the clams back to their home in the sea, which turns out to be the right place for all parties involved. Shijimi is a type of clam found in Asian waters.

Maruki, Toshi. *Hiroshima No Pika.* Out of print. New York: Lothrop, 1980. Age 8 and up.

This landmark picture book recounts the moment and the aftermath of "the flash" (*pika* in Japanese), the explosion caused by the atomic bomb dropped on Hiroshima on August 6, 1945. Maruki's story, a composite of the many stories she heard in the days and weeks afterward, focuses on a family of three eating breakfast when the flash occurs. In an attempt to escape to safety, the mother carries the wounded father on her back, holding the hand of her daughter, who clutches chopsticks in her other hand. Expressionist watercolors reveal the horrors they see en route: burned and incinerated bodies everywhere, including floating down the river. Although the book is no longer in print, it is available on DVD, read in English by Susan Sarandon (First Run Features, 2005).

Nakagawa, Hirotaka. *Sumo Boy.* Illustrated by Hirotaka Nakagawa and Yoshifumi Hasegawa. 978-0-7868-3635-2. New York: Hyperion, 2006. Ages 4–8.

Sumo Boy is a superhero who fights for justice. Like some other superhero characters, he hears a cry for help and he's suddenly flying to the rescue. His moves are all directly out of the sumo wrestler's instruction manual, and the last four pages of the book illustrate many such techniques. Colorful, primitive-style paintings picturing Sumo Boy's dojo and his neighborhood impart a strong Japanese flavor. With minimal text and maximum action packed into its thirty-two pages, *Sumo Boy* may just be every young boy's fantasy—and maybe some girls' too.

Parot, Annelore. *Kimonos.* 978-1-4521-0493-5. Translated by Christopher Francescelli. San Francisco: Chronicle, 2011. Age 4 and up.

Kokeshis are traditional Japanese hand-painted wooden dolls. Annelore Parot, a French artist and textile designer, presents her characters as *kokeshi* dolls, with an emphasis on the patterns and styles of their kimonos. One by one, five Japanese *kokeshi* girls introduce themselves, each challenging readers to find certain items in the picture. For instance, Ayuka notes that in Japan all children wear school uniforms and asks the reader to find the guests in her classroom. In the classroom are signs on the wall listing days of the week in English, Japanese transliteration, and kanji; throughout the book, relevant words are introduced in these three forms. A favorite spread is the gatefold that opens out to show all the members of Yumi's family, with those on her father's side distinguished by a particular fabric pattern and those on her mother's side by another. The reader must figure out who goes with whom—no small task, as the pattern may appear on anything from a bow to a kimono. The book introduces aspects of Japanese culture and encourages children to be visually discerning, but its biggest draw is certain to be the "cute" factor—these *kokeshis* are hard to resist.

Sakai, Komako. *Mad at Mommy*. 978-0-545-21209-0. New York: Scholastic, Arthur A. Levine, 2010. Ages 3–6.

Spare drawings and first-person text capture perfectly a child's feelings of anger, whether justified or not. This particular rabbit child is feeling both neglected and powerless as he recites a litany of Mommy's faults: "You yell for no reason. . . . You always tell me to hurry up—hurry up—hurry up—but then you never hurry up yourself. . . . You're always late picking me up from school." Worst of all is that Mommy sleeps late on Saturdays (past 9:30 in the morning), perhaps the underlying reason for his other complaints, since what he really wants is her attention. Only when he takes action and leaves the apartment is the situation resolved. From the pictures, one sees that Mommy is very aware of her child's every move and, when he returns a minute later to ask if she missed him, Mommy is ready to interact: "SO much," she replies. Some American reviewers see this as a story of unconditional love, while Japanese readers are simply amused at how well the book captures the emotions of childhood.

Say, Allen. *Kamishibai Man*. 978-0-618-47954-2. Boston: Houghton Mifflin, 2005. Age 6 and up.

Kamishibai is a form of picture storytelling that became popular during the 1930s, before the advent of television spelled its demise. *Kamishibai* men strapped large picture boxes to bicycles and went from place to place selling candy and telling stories. Say's *kamishibai* man has been idle for some years but wants once more to ply his trade; when he does, he attracts scores of listeners—the adults who heard him as children. The detailed illustrations capture aspects of both rural and urban Japan, and an afterword notes that as an art form, *kamishibai* followed in the tradition of Kabuki and was a precursor to Manga and anime.

Takabayashi, Mari. *I Live in Tokyo.* 978-0-618-07702-1. Boston: Houghton Mifflin, 2001. Ages 4–8.

In just thirty-two colorful, picture-filled pages, this creative author-illustrator conveys an incredible amount of cultural information about life in Japan and her native city. The book is narrated by 7-year-old Mimiko and structured around the calendar year, beginning with January 1, yet even the half-title and title pages set the scene: readers see the first shoppers of the day greeted by department store workers; a city dense with buildings that stretch into the horizon; the famed Ginza shopping area; the flashy electronics district; and the serene Royal Palace grounds. Mount Fuji is present as the backdrop to a bullet train ride to Mimiko's grandparents' home in Kobe during August. School begins in April, not September, and Mimiko wears a yellow hat that identifies her as a second-grader. The usual holidays and traditions are all covered, but what will interest young readers most are the small details of everyday life.

Tashiro, Chisato. *Five Nice Mice.* Translated by Sayako Uchida. 978-0-698-40058-0. New York: Penguin Young Readers, 2007. Ages 4–8.

Difference and inclusion are the theme of this story of five mice who are not allowed into a frog concert ("Frogs only") and decide to create their own orchestra. They construct instruments out of found objects, then practice and announce their first concert. The concert hall is packed with mice, but attentive viewers will also spy some frogs in the audience, trying to go incognito. The final number is the frog song that inspired the mice to begin with, a sign of welcome that soon has frogs and mice making beautiful music together. Truly, the arts transcend all kinds of borders, including racial, national, and economic.

Early Innovator

Mitsumasa Anno

Mitsumasa Anno's books are truly international, having been trans-lated into Danish, Dutch, Spanish, French, Italian, Taiwanese, and Swedish as well as English. His work exemplifies the best of Japa-nese children's literature in asking children to use their imaginations in help-ing to construct the story and in honing their observational skills. Having been a math teacher for ten years, Anno is also adept at explaining science and math concepts visually, as he does in *Anno's Math Games,* and in repre-senting the physically impossible to challenge young minds, as he does in *Anno's Alphabet.* Anno won the Hans Christian Andersen Award for Illustra-tion in 1984. Most of his books were created three decades ago but remain timeless. Several of Anno's books remain in print; others are usually available in hardcover or paperback at reasonable prices.

Anno's Counting Book. 978-0-690-01287-3. New York: HarperCollins, 1977. Ages 3–7.

On its publication, the *New York Times* called this book "one of the few truly intelligent counting books ever produced—and a work of art besides," an assessment that remains true today. Anno understands the young child's ability to classify and count, and beginning with a bare winter landscape, he adds several details per spread (building, tree, person, and so forth) until by the number twelve he has populated an entire village. That the items are not identical (for instance, for the number 3, the buildings are a church, a

English and Japanese editions of *Anno's Math Games* by Mitsumasa Anno . For the American edition, the original cover illustration was replaced with a piece of interior art that shows children in action.

barn, and a home) and thus must be hunted for and considered by the child adds infinite interest to this counting book.

Anno's Journey. 978-0-698-11433-3 (ppb). New York: Puffin, 1997. All ages.

The first of Anno's journey books, this wordless travelogue takes readers across a Europe that combines impressions from real-life travels with those formed through experiencing Europe's cultural contributions. Observant viewers, especially older ones, will recognize characters from folktales, famous works of art, landmark buildings, and more. Anno has created similar journeys across space and time for Spain, Italy, Britain, and the USA.

Anno's Mysterious Multiplying Jar. Co-authored with Masaichiro Anno. 978-0-698-11753-2 (ppb). New York: Puffin, 1999. All ages.

Anno's mysterious jar contains an ocean, in which exists one island, and on that island are two countries, and in each country three mountains. In just a few pages, he has reached ten, by which time the items number 3,628,800. In this way Anno illustrates how factorials work, and then uses a second visual method, dots on a page, to demonstrate how exponentially the items increase. Math teachers have discovered this book as a way of demonstrating a difficult math concept to students in elementary grades and up.

Tsuchiya, Yukio. *Faithful Elephants: A True Story of Animals, People and War.* Translated by Tomoko Tsuchiya Dyles. Illustrated by Ted Lewin. 978-0-395-86137-0 ppk. Houghton Mifflin, 1997. Age 8 and up.

This story, first written in 1951 and read periodically on Japanese radio, recounts how the animals at Toyko's Ueno Zoo were deliberately killed during World War II. The rationale for this action was that Tokyo was under threat from Allied bombs and were the zoo to be bombed, the loose animals would create havoc throughout the city. The elephants presented a problem, as they would not eat food that had been poisoned and their hides were too tough for syringes. As a last resort, they were starved to death, causing severe anguish all around. Japanese educators see this story as fostering emotion in children and educating them on the horrible effects of war, while some American critics have pointed to its factual inaccuracies and its use as propaganda. While an important book for those involved in peace education, especially as practiced in Japan, this book needs to be read in context and is not an apt choice for casual reading.

Turner, Pamela. *Hachiko: The True Story of a Loyal Dog.* Illustrated by Yan Nascimbene. 978-0-618-14094-7. Boston: Houghton Mifflin, 2004. Ages 4–8.

One of several picture books based on the famous dog that waited for his dead master at the Shibuya train station every evening, this version is exceptional for its spare, evocative illustrations. Hachiko's bittersweet story takes place in the 1920s and '30s and was first publicized in a newspaper, which caused Japanese from all over to come and pet him. A statue of the dog erected in the station has become a standard meeting place, and each year on April 8 a special festival at Shibuya station commemorates Hachiko's death.

Mongolia

Baasansuren, Bolormaa. *My Little Round House.* 978-0-88899-934-4. Toronto: Groundwood, 2009.

The *ger* (yurt in Russian) is a round house that is easily transportable to accommodate the Mongolian herder's need to move his household with the seasons. As Jilu tells his story, the symbolism of the circle becomes evident—his first home is the round belly of his mother, his second a round bed that hangs from the *ger's* frame, and when moving, he is transported in a little round nest atop a camel. His first year of life is one of comforting warmth, from his parents' and grandparents' warm embraces to the *ger's* warm interior to the springtime's warm sunshine. Fascinating folk-art pictures give a strong sense of Mongolian nomadic life and culture.

Nepal

Norbu, Tenzing. *Himalaya.* 978-0-88899-480-6. Toronto: Groundwood, 2002. Ages 7–10.

Opening this book is like stepping into both another land and another time, and yet its setting reflects present-day life in Dolpo, the high, remote region of the Himalayan mountains. The book is based on a story first portrayed in a film by French filmmaker Eric Valli, who has lived in Nepal since 1983. Tenzing Norbu, a lama and painter from Dolpo, has retold and illustrated the story for a young audience. While the film and the book have different looks, both are authentic portrayals. Tenzing Norbu uses the traditional *thangka* art style of Dolpo to convey the harsh beauty of the rocky landscape, the perilous routes through the mountains, and the region's unique architectural styles. The story focuses on the struggle for leadership when a village chief falls to his death on an expedition and the rest of the village must agree on a new chief. The resolution of the struggle involves rash acts, danger, and ultimately wisdom on the part of all.

Philippines

Arcellana, Francisco. *The Mats.* Illustrated by Hermes Alegre. 978-0-916291-86-0. Out of print. La Jolla, CA: Kane Miller, 1999. Ages 4–8.

Francisco Arcellana was an internationally recognized short story writer and a National Artist in Literature; this book adapts one of his classic stories for new generations of both Filipino and American children. Using first-person narration, Marcelina tells the story of the time her father, an engineer who traveled throughout the Philippines inspecting telegraph lines, wrote to his family that he had found a talented mat weaver and had ordered special mats for each family member. Her mother and all seven children were delighted with their mats, each a different color and containing not only their names but also a symbol of their interest or talent. At the end, three mats remained, all dull-colored and blank, save for a name on each—those of their siblings who had died young. 1995 Philippines National Book Award for Children's Literature.

South Korea

Bae, Hyun-Ju. *New Clothes for New Year's Day.* 978-1-933605-29-6. La Jolla, CA: Kane Miller, 2007. Ages 3–7.

As in many Asian countries, New Year's Day in Korea celebrates the beginning of the Lunar New Year and is also the day on which everyone turns a year older. Among the traditions is that one should wear new clothes, and the young girl in this book is excited to don the new clothes that her mother has made for her. Each piece forms part of the traditional Korean dress, and the child narrator explains how each piece is worn and often what it symbolizes. The hat is the final touch, and she goes out the door to wish her friends and neighbors good luck in the New Year. The illustration style reinforces the traditional aspect of the book, and an information page in the back supplies further details about the Korean customs for celebrating the New Year.

Kwon, Yoon-duck. *My Cat Copies Me.* 978-1-933605-26-5. La Jolla, CA: Kane Miller, 2007. Ages 3–6.

Although the child narrator of this story explains the many ways in which her cat copies her, she also sees merit in copying her cat, who is watchful, independent, and brave. The illustrations capture the cat's attitude and antics perfectly, everything from hiding under a newspaper to fighting with a placemat. The artistic style, sumptuous with color and pattern, is both unique and appealing; the girl and cat are of equal size, and little details, such as a similarity between the girl's nose and mouth and the cat's, provide much to discover in repeated readings. The clothing and furniture is a mixture of Korean and Western styles, much what one would expect in a contemporary Korean household.

International Book Artist

Suzy Lee

www.suzyleebooks.com

uzy Lee is a South Korean book artist trained in Seoul and London and now living in Singapore. She has created ten books (four available in the United States) and has quickly made a name for herself internationally. In addition, she has illustrated books written by other writers, including *Open This Little Book* by Jesse Klausmeier (Chronicle, 2013), comprising a series of nested books, so that a character is reading a book about another character who is reading a book, and so forth. In an interview with the literary blog *Seven Impossible Things before Breakfast*, she cites Florence Parry Heide's *The Shrinking of Treehorn* (Holiday House, 1971) as a book that fascinated her as a child, and her own books hold similar mysteries. Although each book is distinctive in its own way, Lee is adept at capturing a child's point of view and emotional state. All four of her wordless books invite readers to participate in the invention of the story.

The Zoo. 978-1-933605-28-9. La Jolla, CA: Kane Miller, 2007.

A little girl recounts the day she and her parents went to the zoo. As she describes what they see, two stories unfold in the illustrations: spreads with blue-gray tones depict the crowd scene, and spreads in bright colors depict activities from her perspective. From the outset, she is intrigued by a peacock wandering the grounds, and while her parents strain to find a bear in its habitat (oddly enough, no animals are visible in any of the places they're supposed to be), she pursues the peacock, finds all the animals at

play, and joins them. At about this time her parents realize she is missing and frantically race around the zoo, eventually finding her asleep on a bench. Beginning with the endpapers, the illustrations contain multiple subnarratives, including escaped animals, a loose balloon, and a missing shoe. The clever illustrations are hand-drawn and often include cutout figures added to the background. Small details, such as the balloon vendor wearing a face mask to protect against germs, schoolchildren dressed alike, and hangul characters on the signage, mark an Asian setting for this very universal story.

Wave. 978-0-8118-5924-0. San Francisco: Chronicle Books, 2008.

This wordless book, which along with *Shadow* and *Mirror* makes up what Lee calls her trilogy, captures the interplay between a young girl and the ocean, with five seagulls echoing her every reaction. When the big wave hits, however, they know better than she how far up the beach it will come. Even being caught up and thrown back on shore by a giant crashing wave does not deter this girl's curious nature. The design of the book is horizontal, enabling the blue of the ocean to creep over from the right-hand page to the left as the waves become stronger, eventually taking over the entire spread.

Shadow. 978-0-8118-7280-5. San Francisco: Chronicle Books, 2010.

This book begins on the left endpaper, solid black save for a white "click!" The page turn reveals a small girl who has just pulled the string on the storage room light, surrounded by miscellaneous items. The book is designed to be read with the spine horizontal, so that each two-page spread consists of a scene on top and its shadow below, separated by the gutter. Lee's illustrations begin as black-and-white drawings, and her introduction of yellow as an aura around the girl's hand-shadow play is almost unnoticeable at first but builds as her imagination takes off, eventually engulfing entire spreads as she becomes lost in her imagination. She is a scary wolf, a dancing ballerina, perhaps even a circus performer. These silhouetted figures call to mind similar images found in H. C. Andersen's paper cuttings, and on one page the animals are stacked like Brementown musicians. But soon it's time for dinner, and the light goes back off. Readers who continue paging through the book will receive a bonus.

Mirror. 978-1-934734-93-1. New York: Seven Footer Kids, 2010.

An illustration from *Mirror* by Suzy Lee

The pattern of repeating Rorschach blots on the front and back endpapers suggests that it is up to readers to see what they want in this wordless story about a girl relating to her own image in a mirror. Lee's black-and-white drawings washed with gold portray a small girl's emotional turmoil. Alone, at first she sits hunched over—is she depressed, sulking, tired? Soon she catches her image in the large mirror resting against the wall and becomes so wrapped up in dancing with her double that she loses herself in the mirror. When she emerges, she and her double have exchanged places, and the double has become independent, no longer mimicking the girl. This angers her, and intending to push her other self, she breaks the mirror instead. In the end, she retreats to the same hunched-over position. Children will be able to supply an endless number of interpretations of this girl's feelings and explanations for her erratic behavior, all drawn from their own feelings and experiences.

Illustrated by Suzy Lee

Klausmeier, Jesse. *Open This Little Book*. 978-0-8118-6783-2. San Francisco: Chronicle, 2013. Ages 3–7.

Book lovers abound in the pages of this book, which is really eight books in one, each a different color and nested one inside the other. Each animal character is reading a book in which another animal character is reading a book, and so on, until the tiniest book belongs to a giant, whose hands are too large to turn the pages. Her animal friends help her, and soon each is closing his book until the largest book, the one in the reader's hands, is also closed. This clever device makes the reader part of the book, on equal footing with the other characters. Don't look for a narrative story here, but revel instead in the experience.

Lee, Hyun Young. *Something for School.* 978-1-933605-85-2. La Jolla, CA: Kane Miller, 2008. Ages 3–6.

Yoon's disastrous first day at school is immortalized in the kindergarten photo that shows her crying because she has been told to line up with the boys. The illustrations tell us why: she is the only girl not dressed in a skirt or a dress. To avoid the same fate the following day, she sneaks out of the house, again wearing the same pants and shirt but also her sister's headband with its long fake ringlets framing her face. The second day is wonderful (she ascribes it to the headband), and she loves kindergarten. The third day, the headband is missing, but no matter—it has already done its job, and she feels accepted for who she is. Lee's illustrations offer a peek at Korean school customs, including the first-day individual and group pictures. Observant children may notice changes in footwear: on the playground each child wears different shoes, but indoors, everyone wears the same white slippers.

Liu, Jae Soo. *Yellow Umbrella.* Music composed by Dong Il Sheen. 978-1-929132-36-0. La Jolla, CA: Kane Miller, 2002. Ages 3–8.

This wordless book offers a stroll to school on a rainy day as seen from above. With each turn of the page, the child with the yellow umbrella meets other children, each with an umbrella of a different color, on a walk that takes them along cobblestone streets, across bridges, down stairs, past the fountain, through the playground, and finally into the school building. The accompanying audio CD includes a seven-minute track that corresponds to the pages, beginning with simple melodies on the piano and becoming more complex as more umbrellas enter the picture. On the jacket flap, author-illustrator Liu notes that "whether they were boys or girls, fat or skinny, tall or short, I realized that under their umbrellas, all those physical differences disappeared.... That is exactly what I wanted to tell in my book."

Taiwan

Chen, Chi-Yuan. *Guji Guji.* 978-1-929132-67-6. La Jolla, CA: Kane/Miller, 2004. Ages 4–8.

Guji Guji is a crocodile hatched out of an egg that ends up in the nest of a mother duck. He learns to waddle like a duck and swim like a duck, and, despite what he looks like on the outside, he feels like a duck. When three crocodiles sweet-talk him into delivering his duck siblings right into their mouths, he proves that nurture outweighs nature, at least in his case. Chen's warmly colored solid illustrations convey the animals' personalities and underscore his theme of interracial adoption, which, he explains, happens in Taiwan as well as elsewhere around the world.

Chen, Chih-Yuan. *On My Way to Buy Eggs.* 978-1-933605-41-8 (ppb). La Jolla, CA: Kane Miller, 2007. Ages 3–5.

At heart, this book is about perception, about seeing the world imaginatively. Shau-yu's father asks her to go to the traditional store to buy eggs, and on the way she walks along a shadow as if it were a high wall; picks up a blue marble and looks through it at an all-blue world; finds a pair of glasses that turns the world blurry and makes her feel like a grown-up. When she enters the store, Shau-yu continues to play that role and the shopkeeper plays along: "Here are your eggs, madam, and maybe your little girl, Shau-yu, would like some chewing gum?" An endnote describes the typical Taiwanese traditional store as places with a little bit of everything, including matchmaking!

Vietnam

Ha, Song. *Indebted as Lord Chom.* Illustrated by Ly Thu Ha. 978-0-9701654-6-6. Gardena: CA: East West Discovery Press, 2006. Age 5 and up, as a read-aloud. Bilingual text in Vietnamese and English.

This legend dates back to the sixteenth century when the Le dynasty was toppled and restored within a decade. Legend has it that before he was killed, the king conceived a child while imprisoned; knowing he was to be killed, the king gave his mistress a jade seal that would identify the child as his heir. The young woman returns to her home village, bears a son who takes after the king, names him Chom (a particularly unpleasant name designed to protect him), and eventually sends him to a temple to be educated. A monk recognizes Chom's cleverness, deduces his parentage, and trains him especially well. Chom returns to his village as a young man, and meanwhile an uprising against the usurpers of the throne is under way, missing only a descendent of the Le dynasty. Twice the leader of the uprising is sent a dream telling him where to find this descendent, and he finally pays attention. Chom is identified, his lineage verified by the jade seal, and he becomes his country's king.

Quoc, Minh. *Tam and Cam: The Ancient Vietnamese Cinderella Story.* 978-0-9701654-4-2. Gardena: CA: East West Discovery Press, 2006. Age 5 and up, as a read-aloud. Bilingual text in Vietnamese and English.

Readers familiar with the Grimms' version of Cinderella (Aschenputtel) rather than the Disney version will recognize similarities in this tale of two half-sisters who are treated differently by their mother, who spoils her younger daughter Cam and makes older stepdaughter Tam do all the hard work. Here Buddha is the spirit that aids Tam by sending birds to separate the rice from the chicken feed and gives her new clothes to wear to the spring festival. It is on the way to the festival that she loses her shoe, which leads to her marrying the king. This represents only half the story, however. On a return to her stepmother's home to observe the anniversary of her father's death, she is tricked into climbing a tree and falls to her death. The balance of the story recounts her reincarnation and journey back to her rightful place next to the king.

Tran, Quoc. *The TET Pole: The Story of the TET Festival.* Illustrated by Bich Nguyen. 978-0-9701654-5-9. Gardena: CA: East West Discovery Press, 2006. Age 5 and up, as a read-aloud. Bilingual text in Vietnamese and English.

Tết Nguyên Đán is Vietnam's most important festival of the year, beginning on the first day of the Lunar New Year and usually celebrated for three days. Tết is a time of renewal, when homes are thoroughly cleaned, disputes put aside, debts paid, new clothing put on, and homage paid to ancestors. The exact origins of this holiday are unknown, but this folktale offers one scenario. It is said that long ago devils took over the land and the people had to work as sharecroppers. In a series of events similar to those in Janet Stevens's *Tops and Bottoms* (Harcourt, 1995), Buddha helps the people regain their crops and their land but allows the devils to return for a few days at the beginning of each year. During this time, the people must be on their guard and their best behavior so the devils do not retake the land.

Chapter 6

Australia and New Zealand

Australia's Picture Book of the Year Award, the counterpart to our Caldecott Award, was established by the Australian Children's Books Council in 1952, but the award was not consistently given until the 1980s. It took a few years for Australia to ramp up its production of picture books, but since then, the country has been producing books that reflect the varied voices and artistic visions of its people. The Australian population is a mosaic of those descended from the early English settlers, subsequent waves of immigrants from Europe and elsewhere, refugees from war-torn countries, and, of course, the country's own Aboriginal people. Eminent professor and critic Maurice Saxby claims that by 1980, Australian picture books had entered their golden age; if so, it is a golden age that is in no danger of ending soon, as the picture book is constantly evolving in the hands of Australia's talented authors and illustrators.

Australian mainstream culture was shaped early on by its relationship to England and its position as a far-flung colony lacking in the amenities of the home country. The attitude of the British toward Australia made Australians feel inferior in every respect (known as "cultural cringe"), and the Australian response was to reject all things English and recast itself in opposition to the British.[1] Whereas the British maintained a rigid class system and rules of etiquette, Australians represented themselves as a classless society and one that flaunted convention and authority. As Rosemary Ross Johnston points out, "much of Australian literature has been obsessed by the nation's search for its identity," and children's literature is a major site for creating and reinforcing national identity among children.[2]

In literature we see the Australian identity emerge both within stories—in the nature of the characters, plots, and settings—and in the narrative approaches. Characters may interact informally and use colloquial language, and the books may openly address topics that the British (and Americans) consider taboo. Several examples come to mind: the home birth pictured in Jenny Overend's *Welcome with Love* (published as *Hello Baby* in Australia); the portrayal of Mary and Joseph as ordinary people in *The Nativity*; and Margaret Wild's *Let the Celebrations Begin!* set in a World War II concentration camp. All three of these books are illustrated by Julie Vivas in her distinctive style, which portrays appealing humans with cherubic faces, often wearing combat boots and baggy clothing, all in a muted color palette.

Another way that Australian artists defy convention is by pushing the boundaries of the picture book as an art form. *The Watertower,* with story by Gary Crew and illustrations by Steven Woolman, was published in Australia in 1994 and came out in the United States in 1998. Although it won the 1995 Picture Book of the Year Award from the Children's Book Council of Australia, it confounded American critics. With its uncanny suggestion of the paranormal delivered primarily through the illustrations, who was it for? *Publishers Weekly* was stumped: "Unfortunately, despite Woolman's able renderings in acrylic, chalk and pencil, the design—which shifts between horizontal and vertical orientations—only underscores the feeling of disorientation raised in the text. This one may well leave even savvy older readers in the dark."[3]

The Watertower was an early example of the trend that has since become known as "picture books for older readers." A slightly later example is *The Rabbits,* with text by John Marsden and illustrations by Shaun Tan, published in Australia in 1998 and in Canada in 2003 (with distribution in the US). This 1999 Australian Picture Book of the Year is an allegory of colonization, with rabbits introduced as a nonnative species that destroys the habitat of the existing native animal species. Drawn in a stylized form that distorts the rabbits so that they look nothing like the soft fuzzy creatures that populate most children's picture books, the illustrations are rich with details that provide many levels of commentary and suggest the plight of the Aboriginal people at the hands of the Europeans.

Early on, the books most likely to be selected for American publication were those in keeping with the American image of Australia, books either set in the outback (although, as Clare Bradford reminds us, most

Australians live in cities) or featuring Australian fauna (exemplified by *Wombat Stew, Koala Lou,* and *Possum Magic*). These books introduced American librarians, educators, and parents to some of Australia's best authors and illustrators of the time—Mem Fox, Marcia Vaughn, Julie Vivas, Pamela Lofts, and others—whose books are still popular in North America today. Margaret Wild's *The Very Best of Friends,* also illustrated by Julie Vivas, came to the US at the same time as Mem Fox's *Possum Magic* and offered a fresh approach to death as a topic in picture books. Not ponderous or sentimental in the least, Wild deftly conveyed her character's depression at losing a life companion and also portrayed the journey back to everyday life.

Mem Fox, a childhood literacy educator as well as an author, developed a loyal following in the US beginning in the 1990s, especially among whole language advocates. Over the course of her many trips to North America, she has spoken at countless national conferences, including those of the American Library Association, the International Reading Association, and National Council of Teachers of English. *Possum Magic* was her first book, though it was the second to be published in the United States. She has written over thirty others, almost all taken for American publication.

Finally, some of the Australian picture books available in the United States contain references to unique elements of Australia's culture and history—the participation of the Australian and New Zealand Army Corps (ANZAC) during World War I at the Battle of Gallipoli; the outback and its cattle drovers, boundary riders, and swagmen; Aboriginal stories; and legendary characters such as the outlaw Ned Kelly. These books are rare, as often books focused on specific Australian historical or cultural events have been deemed "too Australian" for American readers and passed over by American publishers. Yet for the young reader who is intrigued by this country, they are equally important and provide a missing piece in the picture of the "real" Australia.

Although the first children's book published in New Zealand dates back to 1891, until the 1960s most children's books written by New Zealanders were published in England because there were too few buyers in New Zealand to support the local publication of children's trade books. Ironically, since the books weren't always distributed in New Zealand, previous generations of British children may have read more New Zealand authors than their counterparts in New Zealand.

Margaret Mahy, New Zealand's best-known children's author and a winner of the 2006 Hans Christian Andersen Author Medal, is a prime example. Although in 1961 her stories began to appear in the *New Zealand School Journal*, published for children by the Ministry of Education, Kiwi book publishers at the time were not interested in her work, as it was not specific to New Zealand. Mahy later explained that her typically European settings were influenced by the fact that the books she grew up on were set in Europe. Her first stories to be published in book form came out from the American publisher Franklin Watts, and both her picture books and her novels were published overseas rather than by Kiwi publishers. Mahy, who died in 2012, later turned to New Zealand for her settings and stories.

Today both independent publishers and affiliates of international publishing companies are publishing books for children; Scholastic and Penguin are two examples of international companies with editorial offices in New Zealand. Sometimes, but not always, the books originating from international publishers lose their cultural flavor in favor of a more generic one that can be marketed throughout the English-speaking world. The books that speak overtly to the wealth of experiences in New Zealand, including that of the Maori, are often not distributed overseas. The New Zealand Picture Book Collection (www.picturebooks.co.nz) was established to identify picture books with local content for use in Kiwi schools. Although most of these books are not available in the United States, the Internet has made it much easier to locate and obtain such books.

New Zealand-based independent publisher Gecko Press, founded in 2005, publishes children's books originating in New Zealand as well as those in translation (many of which are annotated in this volume under the country headings of their authors). In 2011 Lerner Publishing Group arranged to distribute selected Gecko titles in the US.

NOTES

1. Nimon and Foster, *Adolescent Novel*, 38.
2. Johnston, "Children's Literature Advancing Australia," 13.
3. Review of *The Watertower*.

Australia

Berndt, Catherine. *Pheasant and Kingfisher.* Illustrated by Arone Raymond Meeks. 978-1-87953-164-2. Greenvale, NY: Mondo, 1994. Age 6 and up.

The title page notes that this tale was originally told by Nganalgindja in the Gunwinggu language; it is one of the stories that Berndt, an anthropologist, recorded and translated into English. The pourquoi tale explains how certain rock formations came to be; it was all due to Bookbook and Bered-Bered, two men who come from far in the northwest and journey across the land, burning the dry grass as they go. When they arrive at the place they want, they cut bamboo for spears, hunt, and enjoy their days. Then comes a messenger telling them that a lot of men are planning to kill them for cutting down the bamboo. Pheasant and Kingfisher paint themselves and ready for the fight but are outnumbered, so they transform into their bird shapes and fly off, leaving their enemies to turn into stone below them. A bonus of this book is the explanation by Aboriginal artist Meeks as to how he created his illustrations and the significance of particular elements.

Crew, Gary. *The Watertower.* Illustrated by Steven Woolman. 1-56656-233-3. Brooklyn: Crocodile Books, 1998. Age 8 and up.

The outback setting for this enigmatic story looks like a 1960s Wild West town, with its unpaved main street, two-story wooden buildings, and townspeople dressed as farmers, waitresses, and ranch hands. The main character is the watertower itself, half full of murky water, perched on rusted legs, "casting a long dark shadow across the valley." Two boys seek relief from the dry heat by going up for a swim, and one emerges from the water with an oddly transformed manner. An insignia on the watertower appears on several articles of clothing and equipment in town as well as on the transformed boy's hand. Does the large satellite antenna, whose shape replicates the insignia, have anything to do with the eerie feel of the town? Do the blank stares of the townspeople, often gazing at the watertower, reflect an alien spirit inside? The design of the book, which uses a circular element that echoes the pervasive insignia and at times suggests a reel of film, randomly changes from vertical to horizontal to angular, which contributes to the off-kilter feel generated in the reader.

Fox, Mem. *Koala Lou.* Illustrated by Pamela Lofts. 978-0-1520-0502-3. San Diego: Harcourt, 1989. Ages 2–5.

This story of a mother's love is on its second generation of readers, being given to new babies by those who grew up on it in the 1990s. Koala Lou is the firstborn, and her doting mother constantly coos to her, "Koala Lou, I *do* love you." As more and more babies are born, her mother has her hands full and Koala Lou misses hearing those words, so she sets out to earn her mother's love by winning the Bush Olympics. Although she doesn't win her event, she gains her mother's attention and hears those comforting words again. Readers love the message of unconditional love this story offers and appreciate the colorful, appealing illustrations that represent native Australian animals.

Fox, Mem. *Possum Magic.* Illustrated by Julie Vivas. 978-0-1520-0572-6. San Diego: Harcourt, 1990. Ages 4–7.

With this story, internationally known writer and educator Mem Fox offers a primer on all things Australian. Grandma Poss (short for *possum*) makes "bush magic" that can transform creatures from big to small, from one color to another, from visible to invisible. When little Hush has tired of being invisible, Grandma Poss is unsuccessful in finding the right magic to change her back again, but she remembers that the secret involves "people food." So off they go to eat their way around Australia: Anzac biscuits in Adelaide, Minties in Melbourne, pumpkin scones in Brisbane. From Darwin on, Hush begins to reappear, bit by bit as they eat their way through Perth and Hobart and back home. Like *Wombat Stew* and *Koala Lou,* this was one of the early Australian picture books to catch on in the US.

French, Jackie. *Diary of a Wombat.* Illustrated by Bruce Whatley. 0-618-38136-8. New York: Clarion, 2003. Ages 4–7.

An unimaginative wombat chronicles everyday life, which consists of sleeping, eating, and scratching until a family of humans moves nearby. Then life turns much more interesting as the wombat discovers new activities, such as digging holes in the flower bed and receiving carrots on demand. This book is equally popular at home and in the classroom, where it is used in all kinds of lessons. Spinoffs by the same author and illustrator include

Diary of a Baby Wombat (2010) for the younger reader, and an informational book, *How to Scratch a Wombat* (2009), for any reader in grades 3 through 6.

Germein, Katrina. *Big Rain Coming.* Illustrated by Bronwyn Bancroft. 0-618-08344-8. New York: Clarion, 2000. Ages 4–7.

Weather is a topic of interest no matter where one lives. In the Australian bush—the setting for this book—water is the lifeblood of the people. Old Stephen sees the dark clouds in the south and predicts rain, but it takes almost a week for the rain to arrive. Each day is as hot as the last, and every creature seeks relief—children drag their mattresses outside at night and swim in the billabong during the day, dogs dig deep into the dirt. Drawing on Aboriginal imagery and style to match the setting of the text, Bancroft's illustrations foreground the earth and sky, and the saturated colors positively radiate heat. When rain comes, the horizon line disappears and all is enclosed in the cooling blue and green circles of rain.

Greenwood, Mark. *The Donkey of Gallipoli: A True Story of Courage in World War I.* Illustrated by Frané Lessac. 978-0-7636-3913-6. Cambridge, MA: Candlewick Press, 2008. Ages 8–11.

Jack Simpson was born in England but set out to make his fortune in Australia when he was 17. After trying many different jobs there, he enlisted in the Australian army and was trained as a stretcher bearer, becoming part of the historical ANZAC invasion of Turkey at Gallipoli. Simpson, an actual person of legendary stature in Australia, may be the true subject of this book, but the draw for children will be the eponymous donkey who ferried wounded soldiers down the rugged hills to the waiting medics. Lessac's hallmark folk-art style captures the terrain and coloration of the Turkish landscape; her illustrations contribute greatly to the reader's understanding of the combat situation, which proved a hopeless one for the ANZAC. Jack Simpson's death just twenty-four days into the mission is mitigated by the honor shown him at burial and his lasting fame as a symbol of the courageous soldier who put his life on the line for his fellow soldiers. A welcome aspect of this book is the factual spread at the end that incorporates a Turkish perspective. Greenwood and Lessac are married and live in Australia.

Ingpen, Robert. *The Voyage of* **The Poppykettle.** 978-0-698-40025-2. New York: Penguin, Minedition, 2005. Age 4 and up.

Robert Ingpen is a master at creating worlds, and here he has created a mythical history for Australia that coexists with its actual one. He frames this modern folktale with endpapers that contain a map of the world, the kind that ancient travelers might have used to navigate. The story begins in Peru with a band of tiny people called the Hairy Peruvians who seek a new home after being conquered by the Spaniards. With the help of a pelican and a silver bird, they are led to Machu Picchu, where they find the clay pot that will become their traveling vessel. After outfitting it, they set sail and eventually come to the shores of Australia. The story follows a classic quest pattern, with obstacles to overcome and animal helpers that aid the band. It is also a pourquoi tale, as it explains the appearance of two ancient brass keys found buried on the coast near Geelong, keys identical to those used for ballast on *The Poppykettle*.

Lester, Alison. *Are We There Yet? A Journey around Australia.* 978-1-929132-73-7. Brooklyn: Kane Miller, 2005. Ages 7–10.

What could be a better way to see Australia than on a three-month camping trip with your whole family (minus the dog, cat, and horse, being looked after at home by obliging grandparents)? Eight-year-old Grace, a middle child between two brothers, relates the adventure, and the illustrations supply what her words cannot—the odd geological forms of Murphy's Haystacks, the vast cliffs at Head of Bight, the wavelike stone formation at Wave Rock. The illustrations also include details unmentioned in the text, such as the steering wheel positioned on the right-hand side of the car. Readers are able to trace the family's trip on a large map on the front endpaper as well as smaller maps throughout, and by the end of the trip have a much better understanding of Australia's cultural wealth and diversity; they may also become attached to the family members and wish the trip were not over so soon. *My Farm* (Houghton Mifflin, 1994) by the same writer is a memoir of growing up on an Australian farm where they raised cattle, kept chickens, and grew hay.

Lester, Alison. *Ernie Dances to the Digeredoo.* 0-618-10442-9. Boston: Houghton Mifflin, 2001. Ages 5–8.

Ernie is one of seven friends first introduced by Lester in *Clive Eats Alligators* (1991), a book that shows each child's distinctive tastes and behaviors. Though not made an issue, their ethnicities as represented in the illustrations reflect the diversity of the Australian population. Most of the books in which these friends appear are built around a concept, and in this case it is a series of letters home that recount Ernie's year in Arnhem Land, where his parents will be working in a hospital. Through Ernie's experiences, his friends (and the book's readers) learn about Aboriginal culture and history, something far removed from their own city lives.

Lofthouse, Liz. *Ziba Came on a Boat.* Illustrated by Robert Ingpen. 978-1-933605-52-4. Brooklyn: Kane Miller, 2007. Ages 7–11.

Ziba and her mother are Afghan refugees en route to Australia. On the rough boat trip, Ziba thinks of all that has been left behind—her aunts and cousins, her brick-and-mud house, her mother's loom, the mountains and the river, and not least her father. Ingpen, 1986 Hans Christian Andersen Illustrator Medal Winner, provides lush realistic paintings that transport the reader between the memories in Ziba's mind and the high seas on which the overcrowded fishing boat makes its way. There, Ziba and her fellow refugees are suspended in time between their old life and their new one.

Ormerod, Jan. *Lizzie Nonsense.* 978-0-618-57493-3. Boston: Houghton Mifflin, 2005. Ages 5–8.

Lizzie and her family are pioneers living in the Australian bush, where the closest town is fifty miles away. When Papa takes the horse and cart with a load of lumber to sell, Lizzie, her mama, and the baby are all alone. Lizzie's flights of fantasy seem like nonsense to her mother, who must till the land, do the laundry, scrub the floor, and cook. The Australian animals present in almost every picture remind readers that these pioneers are in the Australian rather than the American heartland.

Spurling, Margaret. *Bilby Moon.* Illustrated by Danny Snell. 978-19291-3206-5. Brooklyn: Kane Miller, 2001. Ages 2–5.

Like the better-known kangaroo, a *bilby* is a marsupial, a class of mammals with pouches for carrying their young; a full-grown bilby is about the size of a rabbit and lives in the Austalian desert. Bilbys are nocturnal, and this young bilby emerges from its burrow to find that part of the moon has disappeared. Concerned, she asks a hopping mouse where it has gone, but the hopping mouse only volunteers to help look for it. Each night more of the moon is missing, and the distraught bilby asks a different desert creature for help. Finally, when the moon has completely disappeared, she comes to the Boobook Owl, who informs her that the moon will come back soon. Sure enough it does, and the animals have a new appreciation of the beauty of moonlight as it illuminates their surroundings. This simple story works in two ways: as a tale of a little one facing the unknown, it captures the emotion of the situation, and as an introduction to some of the animals found in the Australian desert, it portrays them accurately, despite the anthropomorphism.

Vaughan, Marcia K. *Wombat Stew.* Illustrated by Pamela Lofts. 978-0-3820-9211-4. Silver Burdett, 1986. Out of print. Ages 5–9.

This lively offering was among the first wave of Australian picture books to hit American shores and remains a winner, though it is periodically out of print. Indigenous animal characters play the roles in this twist on the stone soup story; Dingo catches a fat wombat and takes it home to make stew, and Platypus, Emu, Lizard, Echidna, and Koala each suggest adding something to the pot before the wombat goes in. Only at the end do readers discover that the animals' goal was not to extend the soup but to save Wombat, which they do. Vaughan's playful, repetitive rhymes, all some variant of "Wombat stew / Wombat stew / gooey, brewy, / yummy, chewy, / wombat stew," live on long after the story is over. Lofts's humorous illustrations bring the animals to life and give them personalities.

Wheatley, Donna. *My Place.* 978-0-196291-54-9. Illustrated by Donna Rawlins. Brooklyn: Kane Miller, 1994. Age 5 and up.

Using the device of tracing back residence on a particular plot of land decade by decade, Wheatley and Rawlins impart an overview of two centuries of Australian history. Everything is here in this microcosm: the waves of immigrant settlers, including a child convict from England (arrested for stealing a coat because he was cold), the impact of the wars on the economy and the population, the rise and fall of manufacturing, the pollution of a nearby canal along with efforts to reclaim it, and the gradual transformation of a rural area into a city. Each child describes his or her family and activities and draws a map showing the area. Children everywhere will enjoy poring over the maps, noticing the differences from decade to decade, and thinking about who or what might have inhabited the same spot where they now live.

Wild, Margaret. *Fox.* Illustrated by Ron Brooks. 978-19291-3216-4. Brooklyn: Kane Miller, 2001. Age 8 and up.

Ron Brooks adopts a much rougher style than usual to suit this stark fable of friendship, jealousy, loneliness, and betrayal. A fire maims both Dog and Magpie—Dog loses sight in one eye, and Magpie loses the use of a wing—but together they compensate for their losses. With Magpie on Dog's back, her eyes see for both of them, and his legs enable her to fly once more. Enter Fox, "with his haunted eyes and rich red coat." Kind Dog welcomes Fox, who betrays him by wooing Magpie away with promises of faster flight; when she finally agrees, he carries her far away, where he abandons her. "Now you and Dog will know what it is like to be truly alone." Brooks's scratchy hand lettering adds to the uneasy feel of the illustrations rendered in hues of reddish-orange, charcoal, and brown. This book challenges notions of what a picture book should look like. Comparing *Fox* with the same duo's *Old Pig* (Dial, 1996) or *Rosie and Tortoise* (DK Ink, 1999) enables readers to see just how versatile both author and illustrator are.

Visionary Artist and Writer

Shaun Tan

Born near Perth and raised in Perth's northern suburbs, Shaun Tan graduated from the University of Western Australia in Perth with joint honors in Fine Arts and English Literature. He writes and illustrates books; has been a concept artist for animated films; worked as a theater designer; and directed an Oscar-winning animated short, *The Lost Thing,* based on his book of the same name. His books have also been the basis for a play and an orchestral performance in Australia. He won the Australia's Picture Book of the Year Award, that country's counterpart to the Caldecott Award, for *The Arrival,* and in 2011 he received the immensely prestigious Astrid Lindgren Memorial Award for his body of work.

Tan has chosen the picture book form as a site of experimentation. Artists such as Tan let their creative vision lead the way and trust that the book will find its own audience. The texts are not difficult, but they are cryptic rather than action-driven, leaving the reader to create the meaning. This process varies according to the extent of the reader's prior knowledge. In the same way that Australian young adult writers have been in the forefront of the crossover movement, creating books that span the young adult/adult market, Tan and other picture book artists are leading a crossover movement in picture books that appeal to all ages, including adults.

"My picture books are essentially an attempt to subversively re-imagine everyday experience.... I'm particularly attracted to realizing fictional places and events that are metaphors for our own, on one hand surreal and on the other strongly resonant and recognizable," says Tan (Haber, "Shaun Tan"). His influences come both from within and outside of Australia—the everyday minutia of life as well as art and literature in all its manifestations. "Half of my attention is fixed upon everyday suburban landscapes, which I often photograph and paint, while much of my time is spent drawing imaginary characters and fictional worlds. I find both equally fascinating," he writes on his website.

The Arrival. 978-0-439-89529-3. New York: Scholastic, Arthur Levine, 2007. All ages.

This wordless book is its own genre, falling someplace between a picture book and a graphic novel. It has chapters but no words. The cover design suggests that the reader will be opening a worn photo album of a time gone by; on the inside, the pictures are square and rendered in tones of sepia and gray, unobtrusively underscoring this impression. The story is reduced to the essence of the immigrant experience: an immigrant leaves his wife and daughter, works hard to establish a place in a new country, and sends for his family. Many of the common experiences are here: the feeling of isolation and disorientation resulting from not knowing the language; the loneliness of being away from family; the search for work; the sharing of stories with other immigrants. All of this sounds rather straightforward, but the world into which Tan has put his characters is like and unlike our own, with surrealistic touches—animals, objects, and landscapes not found in our world—giving readers a small taste of the disorientation experienced by immigrants.

Lost and Found. 978-0-545-22924-1. New York: Scholastic, Arthur Levine, 2011. All ages.

This volume contains three picture books that were published by Simply Read Books in Vancouver and distributed in the US: *The Red Tree* (2002) and *The Lost Thing* (2004), written and illustrated by Tan, and *The Rabbits* (2003), written by John Marsden and illustrated by Tan. The last two have not been available in North America for some time, making this a welcome publication for those readers who first discovered the artist through *The Arrival*.

The Red Tree is narrated by a young red-haired girl sitting in bed, musing that "sometimes the day begins with nothing to look forward to." Above the bed is a framed red maple leaf, but dead brown leaves are falling faster and faster onto her bed and floor. Tan's layered, mixed-media illustrations rely on metaphor to visualize the sense of isolation, despair, and futility that threatens to overwhelm her as the day wears on—she is pictured as lost in a chaotic landscape of ladders and windows, or encapsulated in a bottle, head covered by a diving helmet. One spread is laid out as a board game with the narrator carrying the die on the path leading to a monster. At the end of the day she arrives home to find a blaze-red maple sapling in her bedroom, and for the first time, she smiles. On rereading, one notices a tiny red leaf on every spread, connecting the opening and closing scenes and reminding readers of the narrator's resilience in the face of depression.

The Lost Thing is preceded with a spread of bottle tops, each with a different design, presumably collected by the story's nerdy-looking narrator. On one outing, he spots an enormous sentient creature sitting on the beach, ignored by the human beachgoers, and realizes it is lost. He almost signs it over to the Federal Department of Odds and Ends but for the Thing's whimper and a timely tip that a better place exists. And so it does, a place where many Things of strange shapes and sizes can be themselves. Tan's paintings are framed by a collage of pages from textbooks with mechanical drawings and scientific language, and street scenes are marked by exposed pipes and machines. In this mechanized society, humans are so caught up in their mundane routines that they don't notice what's right in front of them, even something as unusual as a gigantic, red, octopus-legged Lost Thing.

The Rabbits is a straightforward story of colonization told from the perspective of the colonized, with colonizers represented as rabbits and the indigenous population as numbats, a mammal unique to Australia. (Rabbits introduced to Australia by settlers in the nineteenth century soon overran the countryside and ate many plant species into extinction.) Tan's illustrations reference Australian landscape and Aboriginal artwork, from pictographs to the custom of drawing animals with lines showing how they are cut up for eating. The rabbits are portrayed in mechanistic terms, with straight lines and pointy

A sketch by Shaun Tan captures his own desire to explore the unknown.

legs on which they walk upright, in contrast with the rounded, more natural numbats. Numbats are shown in the background communicating with one another and their surroundings, while rabbits are shown working with scientific instruments, weapons, and artillery, creating buildings with no thought to the landscape. This allegorical story, applicable to North America as well as Australia, can easily serve as an introduction to postcolonial theory for young and old.

The Bird King: An Artist's Notebook. 978-0-545-46513-7. Scholastic, Arthur Levine, 2013. All ages.

In the introduction to this collection of sketches and drawings rendered over a dozen years, Tan muses that "drawing is its own form of thinking, in the same way birdsong is 'thought about' within a bird's throat." Included in this 128-page compendium are all sorts of sketches, from rough to almost finished, from black-and-white to full color, from pen-and-ink to pastel. No narrative thread pulls the reader through the sketchbook, but simply curiosity to see what the imaginative and observant eye of the artist comes up with.

New Zealand

Cowley, Joy. *Mrs. Wishy-Washy's Farm.* Illustrated by Elizabeth Fuller. 978-0-399-23872-7. New York: Philomel, 2003. Ages 2–5.

Farming has always been a mainstay in New Zealand, known for its wool and its dairy products. Thus the farm is a perfect setting for Cowley's well-known Mrs. Wishy-Washy, who is intent on keeping everything, including her animals, squeaky-clean. When the cow, duck, and pig have had enough of her soapsuds and run away to the city, they end up covered with paint and thrown in jail. Finally rescued by Mrs. Wishy-Washy, they are thrilled to be home and even happier to jump into the tub. Simple text with ear-pleasing rhymes and representational pictures make this story ideal for preschool listeners. Several other books by this team of New Zealanders feature the same characters, and some are available as board books. Cowley's *The Rusty, Trusty Tractor* (Boyds Mills, 1999), illustrated by American artist Olivier Dunrea, is also set on a farm.

Dodd, Lynley. *Hairy Maclary from Donaldson's Dairy.* 978-1-58246-059-8 (ppb). Berkeley: Tricycle Press, 2001. Ages 4–8.

First published in 1983, the Hairy Maclary books have a devoted following in New Zealand. In cumulative couplets, Dodd tells how Hairy Maclary, a Scottish terrier, goes out for a walk and collects his canine friends along the way: "Schnitzel von Krumm with a very low tum, Bitzer Maloney all skinny and bony, Muffin McLay like a bundle of hay, Bottomley Potts covered in spots, Hercules Morse as big as a horse." These dogs, big and small, strut their stuff through town until confronted by the tomcat Scarface Claw. Suddenly the dogs turn tail, and Hairy Maclary is last seen hiding in his bed.

Mahy, Margaret. *A Summery Saturday Morning.* Illustrated by Selina Young. 978-0-670-87943-4. New York: Viking, 1998. Ages 3–7.

Mahy uses the familiar form of the children's song "Here We Go 'Round the Mulberry Bush," with its repetition and refrain, as a basis for recounting what happens when a group sets out on a walk to the beach "on a summery Saturday morning." Mom (or babysitter), four kids, and two dogs aren't counting on meeting a mother goose and her seven goslings. The dogs chase the geese and the humans chase the dogs until the geese turn on the dogs and the group hightails it back up the hill. Young's colorful cartoon illustrations provide an overview of typical Saturday morning activities on the New Zealand bay and imbue the characters with lots of personality.

Mewburn, Kyle. *Kiss! Kiss! Yuck! Yuck!* Illustrated by Ali Teo and John O'Reilly. 978-1-56145-457-0. Atlanta: Peachtree, 2008, Ages 4–8.

Using the third person, Mewburn sticks closely to the child's point of view as he describes Auntie Elsie's engulfing hugs and kisses (two per cheek) on her weekly visit to her nephew Andy, on whom she bestows such pet names as Andy Apple Pie and Andy Apple Sauce. Despite Andy's attempts to hide, Auntie Elsie always has his number. The boldly colored cartoonish pictures, a mix of digitally treated pencil and collage, show her bulky frame scaling trees and crawling into the pigpen to find him, all the while carrying her crocodile purse. Then comes the week she doesn't arrive because of a broken leg. Weeks pass—enough time for Andy to realize how much he misses Auntie Elsie—and when she does return, it's he who gives the kisses and hugs.

Canada

On average, American children know very little about Canada. If anything, they assume that it is just like the United States, only colder. Few know that Canada is a constitutional monarchy, with Queen Elizabeth as its titular head of state, or that signage in Canada is in both French and English, its two official languages. Like the United States, Canada is home to indigenous people (Inuit and First Nations), descendants of immigrants, and recent immigrants. Canadian faces come in all colors, just as American faces do.

If Canada has a distinct identity today, that was not always apparent. Until the middle of the twentieth century, Canadian culture took a back seat to British and American culture. Books, films, television programs, and other forms of media came from either the United States or England. Representation of the Canadian experience was lacking in all forms of culture, including children's books (with rare exceptions). Imagine if *every* TV show you saw and *every* book you read came from another country. Such a situation could result in a feeling of isolation and diminished importance.

After World War II, a Royal Commission on National Development in the Arts, Letters and Sciences was established to recommend ways to encourage the production of cultural material to strengthen the Canadian national identity. Laws were established for television and radio stipulating that a certain percentage of airplay must have Canadian content (e.g., written, performed, or produced in Canada or by a Canadian). The National Library was founded, as was a program of federal funding for the arts. Children's book publishing programs were slow to take root, however, and not until the late 1960s and early 1970s did all the necessary elements come together to support a viable children's book industry. During this time several independent publishing firms specializing in children's books arose, including Kids Can Press, Groundwood Books, and Annick Press.

Canada's relatively small home market (a tenth of that of the US) does not allow for economies of scale in production, making the publication of picture books a continuing struggle, especially in the face of declining numbers of children, erosion of the school library market, and higher production costs. Through the mid-1990s, publishers were able to reap some income from selling rights to foreign publishers, including Americans. In fact, most of the Canadian books available in the US came by way of American publishers who had bought the rights. Then the American market tightened up and publishers were no longer buying rights. As a result, Canadian publishers took the bull by the horns and began selling their books directly into the American market through distributors.

This new distribution system has had two effects. First, more Canadian children's books are available in the United States than ever before. Second, fewer of these books have overt Canadian content. Many of the picture books that come to mind as rooted in Canadian history or having a strong sense of place were published in the 1980s and 1990s for the Canadian market; some are true stories of growing up in specific parts of Canada during times gone by, which paradoxically renders them timeless.

The all-time best-selling Canadian children's book, Robert Munsch's *Love You Forever* (Firefly, 1986), is a favorite with Americans, including nostalgic mothers who now give it to their children as they go off to college; neither child nor adult realizes that it is anything but American. Nor do American readers know that one of their favorite characters of print and screen, that ubiquitous green turtle Franklin, hails from Canada. More recently, the talented Quebecois author-artist Mélanie Watt has succeeded in gaining a following in the United States with her Scaredy Squirrel books.

Mélanie Watt and Marie-Louise Gay are Francophone artists published by Anglophone firms Kids Can Press and Groundwood Books, respectively. For every book by Watt and Gay, however, there are hundreds of books published by Canadian Francophone publishers that remain unknown to English-language readers because they haven't been picked up for translation by an Anglophone Canadian publisher or by an American publisher. Why not? The simplest answer is that the overall approach to creating picture books differs too greatly between Anglophone and Francophone publishers for the books of one to be marketed successfully to the other.

In *Picturing Canada*, Gail Edwards and Judith Saltman quote Canadian critics, a librarian, and a book designer in their efforts to articulate these differences. The upshot is that the art of Quebecois illustrators, dubbed "the Montreal style,"[1] is less realistic, more conceptual, more avant-garde than that of their Anglophone counterparts. English Canadian artists illustrate in the British tradition, where pictures hew closely to the text. Quebecois artists are influenced by European aesthetics, which favor design and even whimsy over realism. The success of Watt and Gay in the Canadian and American markets suggests that there is room for a bit of both.

Note

1. Edwards and Saltman, *Picturing Canada*, 217.

Canada

Brownridge, William Roy. *The Moccasin Goalie.* 978-1-55143-054-6. Victoria, BC: Orca Books, 1996. Ages 5–8.

Set in the past on the Canadian prairie, this first-person narrative describes young Danny's obsession with hockey, the pickup games he played with his three friends, his position as goalie because of his crippled leg and foot, and the pain of being excluded from the town's start-up hockey team. Of his three friends, only Marcel is chosen. Not Anita, because she is a girl; not Petou, because he is too small; not Danny, because of his leg. Then comes the day that the regular goalie is hurt and Danny is asked to fill in. Not only does he earn himself a place on the team, but he makes sure that his other two friends become part of the team as well. Brownridge's spectacular illustrations capture the icy cold ground and colorful skies of the prairie landscape.

Butler, Geoff. *The Hangashore.* 978-088776-444-8. Toronto: Tundra, 1998. Age 7 and up.

The language of this tale—more short story than picture book text—is rich with the vernacular of its 1940s Newfoundland setting, making it a wonderful read-aloud. The word *hangashore* describes a worthless person who can't fish and is applied to any person deserving pity. When a new magistrate arrives in a small coastal community, he sets himself apart from the "colonials," an attitude symbolized by the act of sitting alone in the front pew every Sunday at church. Irritated by comments by the minister's son John, who has Down syndrome, the magistrate even suggests that John should be institutionalized. Yet when John is quick-witted enough to rescue the magistrate during an accident at sea, the magistrate is forced to rethink who deserves pity and realizes that it's time for him to take the back pew for a change. Butler also wrote and illustrated *The Killick* (1995), set in a Newfoundland fishing village.

Campbell, Nicola I. *Grandpa's Girls.* 978-1-55498-084-0. Illustrated by Kim LaFave. Toronto: Groundwood, 2011. Ages 4–7.

The young girl who narrates this story of a visit to Grandpa's house explains that "Grandpa is a veteran, a cowboy, a rancher, and a businessman." Living nearby are other family members, and going to Grandpa's is a time for the moms to get together and laugh while the cousins swing from the hayloft in the barn, play with the chickens, explore the root cellar, and get into mischief. Best of all, it's a chance to learn about Grandpa as a young man as they explore his trunk in the attic. LaFave's illustrations are bright and upbeat, picturing an enticing rural setting from varied perspectives.

Campbell, Nicola I. *Shi-shi-etko.* 978-0-88899-659-6. Illustrated by Kim LaFave. Toronto: Groundwood, 2005. Ages 7–9.

Shi-shi-etko counts down the days until she must leave to go to an Indian residential school. Each day brings a special activity that will turn into a memory that can sustain her when she is gone. She and her mother go down to the creek where her mother sings a traditional song; aunts, uncles, cousins, and grandparents visit; she and her father canoe across the lake; her grandmother takes her into the woods to collect plant life for her bag of memories, which she leaves tucked in a space between the roots of her favorite tree. Spiritually fortified, she gets on the truck that will take her and other children away from home until the following spring. In an author's note that precedes the story, Campbell asks, "Can you imagine a community without children? Can you imagine children without parents?" It was the law, and parents who refused to comply could be jailed. Canada's last residential school closed in 1984.

Campbell, Nicola I. *Shin-chi's Canoe.* 978-0-88899-857-6. Illustrated by Kim LaFave. Toronto: Groundwood, 2008. Ages 7–9.

This sequel to *Shi-shi-etko* moves from home to school, as Shi-shi-etko returns to the residential school for another year and Shin-chi, her younger brother, attends for the first time. Shi-shi-etko reminds him that they won't be allowed to talk to each other, and that her English name is Mary and his is David. She gives him a small canoe their father has made to remind him of his family; their father has told him that the spring salmon come up the river first followed by the sockeye in the summer. In a bout of homesickness, Shin-chi invests the canoe with all his feelings and sends it down the river to return home in his stead. After a winter of hunger (for which Shin-chi and his friend find a solution), summer finally arrives, and both the sockeye and the children are able to return home.

Carrier, Roch. *The Hockey Sweater.* Illustrated by Sheldon Cohen. 978-088776-169-0. Toronto: Tundra Books, 1984. Age 8 and up.

The rivalry between the Toronto Maple Leafs and the Montreal Canadiens has always been representative of Canada itself, with Anglophone and Francophone cultures sometimes sitting uneasily with one another. This story takes place in 1946 in rural Quebec, where the writer grew up worshiping Canadiens player Maurice Richard; all the boys in town wore Canadiens hockey sweaters with Richard's number. Then comes the day that young Roch's sweater needs replacing and his mother orders a new one from Eaton's catalog. What should arrive but a Maple Leafs sweater! To the detriment of his hockey game, his mother forces him to wear it. When Roch's temper gets the best of him on the ice, the coach sends him to church to pray for repentance—but young Roch prays instead for "a hundred million moths that would come and eat up my Toronto Maple Leafs sweater." Some American readers have called this ending "flat," preferring an on-the-ice triumph not at all in keeping with Carrier's classic tale. The text of this picture book was originally written as a short story, which became the basis for a short animated film shown in elementary classes across Canada.

Croza, Laurel. *I Know Here.* Illustrated by Matt James. 978-0-88899-923-8. Toronto: Groundwood, 2010. Ages 5–8.

The prospect of moving from rural Saskatchewan to Toronto would be daunting to anyone, but it is especially so for the third-grader in this story. Most of her life has been spent in the camp near the dam her father is building—eight trailers on one side of the road, including her family's, and ten on the other. She knows the forest and its creatures, the camp's daily routines, her classroom of nine (two of whom are her siblings). "Have people in Toronto seen what I've seen?" she asks her teacher. Wisely, her teacher suggests she draw a picture of what she wants to remember. James's art is two-dimensional, much as a child's might be, with broad brushstrokes and flat backgrounds, picturing only the important elements.

Gay, Marie-Louise. *Stella, Star of the Sea.* 978-0-88899-337-3. Toronto: Groundwood, 1999. Ages 2–4.

With over seventy books to her credit in both English and French, Gay is well-known across Canada. American readers know her best for Stella and Sam, who made their debut in this book. As the big sister, Stella willingly answers Sam's many questions when they visit the seashore. To his question "Where do starfish come from, Stella?" she inventively explains that "Starfish are shooting stars that fell in love with the sea." Stella urges Sam to come into the water, but Sam is wary and prolongs the moment with question after question, until finally Stella poses her own question, "Are you ever coming in?" to which he answers "Yes!" Gay's training in animation as well as art history results in paintings that exude fresh air and personality. Several more Stella and Sam books follow, including the retrospective *When Stella Was Very, Very Small* (2009).

Ghione, Yvette. *Hockey Opposites.* Illustrated by Per-Henrik Gürth. 978-1-55453-241-4. Kids Can Press, 2010. Ages 2–4.

What could be more Canadian than using hockey to introduce the concept of opposites? Gürth's players are all animals found in Canada, including the *big* bear and the *small* badger. The book begins with the *home* team and the *away* team skating onto the ice, and by the end of the book, one team celebrates a *win* and the other bemoans its *loss*. In between, the exciting game action is easy to follow through pictures that are rendered in a simple, heavily outlined style geared to toddlers.

Granfield, Linda. *In Flanders Fields: The Story of the Poem by John McCrae.* Illustrated by Janet Wilson. 978-155005-144-5 (10th anniversary edition). Markham, Ont.: Fitzhenry and Whiteside, 2005. Age 7 and up.

In the US on Memorial Day, it's not unusual to see VFW or American Legion volunteers soliciting donations and handing out artificial poppies in return. This tradition can be traced directly to Canadian John McCrae's poem, written on the battlefield in Belgium during World War I. Granfield wisely intersperses illustrated stanzas of the poem with informational sections that provided background about World War I, McCrae, and the poem's lasting legacy.

Kusugak, Michael Arvaarluk. *Baseball Bats for Christmas.* Illustrated by Vladyana Krykorka. 978-1-55037-145-1. Toronto: Annick Press, 1990. Ages 8–12.

Repulse Bay is located on the Arctic Circle in Nunavit, one of Canada's three territories. In 1955 when this story takes place, children living in Repulse Bay have no contact with the rest of the world other than the small plane that delivers supplies and Father Didier, who comes to run the mission church. One day not long before Christmas the plane unloads six unrecognizable spindly things—"standing-ups," the children call them, having never seen trees before and lacking a word in their language. With no idea why they are there, they finally decide to trim off the branches and fashion baseball bats. Krykorka's realistic illustrations capture the small community in winter, when the children enjoy sledding and other games and the days are so short that the sun always seems to be rising or setting.

Lee, Dennis. *Alligator Pie.* Illustrated by Frank Newfield. 978-0-06-231346-1. New York: HarperCollins, 2014. Ages 3–8. Also available in Kindle edition.

It would be hard to find a Canadian who is not familiar with Dennis Lee's 1974 collection of verses geared specifically to children. When he wrote this, Lee was already a recognized poet for adults as well as a book editor, and his work was very much grounded in his experiences as a Canadian. He felt that Canadian children should have the chance to hear rhymes and verses that incorporated places and things they knew, rather than only cultural elements from the British tradition. He modeled his new verses after nursery rhymes, as in this short selection: "Wiggle to the Laundromat/Waggle to the sea;/Skip to Casa Loma/And you can't catch me!" This now-classic book paved the way for children's books drawn from the Canadian experience.

Lemieux, Michèle. *Stormy Night.* 978-1-55074-692-1. Toronto: Kids Can Press, 1999. All ages.

A storm is coming, and the young girl in this book prepares for bed but finds she can't sleep. Random thoughts and questions are running through her head: "Is there life on other planets?...When I dream at night, where am I?...Will I always make the right decisions?" Spare line drawings accompany her thoughts, which occur and recur to all humans, young or old.

Lightfoot, Gordon. *Canadian Railroad Trilogy.* Illustrated by Ian Wallace. 978-0-88899-953-5. Toronto: Groundwood, 2010. Age 5 and up.

Lightfoot's now-classic song, commissioned by the Canadian Broadcasting Corporation for Canada's centennial in 1967, describes the construction of the Canadian Pacific Railway. Built to connect eastern and western Canada, the Canadian Pacific has always served as a symbol for Canadian nationalism, and Andrews's panoramic illustrations add another layer to Lightfoot's song with historical details not mentioned in the lyrics. Building the railroad was a heroic feat, yet it also had enormous cost in lives, lands, and livelihoods. The music is reproduced in the back, as are lengthy illustrator notes that explain the allusions in each illustration. With something to offer every level of reader, this book and its reader can grow together. Ian Wallace has illustrated many other books that deal with Canadian culture and history, including Jan Andrews's *Very Last First Time* (1985, 2003), about the Inuit; Wallace's own *Boy of the Deeps* (1999, 2005), set in Nova Scotia; and *Duncan's Way* (2000), also by Wallace, set in Newfoundland.

McGugan, Jim. *Josepha: A Prairie Boy's Story.* Illustrated by Murray Kimber. 978-0-88995-142-6 (ppb). Calgary: Red Deer Press, 2003. Age 6 and up.

In the Old Country, Josepha's family had a shop, but on the plains of Canada in 1900 they are trying to eke out a living as farmers. Tall lanky fourteen-year-old Josepha must sit alongside the small children in the one-room school house until he learns English. His frustration at not being to express himself is evident, but his general good nature manifests itself in protecting the little kids from the older bullies. His story is told from the perspective of a young classmate whom he has befriended, and an early illustration that shows Josepha larger than life reflects the narrator's perception of him. His teacher sees that he is bright and tries to talk him out of quitting school, but the immediacy of contributing to the family income by bagging wheat—a dollar a day for *baggink!*—outweighs the long-term benefits of education. At parting Josepha gives the narrator his only possession, the pocketknife with which he has whittled many a toy and keepsake, and in return the narrator gives Josepha his prized pair of too-big boots to cover Josepha's bare feet. Kimber's expressionist illustrations capture the desolation of life on the prairie for early settlers.

Moore, Yvette. *A Prairie Alphabet.* Illustrated by Jo Bannatyne-Cugnet. 978-088776-937-5 (ppb). Toronto: Tundra Books, 2009. Ages 7–11.

First published in 1992, this rich alphabet book offers a glimpse of life on the Canadian prairie, which ranges across Alberta, Saskatchewan, and Manitoba. These wide-open spaces are not unlike their counterparts in the Dakotas, Nebraska, Kansas, and neighboring states where people rely on farming for their livelihoods. On the prairie, neighbors help one another. Whole families work on the farm but also enjoy themselves at the rodeo or sledding during the winter. On each page, a sentence uses words beginning with the featured letter and the illustration contains many objects beginning with the letter in addition to those named, providing an "I spy" activity. Details situate this prairie in Canada: the Canadian flag on signage; the Canadian Pacific Railway transporting grain; Canada Air planes in the sky. The back matter lists the objects in the pictures and uses each picture as an impetus for further commentary about life on the prairie.

Oberman, Sheldon. *The White Stone in the Castle Wall.* Illustrated by Les Tait. 978-0-88776-386-1 (ppb). Toronto: Tundra Books, 1996. Ages 7–11.

While many readers can enjoy this story of a hard-working young boy whose efforts pay off, its focus on the Casa Loma mansion in Toronto gives it special significance. Sir Henry Pellatt is building a stone wall around Casa Loma in the early 1900s, and Young Tommy Fiddich hears that Sir Henry will pay a silver dollar for each stone that meets his standards. Tommy loads his large white stone into a wheelbarrow and pushes it up the long hill to the castle, only to find it rejected by the foreman as too white. After all that work, the stone has value for him, so he offers to give it to the gardener rather than see it thrown away. The gardener turns out to be Sir Henry himself, who appreciates Tommy's work ethic and not only pays him the dollar but offers him a job as gardener. Although the story behind the white stone is fiction, the castle still exists, as does the wall with the one white stone. Children growing up in this century might do well to view the investment of themselves in their work as an intrinsic reward added to the extrinsic reward of monetary gain.

Pendziwol, Jean E. *Marja's Skis.* Illustrated by Jirina Marton. 978-0-88899-674-9. Toronto: Groundwood, 2007. Ages 4–9.

During the nineteenth century, Finnish immigrants settled in northern Ontario (as well as northern Minnesota and Michigan), where they found work in mining and forestry. Marja's father is a logger; when he dies in a logging accident, the family takes in boarders to make ends meet. Marja, who skis to and from school, comes upon one of the boarders who has fallen through the ice and, bearing in mind her father's lesson to stay strong inside, she manages to ski out far enough to hand him her ski poles so that he can pull himself out. Pendziwol's text appeals to all the senses—the swish of skis on snow, the crisp clean air, the smell of hay in the barn, the warmth of the sauna. Marton's impressionistic illustrations are equally evocative.

Pendziwol, Jean E. *Once Upon a Northern Night.* Illustrated by Isabelle Arsenault. 978-1-55498-138-0. Toronto: Groundwood, 2013. Ages 4–7.

Softness pervades this northern lullaby, set deep in winter when snow blankets the world and the northern lights shimmer in the night sky. Only the animals are out and about to witness nature's stark beauty. The voice of a parent describes these scenes to a sleeping child, while full-page illustrations, each with a single color overlaying the black-and-white scene, harken back to an earlier, simpler time. This quiet, beautifully written and illustrated book transforms a cold Canadian night into something to be cherished.

Schwartz, Roslyn. *The Complete Adventures of the Mole Sisters.* 978-1-55037-883-2. Toronto: Annick Press, 2004. Ages 2–4.

A popular animated TV series based on Schwartz's small preschool books have made the Mole sisters favorite characters throughout Canada since 2003. Originally published individually, all ten stories have been collected in one volume that stars two independent, somewhat dreamy sisters who see the good in everything. In "The Mole Sisters and the Blue Egg," for example, the sisters are not sure what they're looking for, but they'll know when they find it. After an adventure climbing up a tree, seeing what it is like living in a bird's nest, and sliding back down to earth, they find two halves of a blue eggshell. Observant toddlers will know where the eggshell came from, although the sisters don't. Instead, the Mole sisters see what the halves can be—two bucket seats for swings.

Service, Robert W. *The Shooting of Dan McGrew.* Illustrated by Ted Harrison. 978-1-55074-608-2. Toronto: Kids Can Press, 1986. All ages.

Canadian children have grown up memorizing this poem in school, along with Service's "The Cremation of Sam McGee." Both poems speak to the wild and woolly Gold Rush days in the Yukon Territory. Artist Ted Harrison is a Canadian immigrant who settled in the Yukon, where he became famous for his paintings of the Far North landscape. He brings to Service's poem his distinctive style, with its heavy outlines and bold palette of colors. Each page is truly a frameable piece of art.

Setterington, Ken. *Mom and Mum Are Getting Married.* Illustrated by Alice Priestley. 978-1-896764-84-3. Toronto: Second Story Press, 2005. Ages 4–8.

The point of this book, clearly, is to show a situation in which the families of a same-sex couple greet their marriage announcement as they would any joyful event in the family. Told in the voice of the couple's daughter, who is to be the flower girl (there will be no bridesmaids), the slight plot revolves around the fear that the rings may get lost, and the daughter's solution in tying them to the baskets that she and her younger brother carry. Realistic pencil drawings portray the extended family on both sides in groupings that represent all configurations of family. Published on the heels of the legalization of same-sex marriage in Ontario in 2003 and in the same year that same-sex marriage became legal throughout Canada, this book anticipated the need some children will have to see their lives affirmed in a book.

Slodovnick, Avi. *The Tooth.* Illustrated by Manon Gauthier. 978-1-935279-72-3. La Jolla, CA: Kane Miller, 2010. Ages 5–8.

Marissa's tooth aches, and so her mother takes her downtown to the dentist, where among the skyscrapers and rush of people Marissa spots a homeless man sitting on the sidewalk with a box of coins. The dentist pulls Marissa's tooth and gives it to her in an envelope to take home for the tooth fairy, but when she gets outside she drops the tooth in the homeless man's box, telling him to put it under his pillow that night "and there will be money there tomorrow." Throughout, only Marissa acknowledges the man; her mother pulls her away, and passersby willfully ignore his existence. Soft-hued, edgy illustrations underscore this contrast by showing only Marissa, the man, and her mother in color, with the balance of the street scene in gray tones. Through understatement, illustrator and artist capture perfectly the impact of a child's first encounter with social inequity.

Teevee, Ningeokuluk. *Alego.* 978-0-88899-943-6. Toronto: Groundwood, 2009. Ages 4–7.

Set in the northernmost part of Canada on Baffin Island, this bilingual book (Inuktitut and English) recounts a young Inuit girl's first experience going clam digging with her grandmother. They go when the tide is out, leaving the ocean's bounty on the sand; Alego cannot resist collecting the many forms of sea life she discovers—from sculpins to starfish to snails to other creepy-crawly things. While Alego comes home with a full bucket but few clams, her grandmother has collected enough clams to prepare a feast. Teevee's pen-and-ink drawings provide a strong sense of this Inuit community, from a bird's-eye view of the village to close-ups of the sea creatures; front and back endpapers pinpoint Baffin Island's location in North America. The Inuktitut text will fascinate some readers, as the writing system uses signs that represent sounds. Interspersed within the English text are a few transliterated Inuktitut words that give readers an idea of the sound of the language.

Trottier, Maxine. *Migrant.* Illustrated by Isabelle Arsenault. 978-0-88899-975-7. Toronto: Groundwood, 2011. Ages 4–8.

In many parts of North America—Canada as well as the United States—farms depend on migrant workers to harvest seasonal crops. Some very unusual migrant workers are the Mennonites who settled in Canada and then moved to Mexico in the 1920s when Canada passed a law mandating that they send their children to public schools. During recent difficult economic times, they have been returning to Canada during the summer to work in the fields. Told in third person, this is the story of one such family through the feelings of their youngest daughter, which are consistently expressed in animal terms. She feels like a jackrabbit coming to live in an abandoned burrow, for instance, and at night she and her sisters cozy up like kittens under one blanket while her brothers fidget like puppies in the other room. Arsenault's modern, surrealistic illustrations expand on these metaphors while simultaneously capturing the Old World feel of the family.

Van Camp, Richard. *A Man Called Raven.* Illustrated by George Littlechild. 978-0-89239-144-8. San Francisco: Children's Book Press, 1997. Ages 6–9.

Two boys are hitting a raven with hockey sticks when a foreboding man suddenly appears before them. He makes them take him to his parents, and then he tells the story of a man who hurt ravens and became one as punishment. The boys are suitably chastised, and one asks if the man ever got to be human again. "Sometimes, when there was something the people were forgetting, he would change back, but not for long," he responds, and disappears in a rush of wings. Littlechild's abstract, boldly colored illustrations give energy and an otherworldly power to this story that reminds the reader that all life is connected. Van Camp, from the Dogrib Nation, and Littlechild, a Plains Cree, have collaborated on another picture book, *What's the Most Beautiful Thing You Know about Horses?* (1998) that is no longer in print.

Warner, Jody Nyasha. *Viola Desmond Won't Be Budged!* Illustrated by Richard Rudnicki. 978-0-88899-779-1. Toronto: Groundwood, 2010. Ages 6–10.

Although Canada abolished slavery a good thirty years before the United States did, discrimination against African Canadians continued well into the twentieth century. Viola Desmond was born and raised in Halifax, Nova Scotia, and owned a popular beauty salon there. In 1946, en route to a meeting in another city, she had car trouble and stopped in New Glasgow to have her car repaired. With several hours on her hands, she went to a movie at the local theater and bought a ticket. When she sat down, the usher told her to move to the balcony: "You have a cheap upstairs ticket." She was not allowed to pay a penny more for the main-floor, whites-only section. In a protest that preceded that of Rosa Parks, Viola Desmond refused to move and was arrested, jailed overnight, and fined for not paying the proper price. When the case was taken to the Nova Scotia Supreme Court in 1947, the judge dismissed it, ignoring the racist policy by framing it as a case of tax evasion. Rudnicki's realistic acrylic paintings capture the look of the 1940s and the stylish Viola's strength.

Watt, Mélanie. *Scaredy Squirrel.* 978-1-55337-959-1. Toronto: Kids Can Press, 2006. Ages 5–8.

The fake smile on Scaredy's face tells it all: he's afraid of everything and everyone, including readers who may have germs. It's so much easier to stay in his tree and plan for every eventuality; thus he has his first-aid kit and his emergency exit plan. But life has a way of ignoring the best-laid plans, and his panic at the sight of a killer bee causes him to fall from the tree. That's how he finds out he is a *flying* squirrel. This is the first of a series about Scaredy, who is also the basis for a cartoon series of the same name created in Canada and airing periodically in the US on the Cartoon Network.

Watt, Mélanie. *You're Finally Here!* 978-1-4231-3486-2. New York: Disney Hyperion, 2011. Ages 4–7.

Who is the *you* of the title? Why, the reader, of course. A cocky cartoon rabbit rejoices at the reader's presence yet cannot help but scold the reader a bit for keeping him waiting inside the book. It's boring, unfair, annoying, and rude, and he has all kinds of examples to prove it. When the rabbit finally makes sure the reader will stay, his phone rings—and he doesn't hesitate to answer it. "No, I'm not busy at all." He gets a second call on top of the first, begins chatting away, and suddenly realizes that the reader has turned the last page and is on the way out. "Wait! Where are you going? Was it something I said?" This egocentric rabbit rivals Mo Willem's pigeon when it comes to making young readers and listeners feel like an important part of the book.

Wheeler, Bernelda. *Where Did You Get Your Moccasins?* Illustrated by Herman Bekkering. 978-1-895411-50-8 (ppb). Winnipeg: Peguis, 1992. Ages 3–6.

In this cumulative tale, a young boy answers the title question, only to be asked another question, and another, and another. In a series of answers he explains that his *kookum* (grandmother) made his moccasins, using leather that she made from a deer hide that she got from his dad when he went hunting. The final question his classmates ask is where his *kookum* got the beads that adorn the moccasins, and his answer is a surprise: from the store! Realistic pencil illustrations in black-and-white show a contemporary elementary school setting with a diverse student population, with background images of the boy's *kookum* and the steps that went into making the moccasins. Although this staple-bound book is not showy, both text and illustrations are solid and gain more appeal with each reading.

Yee, Paul. *Roses Sing on New Snow.* Illustrated by Harvey Chan. 978-0-88899-217-8 (ppb). Toronto: Groundwood, 2003. Ages 4–8.

Maylin's culinary skills have made her father's Chinese restaurant "well known through the New World," but her two lazy brothers get all the credit because she is female. Chan's realistic watercolor illustrations reveal a Chinatown of old, when streets were unpaved and used by horses, set against

Looking Forward

Cybèle Young

C ybèle Young is a rising star on the Canadian children's book scene but an established planet in the art world, where she is known for her miniature sculptures made of Japanese paper. She is also a printmaker, and these two art forms combine naturally in her books for children. She has illustrated several children's books, including *Pa's Forest* by Jan Andrews, *Daughter of the Great Zandini* by Cary Fagan, and *Jack Pine* by Christopher Patton, but in 2011 she made her debut as an author-illustrator with two innovative picture books that both won acclaim. *Ten Birds* (Kids Can Press) and *A Few Blocks* (Groundwood) couldn't be more different in look, style, or tone, and yet both evidence Young's background in printmaking and sculpture.

Ten Birds. 978-1-55453-568-2. Toronto: Kids Can Press, 2011. All ages.

Ten birds are presented with the problem of crossing a river (this premise requires the reader to suspend disbelief that the birds cannot fly across). The first nine, each of whom is considered intellectually gifted, devise ingenious modes of transportation using elements from the collection of odd wooden and iron machines at hand: one catapults herself, another uses stilts, another drifts across in a basket carried by balloons, and so on. The tenth bird, known as "Needs Improvement," simply walks across the bridge. The text and illustrations both follow a pattern. For instance, one spread reads: "The one they called 'Magnificent' had an idea. Swooshing, he left SEVEN behind." From the illustration on the right, readers see that Magnificent has flown over in a kite, and underneath the text on the left is the numeral 7 formed by the leftover kite-building materials. Perhaps it is the use of black-and-white illustrations, or the surrealistic, sculptural quality of the art, or the inherent irony and social commentary of the text that suggests the work of another sculptor-turned-book-creator, Chris Van Allsburg.

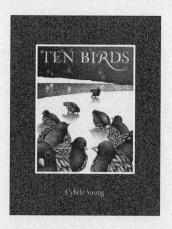

A Few Blocks. 978-0-88999-995-5. Toronto: Groundwood, 2011. Ages 4–7.

What's a sister to do when her younger brother doesn't want to go to school? Viola knows Ferdie's penchant for imaginative play, and so she creates one scenario after another to coax him on his way. His coat becomes a superfast cape, and they fly over the city conquering evil; a leaf becomes a ship that takes them across the ocean in search of treasure; a piece of cardboard becomes a knight's shield that helps him defeat the dragon and save the princess Viola. But big sister becomes tired of this game and turns the tables. Now it is Ferdie's turn to coax Viola the rest of the way to school. Delicate one-color pen-and-ink illustrations chronicle the realistic part of their journey and segue into pastel-hued scenes created with etched-paper assemblages. As they walk the remaining block to school, real and imaginary worlds converge: they are entering a place that will stoke their imaginations. Viola and Ferdie return in a second book, *A Few Bites* (2012), in which Viola uses her storytelling skills to convince Ferdie to eat his vegetables.

a backdrop of mountains. When the governor of South China comes to town, each restaurant brings its best dish to a banquet, and Maylin sends a dish she names Roses Sing on New Snow. The secret is out when the governor pronounces it the tastiest and asks how to make it; further, Maylin has the audacity to tell him that he can't possibly make the same dish. "If you and I sat down with paper and brush and black ink, could we bring forth identical paintings?" she asks him. Yee and Chan's first of many collaborations is a subtle reminder of the role Chinese immigrants played in early Canadian history.

Yerxa, Leo. *Ancient Thunder.* 978-0-88899-746-3. Toronto: Groundwood, 2006. Age 4 and up.

Yerxa's descriptive poem, circular in structure, celebrates the beauty and strength of the horse as it carries man across the plains "on hooves of ancient thunder." Collage illustrations simulate fringed buckskin clothing in the Plains style painted with figures of running horses similar to those found in Lakota ledger books. On the front endpapers, individual horses of painted cut paper run against a dark background, anticipating the poem's first line, "At the rise of the Strawberry Moon," explained in a note as June. These same horses appear throughout the book, under or alongside the clothing or simply against a white background. Finally, they run across the back endpapers, this time against a light background, out of the book and into endless time. Yerxa has created a book that envelops the reader's sense of touch, sight, and sound.

Europe

By far the greatest number of children's books coming to the United States originate in Europe, more specifically in the United Kingdom. British books have several things going for them in the United States: the English language, give or take usage differences; a shared history of children's literature through the early twentieth century; and a similar artistic aesthetic. American editors can read British books and make an acquisitions decision without relying on a translator's synopsis or recommendation. British attitudes toward the body and its functions are also similar to American ones, so that one rarely encounters images of breastfeeding mothers or partially clothed adults in British books as one might in books from continental Europe.

Post-World War II British picture books were revolutionized by the advent of the offset printing process that enabled illustrators to work in full color. As Douglas Martin mentions in his study of fifteen British artists, *The Telling Line,* "Britain was in the forefront of this initiative, its publishers ready to invest in the development of original talent as well as to encourage their established artists to make full use of the new resources."[1] This initiative produced Brian Wildsmith, Charles Keeping, Shirley Hughes, and a host of other artists who got their start in the 1950s; some continue to create new books today. The 1970s and 1980s saw the full flowering of lush, detailed color illustrations that often accompanied forgettable text. Today's British picture books represent all points on the artistic spectrum, from Quentin Blake's quirky cartoon figures to Anthony Browne's surrealistic primates to Emily Gravett's postmodern book designs. Most of the books that win the Kate Greenaway Award, the UK's annual award for best illustrations in a children's book, are acquired for US publication.

The number of books from other European countries is a drop in the bucket compared to the number from the UK. In fact, in any given year, translated books from *all the countries in continental Europe combined* add up to only about a quarter of what comes from England alone.[2] Included in this small number of books are acquisitions from Germany, the Scandinavian countries, France, Belgium, and the Netherlands, with occasional books from Spain and Italy. A Swiss publisher, NordSüd, works with writers and artists from throughout Europe, and many of their picture books are taken for publication by their American sister company North-South Books.

NordSüd is just one of many publishers working in the German language. Within Europe, German is spoken not only in Germany but also in Austria, Liechtenstein, and parts of Switzerland, Italy, Luxumbourg, and Belgium. German-language publishers work across national borders—it is not uncommon for, say, a German writer to be published by an Austrian publisher or a Swiss illustrator to work for a German publisher. The German-language publishing industry is robust, and the picture books that come to the US are a very small sampling of the creativity to be seen in German-language picture books. Most of the picture books acquired for US publication are safe choices both in terms of illustration style and content. Some, in fact, are illustrated editions of the Grimms' fairy tales, which can be problematic, since the texts are original and have not been sanitized to many Americans' liking. The idea of Cinderella's sisters cutting their toes or heels off to fit into the glass slipper is always a rude shock to those who have grown up on the Disney version of the story.

A few years ago the German press ran an article about an American publishing firm that had contracted for a book by Rotraut Susanne Berner, an internationally recognized German author-illustrator. The article was entitled "Ein fall von zensur" [A case of censorship][3] and explained that the American publisher had asked Berner to change two illustrations in the book. One of these involved a person smoking in a café, and the other showed a nude woman in a painting along with a small sculpture of a nude man, two of seven items in an art museum. Berner refused, and the contract was canceled. In the end, another American publisher brought out this book without any changes, and judging from customer reviews of the book, it is the rare parent who objects to these scenes. Most rave about how much their young children enjoy following the characters in the illustrations again and again. Herein lies one of the difficulties some continental European publishers have trying to place their books in the American market. What's perfectly common in some countries is not socially acceptable in some parts of the US, and therefore in an effort to offend no one, most American publishers play it safe by rejecting outstanding books. It is usually the smaller independent publishing houses that are willing to take risks on books that are culturally authentic in these kinds of ways.

One such American publisher is Kane Miller, which has been responsible for bringing books to the US that we might never otherwise see. A prime example is *Standing Up* by Marie-Anne Gillet and Isabelle Gilboux (2005), no longer in print. First published in the Netherlands and set in Brussels, Belgium, it is the story of a toddler who sees the famous fountain Manneken-Pis and is inspired to pee standing up like the statue does. The book chronicles the boy's attempts—at first faulty, as his aim is not good and he doesn't restrict his attempts to the bathroom toilet. The book is hysterically funny to adults and children alike and can even be useful for toilet training, but those positive aspects could not overcome the negative reactions of the adults who railed at the inappropriateness of the subject matter. On the other hand, many of Kane Miller's risky acquisitions do remain in print.

If the UK is at the top end of the scale in terms of number of books taken for US publication, the Netherlands might well be at the low end, with only a handful of picture books, if that, coming to the US annually. This is the country that gave us Dick Bruna's Miffy books and Max Velthuijs's much-loved series about Frog and his friends, but also *Standing Up*. As the latter demonstrates, some Dutch books are simply too far out there for American tastes. When writing about Dutch culture and Dutch children's books, British critic Aiden Chambers commented, "The people of the Low Countries protect their children very conscientiously, which means protection of the right to know as well as protection from abuse and exploitation. . . . Few other nations take such an open-minded view of what children are capable of comprehending."[4]

The same might be said of the Scandinavian countries. More than a century ago Denmark gave us Hans Christian Andersen, whose tales do not always end happily in the eyes of American readers. The ugly duckling turns into a swan, it is true, but there is no way around the fact that the little match girl freezes to death. Denmark, Finland, and Norway each have half the population Sweden has, which means half the readers, half the book-buying public, and half the number of picture books published each year. Thus it makes sense that we see more books from Sweden than from any of the other Scandinavian countries, although Norway does provide grants supporting the translation of Norwegian children's books into other languages. *Garmann's Summer* by Stian Hole was supported this way and was named a Batchelder Honor Book in 2009. Not only does the book not gloss over a child's fear, it also intensifies Garmann's uneasy feeling through the use of surrealistic illustrations.

Sweden's most famous literary export is *Pippi Longstocking*, which paved the way for further translations in the last half of the twentieth century. With their colorful, child-centered illustrations, most Swedish books have a look that appeals to American aesthetic tastes. Enough Swedish picture books have been published in English that one can begin to identify cultural patterns. Contrary to the stereotype, not all Swedes are blond-haired and blue-eyed. The playground and school scenes are ethnically diverse, reflecting the fact that one in four Swedish children has roots in another country, either as an adoptee or as a child of immigrants. Day care is a frequent setting for picture books, perhaps because 80 percent of Swedish mothers work.

During the last decade, discussion about gender representation has led to better representation of strong girls in Swedish picture books. Many of these books address the fears and emotions of children, often with humor or even fantasy. Children immediately respond to these stories, but literal-minded adults are often puzzled by them; consequently, some of the most inventive Swedish picture books don't stay in print long.

Finally, while France has had a long-standing tradition of publishing books for children, until recently few American children have had the opportunity to see them. An exception is the Babar series by Jean de Brunhoff, which began with *The Story of Babar* in 1931, published in translation in the US and the UK in 1933. That was the beginning of an era in which American children's book publishers were receptive to European books. "Early last century the children's rooms of American's major public libraries stocked picture books imported not only from Mother England but also from France, Germany, Sweden, Russia, and Czechoslovakia," notes children's literature historian Leonard Marcus. "They did so as a service to their immigrant populations but also to give native-born children their first window onto 'other lands.'"[5] Laurent de Brunhoff continued the series after his father's death, and Babar books continue to have staying power;

a children's TV series was created in the 1990s and appears frequently in reruns. The other famous French children's book character in America did not come from France at all. Ludwig Bemelman's *Madeline* and its sequels were created after he immigrated to New York from Austria in the early twentieth century.

Perhaps the children's book character most identified with France is Astérix, "the biggest comic-book star in France these days, [and] in the whole of Europe," but virtually unknown to American children.[6] For fifty years, Astérix and his fellow Gauls have been lodged in a small corner of France resisting the Roman conquest. That the thirty-four books in the series have been translated so widely is a testament not only to their popularity but to the abilities of the translators, since the books are filled with puns that work only in the French language. The British translators, Anthea Bell and Derek Hockridge, did a masterful job finding equivalents that carried the same sense of fun if not of meaning.[7] Forty years ago an American publisher released the first three books in the series, but they didn't sell well, and today the books are available in the United States only as British imports.

Notes

1. Martin, *The Telling Line*, 24.
2. Stan, "A Study of International Children's Picture Books Published in the United States in 1994," 261–275.
3. "Ein fall von zensur."
4. Linders and de Sterck, *Behind the Story*, 11.
5. Marcus, "Outside over Where?" 49.
6. Cendrowicz, "Astérix at 50."
7. Bell, "The Translator's Notebook," 129–139.

Austria, Germany, and German-Speaking Switzerland

Bauer, Jutta. *Grandpa's Angel.* 978-0-7636-2743-0. Boston: Candlewick, 2005. Ages 7–11.

As he lies in a hospice, a grandfather tells his visiting grandson stories of his life, up to, through, and after World War II. The straightforward text is paired with pictures that show an angel consistently watching over Grandpa and saving him from harm—a wonderful example of dramatic irony. By the time Grandpa finishes his story and notes that he has been very lucky, the reader realizes that Grandpa doesn't know the half of it. Grandpa's story is framed by the boy's first-person narration at the beginning and the end, distinguished by a different typeface. Details in the illustrations such as a Nazi armband, a yellow star, and signage show a German setting. When the young narrator leaves the hospice, Grandpa's angel follows him out, a sign perhaps that he too will lead a lucky life.

Bauer, Jutta. *Selma.* 978-1-929132-50-6. La Jolla, CA: Kane Miller, 2003. All ages.

What is happiness? The wise ram tells the story of Selma, a sheep with a satisfying life. Each day, Selma plays with her children, munches grass, exercises, chats with her neighbors, and sleeps well. When asked what she would do if she had more time or more money, she says she would do exactly the same. This profound tale housed in a postcard-size book speaks to each age group in a different way and appeals equally to a 5-year-old and a 50-year-old.

Berner, Rotraut Susanne. *Hound and Hare.* Translated by Shelley Tanaka. 978-0-88899-987-0. Toronto: Groundwood, 2011. Ages 6–8.

In this beginning chapter book, a long-standing feud between families, the Hounds and the Hares, is resolved when their school-age sons, Hugo and Harley, go missing during a lightning storm while running in the village's Big Race. The boys combine their specialized knowledge to save themselves—and the missing Pippa Pig—and share the podium for first place. The ridiculous slurs hurled by the parents against one another will amuse children but also point up the baseless foundation of prejudice. Berner exhibits yet another illustration style here, different both from the book listed below and her illustrations for Jutta Richter's book for older readers, *Cat, or How I Lost Eternity* (Milkwood, 2008).

Berner, Rotraut Susanne. *In the Town All Year 'Round.* 978-0-8118-6474-9. San Francisco: Chronicle Books, 2008. All ages.

Individual stories abound in this wordless book of small-town residents and their activities throughout the seasons. Every page is crammed full of people—young, old, families, singles, couples, and pet owners—and each has a story that emerges over the course of the seasons and the year. The same seven scenes are shown for each of the seasons, and cutaway buildings offer even more opportunity to see what the characters are doing. Readers will continuously find themselves flipping back and forth to look for missed details. A German setting is reflected in some of the architecture as well as in the densely packed buildings, open plazas, outdoor kiosks, the public transportation system, and the kind of stores (e.g., green grocer).

Grossman-Hensel, Katharina. *How Mommy Met Daddy.* Translated by Rachel Ward. 978-073582176 New York: North-South Books, 2008. Ages 5–8.

Mommy is big, colorful, and messy. Daddy is tall, thin, and tidy. How these two characters met and fell in love is the subject of their child's tale. Each opened a store on the same street opposite the other, but neither was successful. Mommy's store was full of clothes that she made herself, while the shelves in Daddy's store were stacked with items in only black or white. Only after they accidentally crash into each other and experience love at first sight do they merge their stores and find retail success. The child narrator is a happy combination of both, wearing colorful shoes and socks with a black-and-white top.

Hächler, Bruno. *Anna's Wish.* Illustrated by Friederike Rave. 978-0-7258-2207-8. New York: NorthSouth, 2008. Ages 3–7.

Anna's wish is for snow, which she has never seen; the last snowfall occurred during her mother's childhood. Passing by the bakery, Anna feels a tiny brush of cold and is inspired to retrieve the old sled from the basement. Her sleep is filled with dreams of snow, and the following morning she returns to the bakery to wish on the sparkling white horse that adorns a cake. Whether this book is a cautionary tale or a realistic one, it succeeds in conveying the magic of a first snowfall. Climate change is a growing concern in Switzerland, where the snow line in the Alps has visibly receded.

Janisch, Heinz. *The Fantastic Adventures of Baron Munchausen.* Illustrated by Aljoscha Blau. 978-1-59270-091-2. New York: Enchanted Lion, 2010. Age 6 and up.

Baron Munchausen's tales disappeared in the US over the last century and are now unknown to most Americans, but this slim volume may begin a resurgence. The eleven tall tales presented here, especially as retold by Janisch, are compact and wonderfully entertaining, and each is accompanied by an illustration that shows the Baron in eighteenth-century dress while the rest of the world has moved on in time. Baron Munchausen was a real person who apparently loved to embellish his exploits in the retelling, but the collection of tales attributed to him has grown since his death in 1797, and an enigmatic foreword to this edition suggests that Janisch has added a few tales of his own in keeping with the tradition.

Janisch, Heinz. *"I Have a Little Problem," Said the Bear.* Illustrated by Silke Leffler. 978-0-7358-2235-1. New York: NorthSouth Books, 2009. Ages 3–7.

Here is a lesson on how *not* to be a good listener. Bear barely mentions that he has a little problem, and each person he addresses won't let him finish but tells him his problem and hands him a solution: wings to make him lighter, a scarf to keep him warm, and so on. Just when he has given up hope, a fly alights near him and asks what's wrong. "I don't want to talk about it," he says. "No one listens to me anyway." The fly, however, is a good listener, and when Bear explains that he is afraid of the dark and doesn't want to sleep in his cave alone, she volunteers to move in with him. Problem solved. Why the bad listeners are human and the good listener is part of the ecosystem is something to ponder.

Johansen, Hanna. *Henrietta and the Golden Eggs.* Illustrated by Käthi Bhend. Translated by John S. Barrett. 978-1-56792-210-4. New York: Godine, 2002. Ages 6–9.

Henrietta is a young chicken with big ideas living in a factory farm where 3,333 chickens are packed into a small space. She alone has the curiosity to peck her way out of the chicken house into the fresh air, and when the hole is large enough, all the big chickens follow her. This scenario is repeated two more times until the farm owners wise up and build a large chicken house with ample room for all. Bhend's humorous pen-and-ink illustrations imbue the animals with character and show the chaos that Henrietta manages to cause. Some will like this story simply for its plucky heroine, while others will recognize the implicit criticism of industrial-sized poultry farms.

Könnecke, Ole. *Anthony and the Girls.* Translated by Nancy Seitz. 978-0-374-30376-2. New York: Farrar Straus Giroux, 2006. Ages 4–7.

Everyone knows someone, adult or child, who thinks having bigger, better toys ensures him (or her) a place in the sandbox. Anthony (Anton in the original German) is one such child, but he fails to win the attention of the two girls who are happily playing in the sand. They are not interested in his toys or in his attempts to show how high he can jump or how brave he is on the slide. Finally, he resorts to piling things atop one another to build the biggest house in the world but slips and falls. His tears catch the girls' attention, and before long, he is playing with them in the sandbox. Then along comes Luke hauling even bigger toys, and readers are left to guess what social dynamics may come into play. The text is spare and the illustrations uncomplicated, but the story is complex.

Könnecke, Ole. *Anton Can Do Magic.* Translated by Catherine Chidgey. 978-1-877467-37-0. Wellington, NZ: Gecko Press, 2011. Ages 4–7. Distributed by Lerner Publishing Group.

The same small boy we met in *Anthony and the Girls* reprises his role as someone who likes attention. Here he has been given the same kind of turban worn by magicians, and he sets out to do magic. When he can't make a tree disappear, he focuses his attention on a bird, which conveniently flies off while his eyes are covered. Convinced that the hat works, he next tries it out on Luke, who walks away (disappearing from Anton's view). In a fortuitous set of events, Anton tries to bring back Luke but finds a bird instead, covers it with the hat, puts the hat on his head. Ta-da! Greta comes looking for her lost bird, and Anton produces it. A bit of male rivalry is apparent in Luke's assertion that Anton cannot do magic and his facial expression when Anton produces the bird.

Charting New Territory

Wolf Erlbruch

Since 1985, Erlbruch has been blazing trails in the picture book genre, in the area not only of book illustration and design but also of content. Whether illustrating his own stories or those of others, he manages to push the envelope. Perhaps part of the reason is that he doesn't distinguish between adult and child readers when working on a book. He takes on assignments that others might shy away from—a story about an ogress who eats children (not taken for US publication, predictably), a book about animal excrement (in print for over twenty years in the US, surprisingly). The books he both writes and illustrates take on big topics: death, the desire to parent, the meaning of life.

Erlbruch's illustrations are readily recognizable. His characters vary from book to book but all belong to the same family. His human characters usually look a bit as if they were being reflected in a fun-house mirror, with elongated heads or stout waistlines, and his animal characters are equally distorted. Always, however, they engender feeling in the reader. Erlbruch's choice of media varies as well, including some combination of pen, pencil, and pastels as well as items at hand—old maps, bills, wrapping paper, notebook paper. Sometimes his characters are set in context, while other times they float against a white background.

Wolf Erlbruch is a recipient of the 2006 Hans Christian Andersen Illustrator Medal and the 2003 Sonderpreis, a lifetime achievement award given once every three years to a German children's book artist (the prize alternates between author, artist, and translator). He has influenced a whole generation of illustrators, those who have come in contact with his work in picture books, art exhibits, and editorial illustration as well as those who have studied with him at the University of Wuppertal.

Illustrated by Erlbruch

Holzworth, Werner. *The Little Mole Who Went in Search of Whodunit.* 978-0-81091-641-8. New York: Abrams, 2007. All ages.

A big turd lands on Little Mole's head and he asks each animal in turn if it is his. "No, I do mine like this," each responds, and readers see clearly from the illustration what he means. While the conventional wisdom is that we Americans are much more uncomfortable talking and reading about bodies and bodily functions than Europeans are, when this book appeared in Germany in 1990 it "caused a considerable stir among adult mediators and book buyers, and neither objections to nor praise for the book have diminished yet" (Künnermann, "How Much Cruelty Can a Children's Picturebook Stand?" 16). The same can be said for its reception in the United States, where people find it either hilarious or totally inappropriate. In contrast, the Dutch National Library developed a list of classroom activities to go along with the book. This is the best-known internationally of Erlbruch's books—and the best seller.

Hopkins, Lee Bennett, ed. *Oh No! Where Are My Pants?* 978-0-688-17860-X. New York: HarperCollins, 2005. Ages 5–10.

The sustaining idea for this collection of fourteen poems is disaster in all its childhood forms—missing the ball during the big game, having your best friend move away, mispronouncing a word during class, arriving pantless at the dance. Although a couple of the poems have been collected elsewhere, most are being published here for the first time. The poems are not layered with meaning, nor are Erlbruch's illustrations, yet both are masterful at capturing the emotion of the moment.

Written and Illustrated by Erlbruch

The Big Question. Translated by Michael Reynolds. 978-1-933372-03-7 (ppb). New York: Europa Editions, 2005. All ages.

We all grapple with the Big Question at times in our life with different answers at different stages of life. The question is never stated, but the answers, which come from all quarters and reflect their speakers' lives, reveal it: why are we here? Some people believe they are on earth to pursue their dreams, desires, or vocations; others, like the rock, are more Zen-like: "You're here simply to be here." The family members of this boy, however, know that he is here to love and to be loved. This beautifully produced paperback uses the European format of wide front and back flaps attached to the cover.

Duck, Death and the Tulip. Translated by Catherine Chidgey. 978-1-877579-02-8. Wellington, NZ: Gecko Press, 2011. All ages. Distributed by Lerner Publications Group.

This book exemplifies Erlbruch's assertion that he does not distinguish literature for adults from that for children. Long-necked, short-legged Duck notices that she is being followed by Death, who is rather stylish in a long checked coat with short feet poking out. It turns out Death has always been near, "just in case." They go to the pond, where Duck has a wonderful time but Death finds the water too chilling. In a moving scene, Duck warms Death by covering him with her wings. They spend the summer together, but then it is Duck's turn to be cold, and one day she stops breathing. Death carries her to the river, places the tulip on her body, and sends her downstream. "He was almost a little moved. 'But that's life,' thought Death." Erlbruch's approach to death here is matter-of-fact, acknowledging that life and death are two sides of the same coin. Adults who recognize their own mortality will see themselves in Duck, in turns frightened and comfortable, but children who are seeing an older relative on the verge of death may also find a kind of comfort in Erlbruch's allegorical tale.

The Miracle of the Bears. Translated by Michael Reynolds. 978-1-933372-21-4 (ppb). New York: Europa Editions, 2006. All ages.

Coming out of hibernation, a bear has one thing on his mind—to replenish his store of fat. That done, his thoughts start turning to how to become a papa bear. The picture accompanying this thought is hilarious—posed on his side, legs crossed, he is a beefcake parody. Not sure how to achieve his goal, the bear asks a series of animals and each provides a different answer: babies grow in turnip fields; babies come from eggs; the stork brings babies (the stork roundly refutes this old myth). Then along comes a female bear, who senses what he wants and knows how he can get it. Off they go into the woods, leaving readers to figure out the rest for themselves. What might be a birds-and-bees story, judging from the bees on the cover and appearing throughout, turns into a story of courtship between a good-hearted but rather dense male bear and a female bear with an agenda. This paperback is bound in the European style with wide front and back flaps attached to the paper cover.

Loth, Sebastien. *Remembering Crystal.* 978-0-7358-2300-6. New York: North-South, 2010. Ages 3–6.

Zelda and Crystal both live in the garden. Zelda is a young goose and Crystal an old turtle, yet they have become best friends through the many activities they share. When Crystal dies, Zelda refuses to believe it and takes a trip in search of her, finally returning home to mourn her friend and cherish her memories of their time together. This simple story with its spare illustrations plays out the metaphor of the grief journey, beginning with denial and ending with acceptance.

Müller, Birte. *Giant Jack.* 978-0-7358-1620-6. Translated by J. Alison James. New York: North-South Books, 2002. Ages 4–7.

Jack is having trouble fitting into the family since he is so much larger than his mouse sisters. His mother finally addresses his unhappiness by explaining that she found him as an infant and that he is actually a rat, but she loves him as her own. From that point on, Jack's attitude changes; he feels better about himself, and his relationship with his sisters blossoms. More than a book about interspecies (read: interracial) adoption, this is a book about the importance of self-identity, for without knowing why he was different, Jack was unable to cope with his difference. Müller's illustrations are suffused with emotion—one can feel the love mother has for son.

Pin, Isabel. *When I Grow Up, I Will Win the Nobel Peace Prize.* Translated by Nancy Seitz. 978-0-374-38313-8. New York: Farrar, Straus, Giroux, 2006. Ages 7–9.

Germans have a fascination with American Indians and the American West, evident in the frequent appearance of "playing Indian" in the illustrations of German picture books. In this book, a brother plays the cowboy giving chase to his sister, the Indian, as they race across the title page and into the first spread, where he lounges on the bed listening to a book read by his mother (or perhaps she's the babysitter) while his sister lies tied up underneath. This may be reason enough for some people to give a pass on this book, although for others, the dramatic irony caused by the disparity between the text and pictures makes this a fun book to read and discuss. The text, voiced by the boy, states his intentions to share with the poor, help people in need, and perform other acts of kindness, while the illustrations show him engaged in classroom shenanigans, failing to help an older woman with her heavy shopping bags, and so on. When he imagines being awarded the Nobel Peace Prize for his saintly behavior, the illustration shows Mother Teresa, Nelson Mandela, and the Dalai Lama awarding him the prize. On the last spread, he carries scissors to untie his sister, and beyond the back matter is a small picture of the brother and sister in a hug that rounds out the unspoken narrative at work in the illustrations.

Schubert, Ingrid and Dieter. *The Umbrella.* 978-1-9359-5400-2. New York: Lemniscaat USA, 2011. Ages 1–4.

There are two kinds of wordless books: those packed with myriad details that cause you to examine and reexamine the pictures, and those that tell a simple narrative with one large image per spread. This is the latter kind, beginning on the endpapers when a small black dog finds a red umbrella. A gust of wind sweeps him up in the air, away from his home and the house cat, and carries him around the world across every kind of terrain and climate imaginable. The umbrella becomes a boat, a plane, a sled, a parachute; eventually it brings him right back to his starting point. The back endpapers show the house cat about to pick up the umbrella, and one imagines that the story could begin all over again. Entrancing illustrations offer elements that very young children will be able to identify.

Waechter, Philip and Moni Port. *Bravo!* Translated by Sally-Ann Spencer. 978-1-877476-71-4. Gecko Press USA, distributed by Lerner Publishing Group, 2011. Age 7 and up.

Helena's father is a shouter ("Everything he said came out in a roar"). Helena can take it no more, and so she leaves home and knocks on the door of a house she comes across; when the woman asks about her parents, she need only explain that her father is a shouter and the woman takes her in. The penitent father searches for Helena and announces that he will stop shouting if only she will come home. Some time later, he sees a poster for a trumpet concert featuring Helena; he, Helena's mother, and her young brother all attend, and over the applause Helena hears a welcome shout, "Bravo!" The image of their reunion is surprising: instead of a warm hug between Helena and her father, Helena and the woman face the other family members. American readers will probably find this book problematic as so much is left out, but clearly shouting is emblematic of worse behavior, and as such the book can introduce the subject of the abusive parent and the mother who sits by.

Wolfsgruber, Linda. *A Daisy Is a Daisy Is a Daisy (Except When It Is a Girl's Name).* 978-1-55498-099-4. Toronto: Groundwood Books, 2011. Ages 6–9.

Along with a diverse population comes a proliferation of unfamiliar names, and this appealing book will be useful in introducing some of them to a wider audience. As it happens, many girls' names denote flowers and have linguistic cousins in languages around the world. Thus Flora, Lore, Hana, and Zvetana all mean *flower* and come from Latin, Basque, Japanese, and Bulgarian respectively. Imaginative, airy illustrations create sprites out of flowers (somewhat like the hollyhock dolls children make) or show scantily clothed sprites, almost as if in a sketchbook. This book evokes summer, little girls, and free time to draw.

Belgium

Ashbé, Jeanne. *What's Inside?* 978-0-916291-97-9. La Jolla, CA: Kane Miller, 2002. Ages 2–4.

This novel approach to impending siblinghood uses the concept of inside/outside and a lift-the-flap design to inform children about what happens inside a mother's body. Some things, such as a suitcase, one can open; other things, such as a teddy bear, can be opened but not so easily put back together again. Mommy's tummy is different—we can't open it to see inside, but under the flaps are cutaway pictures showing three stages of the baby within. This book keeps it simple, not mentioning how the baby got there or how it will get out.

De Kockere, Geert. *Willy.* Illustrated by Carll Cneut. 978-0-8028-5395-0. Grand Rapids, MI: Eerdmans, 2011. Ages 5–8.

Willy makes the most of his elephantine attributes to be a good listener, help his friends as needed, and participate in his community. Still, he is not immune to the odd uncharitable remark about his appearance, but his friends always rally around him to dispel the hurt. The narrator addresses readers who may happen to have any of Willy's attributes, advising them to think of Willy; implicit is the idea that attitude can make the difference between a perceived deficit (big ears, legs like pillars) and a true attribute. Stylized illustrations in tones of red and gray add heft and dignity to this wonderful story.

Robberecht, Thierry. *Back into Mommy's Tummy.* Illustrated by Philippe Goossens. 978-0-618-58106-1. New York: Clarion, 2005. Ages 2–5.

In first-person narration, a small girl celebrating her fifth birthday declares that she wants to be back in her mommy's tummy so she can be close to her all the time. Her clever mother reminds her daughter of all the things she wouldn't be able to do, including being at her own birthday party. Mommy realizes that the source of the problem is the new baby she is carrying, and when she asks her daughter if she is jealous that her little brother is in her tummy, the girl replies with honesty: "He's so close to you. I'm afraid you'll love him more than you love me." Most stories on this theme focus on the attention the new baby takes away from an older sibling after it has been born, but this one addresses just as real a concern. The round shapes in these illustrations, from Mommy's tummy to the girl's head, provide visual comfort to reinforce Mommy's words of love.

Robberecht, Thierry. *Sam's New Friend.* Illustrated by Philippe Goossens. 978-0-618-91448-7. New York: Clarion, 2007. Ages 4–7.

Sam's belief that as a boy (of the canine variety) he is strong and brave and never plays with girls is challenged when his mother tells him that the new girl in class will be spending the night at their house. Only after he finds her crying—her parents may be getting a divorce—and befriends her does he realize that gender should not be a barrier to friendship. The next day on the playground he demonstrates this lesson to others by playing with her. This story of gender identity and resisting peer pressure is not at all heavy-handed. Other books by the same duo include *Sam Is Never Scared* (2006), *Sam Tells Stories* (2007), and *Sam Is Not a Loser* (2008).

Van Mol, Sine. *Meena.* Illustrated by Carianne Wijffels. 978-0-8028-5394-3. Grand Rapids, MI: Eerdmans, 2011. Ages 5–8.

Children everywhere can let their imaginations get out of hand when it comes to older neighbors with odd behavior. In this case, three neighborhood children are convinced that Meena is a witch, and they conspire to drive her away by chalking *witch* on sidewalk and warning the girl who visits her periodically. Even when the girl explains that Meena is her grandma, they assume that she must be under Meena's wicked spell. For them, the juice from cherry pie turns into blood, and the pie that Meena offers them is certainly deadly. It takes one brave soul to taste the pie, another to follow him, and the third to see that her friends are still alive to change their minds about their neighbor.

Verplancke, Klaas. *Applesauce.* Translated by Helen Mixter. 978-1-55498-186-1. Toronto: Groundwood, 2012. Ages 4–8.

Nobody is perfect: neither a father who has warm hands and can make delicious applesauce, nor a child whose actions bring out his father's ire. True to the child narrator's perspective, the reader sees only the father's varying moods and never the actions that may have prompted these responses. Like the text, the illustrations also reflect the child's perspective, showing the playful daddy as handsome and strong, and the stern one, known as "thunder daddy," as huge and ominous. Sent to his room, Johnny has a Wild Things moment as the bannister leading upstairs becomes a forest, but rather than becoming King of the Wild Things, he must listen to the forest trees singing the thunder songs of his father: do your homework, pick up your shoes, turn down the TV. When the smell of applesauce eventually lures Johnny back into the kitchen, the wordless pages show how his father gently coaxes Johnny out of his bad mood and back into their normal, close relationship.

Zidrou. *Dounia.* Illustrated by Natacha Karvoskaia. 978-0-916291-58-7. La Jolla, CA: Kane Miller, 1995. Ages 2–5.

The story may be slight, but the illustrations suffused with yellow reflect the warm feelings in this transnational adoption story. A small girl from an unspecified African country travels by plane to Belgium, where she is met by a couple who will be her new parents. The details—Dounia's country of birth, how her parents died—are deliberately fuzzy, as are the illustrations. The third-person story is recounted from her perspective, where she sees in her new home "a kitchen like grocery shelves, a living room like a bookshop." The lack of detail means that the book has not become dated, and it is one of few books available that show adoptions from Africa rather than Asia.

Czech Republic

Pacovská, Květa. *The Little Flower King.* 978-0-698-40054-2. New York: Minedition/Penguin, 2007. Ages 3–6.

When creating a book, Czech artist Pacovská approaches it as architecture, "a given sealed space into which painted written and empty pages I compose." This second edition of *The Little Flower King* is identical to the first in content but is about 20 percent larger with new cover artwork. The simple story of a very small king who finds his princess in a tulip is illustrated with modernist, often abstract pictures created through a mixture of paints, collage, and pencil. Die cuts on the covers and inside pages frame the king alone on the front and the happy couple on the back. Here is a princess story stripped of its sappiness, with much to look at on every page, sized and shaped for young viewers.

Sís, Peter. *Three Golden Keys.* 978-0-374-37525-6. New York: Farrar, Straus, Giroux, 2001. All ages.

Originally published by Doubleday under the editorship of Jacqueline Onassis, this homage to Prague is replete with cultural allusion, symbolism, and the magic of Sís's native city. As with most of his work, this is a book that repays rereading and grows with the reader. His story follows the journey pattern, where the young Peter finds his front door padlocked and must collect the three golden keys to gain entry. Each key is found at a site important to Prague and comes with a tale that forms part of Prague's history and culture. The journey is linear in space but not time; although it takes just a night, it encompasses all four seasons, each triggering a different set of childhood memories. The illustrations layer images on top of one another in the same way that recent memories sit atop older ones. Some illustrations are mazes, others contain hidden pictures or symbols, and yet others reference classic works of art. Woven throughout is the motif of the black cat as guide.

Denmark

Drummond, Allen. *Energy Island.* 978-0-374-32184-0. New York: Farrar, Straus, Giroux, 2011. Age 7 and up.

Drummond, a British artist living and teaching in the US, describes the process by which the Danish island of Samsø became completely independent of nonrenewable energy sources, relying instead on electricity generated by wind turbines, on heat from burning straw, on solar power, and on biofuel. No longer does the tiny island in the middle of Denmark import oil or buy electricity from the mainland. Sidebars explain concepts in greater detail, while the main narrative, consisting mostly of illustrations with a sentence or two of text, emphasizes how the initial skepticism of the islanders changed to enthusiasm as they began to see positive results from their efforts.

Rasmussen, Halfdan. *The Ladder.* Illustrated by Pierre Pratt. Translated by Marilyn Nelson. 978-0-7636-2282-4. Cambridge, MA: Candlewick, 2006. Ages 4–7.

Rasmussen was one of Denmark's national poets and known for his literary nonsense verse for children, and it is fitting that Marilyn Nelson, an American poet, should translate this text. A carpenter builds a ladder, climbs it to the sky, and disappears, whereupon the ladder takes the opportunity to explore the countryside. Various people it encounters climb it into the heavens—a farmer, a marching band, a chauffeured limo, some animals chasing one another, a romantic couple. Suddenly the sky darkens and down a bolt of lightning comes the farmer followed by the others. The intricate book design includes flaps that fold up and out, adding enjoyment to this quirky narrative.

Finland

Jansson, Tove. *The Book about Moomin, Mymble, and Little My.* 978-1-897299-95-1. Montreal: Drawn and Quarterly, 2009. Ages 3–6.

Jansson's picture book, featuring the same beloved characters as in the longer Moomin books, was first published in 1952 in Finland, published in the US in 1996 (Blue Lantern, out of print) and is now available from the Canadian publisher. Die-cut openings and a refrain of "What do you think happened then?" propel this adventure of Moomintroll, who sets out to bring Mother a can of milk but encounters obstacles, friends, and foes along the way. Jansson's brilliant design and text involve children in not only anticipating the next event but in second-guessing what they see through the die-cut windows. Also available from Drawn and Quarterly is Jansson's *Who Will Comfort Toffle?* the story of a shy wallflower who finds his voice in helping another introvert.

Jansson, Tove. *Moomin and the Birthday Button.* 978-0-374-35050-5. New York: Farrar Straus Giroux, 2011. Ages 2–4.

This is one of several picture books for the very young that have been created using Jansson's original artwork, which has been colorized and digitally manipulated, with text based on episodes from the Moomin series. In this story, Moomin receives a shiny gold button for his birthday and rushes off to show his friends, who are all too busy to take notice and even forget to wish him a happy birthday. Soon, however, they are at the door with a present for him that each has helped to make—a treasure chest in which to put his new button. The new picture books work well as a good introduction to Finland's best-known character for those not quite ready for Jansson's now-classic books.

Peltola, Anne. *Boing Boing.* 978-1-59270-085-1. New York: Enchanted Lion, 2009. Ages 3–7.

Finland is known for its design, everything from fabric to architecture. This small square book is at its heart all about design—the uses to which a round red circle, called Boing Boing, can be put. Drawn by a child, the circle becomes a clown nose, a car wheel, a plate, and loads of other functional items before returning home to its creator. Endpapers show red circles drawn by people of all ages, from 5 months to 86 years.

Stamp, Jørgen. *Flying High.* 978-1-59270-089-9. New York: Enchanted Lion, 2009. Ages 6–9.

If this book is any indication, Jørgen Stamp could easily be Finland's Dr. Seuss. Using exaggerated cartoon animals, he has created an exciting story with a clear moral: friendship is as friendship does. Walter the giraffe builds an airplane but informs his friend Sonny the turtle, who wants to fly with him, that he would not be able to tolerate such speed. Walter is a bit too cocky for his own good and ignores the threatening storm; his plane is hit by lightning, and he falls into a nearby lake, where Sonny saves him from drowning. Lesson learned—Walter's next plane has a cockpit for two.

France and French-speaking Switzerland

Badescu, Ramona. *Pomelo Begins to Grow.* Illustrated by Benjamin Chaud. 978-0-59270-111-7. Brooklyn: Enchanted Lion, 2011. Ages 6–8.

Pomelo lives in a garden, and his surroundings seem smaller than they used to—he discovers that he is growing. This causes him to ask all sorts of questions about his body and his future: Will he grow evenly? Will he forget things he used to know? What happens inside his body when his outside grows? He finds he likes foods he didn't used to like and is braver than he used to be. Throughout, this little pink elephant interacts with animated potatoes, giant tomatoes, and assorted other garden denizens, all drawn with a Seuss-like quality. This combination of the wacky and the serious is appealing to children, who like Pomelo are changing, questioning, and learning every day.

Banks, Kate. *The Cat Who Walked across France.* Illustrated by Georg Hallensleben. 978-0-374-39968-9. New York: Farrar Straus Giroux, 2004. Ages 4–8.

Any story of a relocated pet who finds his way home tugs at the heartstrings, yet Banks manages to tell this one without sentimentality. When the cat's owner dies, her belongings, including the cat, are shipped from

St. Tropez north to Rouen. With no one to care for him, the cat's thoughts returned to the house by the sea, and so he sets out with only his nose to guide him. The illustrations form a visual travelogue with landmarks of his journey—the great gothic cathedral of Rouen, the Eiffel Tower of Paris, the royal chateaus of Chambord, and more, all labeled on a map of France on the back cover. This is a book for animal lovers and Francophiles; the American-born writer and German-born artist are both French residents and frequent collaborators.

Boisrobert, Anouck, and Louis Rigaud. *Popville.* 978-1-59643-593-3. New York: Roaring Brook Press, 2010. Age 7 and up.

The pop-up format is a perfect vehicle for illustrating how an isolated building surrounded by farmland and trees develops over time into a full-fledged city, with all the buildings needed to provide places for its residents to work, live, attend school, and socialize, along with the utilities needed, such as a power plant. In an afterword, the creators challenge readers to consider what they might add if they were building a city.

Boisrobert, Anouck and Louis Rigaud. *Wake Up, Sloth!* 978-1-59643-712-8. New York: Roaring Brook Press, 2011. Age 7 and up.

This engineered companion to *Popville* brings attention to the destruction of a forest habitat and its reforestation. Throughout, the text points readers to various forest creatures who flee as the machines begin clearing the land; the sloth is the last to leave. When it appears that all is lost, one person arrives to plant seeds, and by pulling on a tab, the reader can see the young seedlings that mark the beginning of a new forest and the return of the sloth.

Brami, Elisabeth, and Anne-Sophie Tschiegg. *Mommy Time!* 978-1-929132-22-5. La Jolla, CA: Kane Miller, 2001. Ages 4–6.

This small book, told from a child's perspective, considers what mothers do all day when their children are in school. The options range from what a child knows of a parent's activities to what a child can dream up, that is, anything from housework to a trip to Mars. What it's all leading up to, however, is the question of whether Mommy will be there when school gets out. The illustrations combine patterns of circles and squares with a very modern Mommy. The French title, *Drôle de Maman,* is more sugges-tive of the odd and comical scenarios imagined by this boy.

Brun-Cosme, Nadine. *Big Wolf and Little Wolf.* Illustrated by Olivier Tallec. Translated by Claudia Bedrick. 978-1-59270-084-4. New York: Enchanted Lion, 2009. Age 3 and up.

Although in picture book format, this story resonates with everyone who has ever loved, lost, and loved again—whether friend, family member, or romantic interest. Big Wolf thinks he is content living a life of isolation under his tree until Little Wolf comes along. Little Wolf does everything Big Wolf does, only not as well. When Big Wolf goes for a long walk, Little Wolf stays under the tree, but when Big Wolf finally comes home, Little Wolf is gone. Heartache ensues: "For the first time, he said to himself that a little one, indeed a very little one, had taken up space in his heart." Happily, Little Wolf does come back, and both agree that without each other, life is lonely. But friendship is never static, and the next two books of the trilogy explore what it means to be a friend: *Big Wolf and Little Wolf: The Leaf That Wouldn't Fall* (2009) and *Big Wolf and Little Wolf: Such a Beautiful Orange* (2011).

Cali, Davide. *The Enemy: A Book about Peace.* Illustrated by Serge Bloch. 9780987109965. New York: Wade and Schwartz/Random House, 2009. Age 5 and up.

Two foxholes, two soldiers on opposite sides of the front. Each believes that the other—the enemy—is monstrous and will destroy their families and villages if given a chance. Simultaneous forays by each into the other's territory show them that the enemy *is* human after all. "I wasn't expecting him to have a family. And what's this? A manual just like mine. But there is a difference: in this one, the enemy has my face." Simple text and spare line art on a white background convey the elemental message that humans are more alike than different.

Desbordes, Astrid. *Daydreams of a Solitary Hamster.* Illustrated by Pauline Martin. 978-1-59270-093-6. Brooklyn: Enchanted Lion, 2010. Age 6 and up.

Hamster thinks quite a bit of himself and doesn't doubt for a minute that the rest of the animals agree. In short one- to two-page comic strips, the reader is privy to the thoughts and everyday lives of Hamster and his friends Mole, Snail, Hedgehog, and Rabbit. Their insecurities, kind acts, and musings on such topics as true friendship resonate with readers of all ages, and Hamster's upcoming birthday party— an ongoing topic throughout—will keep young children interested.

Doray, Malika. *One More Wednesday.* 978-0-09-029589-9. New York: Greenwillow, 2001. Ages 4–7.

Spare pictures rendered in broad black brushstrokes highlighted with a touch of flat color accompany the first-person narrative of a bunny child who recounts her (or his) weekly Wednesday visits to Granny. Then comes the Wednesday that visits stop; Granny is in the hospital and dies soon after. The bunny attends the funeral but doesn't understand: "Did this mean that my granny was gone forever?" How the parents respond is the crux of the story, handled honestly and without sentimentality.

Faller, Régis. *The Adventures of Polo.* 978-0-59743-160-7. New York: Roaring Book Press, 2006. Ages 3–7.

Meet Polo, a resourceful dog who leaves his island treehouse to see the world (and beyond), making friends along the way. His adventures are told in the form of a wordless graphic novel, long enough for several bedtimes' worth of "reading." Five more volumes follow this introduction, one this length and four shorter stories. Polo has his own website (www.chezpolo .com) with activities that relate to Polo's world; to date, instructions are in French.

Fromenetal, Jean-Luc, and Joëlle Jolivet. *Oops!* Translated by Thomas Conners. 978-0-8109-8749-4. New York: Abrams, 2010. Age 5 and up.

"Oops!" is an understatement. When a bar of soap slips out of Aunt Roberta's hand and into the street, it causes a chain of catastrophes that prevents her family from catching their flight at the airport. Aunt Roberta is at the apartment to take care of the pets while this family of four is vacationing in Djerba. Their mad rush to the airport begins with a taxi that crashes into a mailman whose bike slipped on the soap, and it continues through every form of transportation available in Paris and past many of the city's iconic landmarks. They finally arrive at the airport to find that they have just missed their flight, so home they go. There Aunt Roberta is entertaining a couch-full of extraterrestrials, who have returned the bar of soap and offer to take the family to the Tunisian island in their flying saucer. A final page traces the chain of events, exemplifying the extraterrestrials' claim that "every cause has its effect, and every effect has its cause."

Lacomb, Benjamin. *Cherry and Olive.* 978-0-8027-9707-0. New York: Walker, 2007. Ages 5–9.

Cherry (a direct translation of Cerise in French) is overweight, shy, and friendless, living alone with her father in an apartment across the street from the animal shelter where he works. The mean girls at school mock her, and her only comfort is the dog she befriends at the shelter, but her father warns her not to become too attached in case the owners come to claim the dog. She does, and they do, but happily, her care for the dog leads to her making friends with the owners' son, a boy her age. Lacomb's illustrations emphasize Cherry's pain, isolation, and use of food as a consolation. They suggest that obesity might run in the family, as her father too is overweight, or perhaps both are eating to fill the hole created when Cherry's mother left them.

Moundlic, Charlotte. *The Bathing Costume.* Illustrated by Olivier Tallec. 978-0-59270-141-4. New York: Enchanted Lion, 2013. Ages 7–11.

A strong French setting marks this story of an eight-year-old boy, Ronnie, who is sent to live with his grandparents in the countryside while his parents move their Parisian household. His older brother won't be joining him, but it turns out his cousins will. What Ronnie anticipates will be a disaster turns out to be a chance for him to come into his own—he finds he likes his grandpa rather than fearing him, he bonds with his cousins, he overcomes the shame of having to wear a swim suit ("bathing costume," as Grandma says) that's too big for him, and he meets the challenge of the high diving board. Illustrations show all swimmers wearing swim caps, which are *de rigueur* at French public pools.

French Artist Extraordinaire

Olivier Tallec

Olivier Tallec was born in the French province of Brittany and graduated from the Duperré School of Applied Arts in Paris. The diverse training he received is reflected in his body of work, which ranges from editorial and advertising illustration to children's book illustration to molded and carved sculptures and dioramas. His work in children's books shows that he is equally adept in a variety of styles and media. Although he has written and illustrated one book, he seems most at home illustrating the work of others. To date, his list of illustrated books numbers over sixty, of which twelve have appeared in English. He has won numerous prizes in France, and his illustrations have elicited high praise from American reviewers.

Tallec may be best recognized in the United States for his illustrations in Nadine Brun-Cosme's Big Wolf and Little Wolf trilogy, published by Enchanted Lion Books. *Big Wolf and Little Wolf* (2009), *Big Wolf and Little Wolf: The Leaf that Wouldn't Fall* (2009), and *Big Wolf and Little Wolf: Such a Beautiful Orange* (2011) together tell the story of a friendship that grows and changes over time. Adults will read it as a love story; youngsters will see the pair as best friends. In writing about Tallec's artwork in *Such a Beautiful Orange*, Barbara Elleman notes that Tallec's "beautifully composed spreads, rich with blues, greens, and yellows, are a marvel

"It's raining outside." Original drawing by Olivier Tallec

of soft, richly applied hues and dark swaths of color for contrast." Tallec has a talent for imbuing his characters with emotion. Big Wolf is rendered in scribbled black crayon, set against a painted background of highly saturated colors; he shouldn't feel real, and yet he does. Little Wolf is a third the size of Big Wolf and painted in blue, but with the same elongated snout. All emotion is carried by the characters' eyes, body positions, or placement on the page, as they have no mouths turning up or down to show joy or sadness.

At the other end of the spectrum are Tallec's minimalist cartoon illustrations for Jean-Philippe Arrou-Vignod's series of books about Rita and her dog Whatsit. In 2009 Chronicle Books published *Rita and Whatsit*, *Rita and Whatsit at the Beach,* and *Christmas with Rita and Whatsit.* In these simple stories, Tallec's black-and-white line drawings effectively capture the personalities of Rita and her anthropomorphic terrier. In the tradition of the best cartoonists, Tallec is able to conjure up a whole landscape with just a line or two, and the slightest stroke of the pencil creates a smiling dog or a confident Rita. The only touches of color come in the orange-red accents of Rita's clothing and Whatsit's spot. Tallec returns to this style for *Waterloo and Trafalgar*, a wordless picture book about the absurdity of war.

Falling somewhere in between the above two illustrative approaches are Tallec's pictures for *The Scar* by Charlotte Moundlic, published in 2011 by Candlewick Press. With his outsized round head perched on a small body, the young boy of the story could be related to Rita. He, however, is fleshed out with color and variously positioned in the page—sometimes in continuous action against a white background and other times within an entire painted scene, more in keeping with the composition in *Big Wolf and Little Wolf. The Scar* recounts a young boy's grieving process when his mother dies, and none better than Olivier Tallec to express these feelings through art.

See the bibliography for the following books illustrated by Tallec: *Big Wolf and Little Wolf* by Nadine Brun-Cosme; *The Scar* by Charlotte Moundlic; *The Bathing Costume,* also by Charlotte Moundlic; and *Thumbelina of Toulaba* by Daniel Picouly.

Moundlic, Charlotte. *The Scar.* Illustrated by Olivier Tallec. 978-0-7636-5341-5. Somerville, MA: Candlewick, 2011. Age 4 and up.

A young boy narrates this story in the aftermath of his mother's death as his feelings ricochet between denial, anger, and pain. His reactions are understandably irrational—to keep his mother's smell in the house, he shuts all the windows, and he sees it as his job to take care of his father. When he falls and scrapes his knee, his mother's soothing voice comes into his head and he associates his wound with her presence. Then his grandmother comes to visit and opens all the windows, and he lets go of all his pent-up fears and emotions. Grandma puts her hand on his and guides it to his heart; his mother will always be there. The wound on his leg heals into a scar, and when he wants to feel his mother's presence, he has only to become aware of his heart beating. Tallec's cartoon illustrations overflow with red and punctuate the text, reinforcing the emotional truth of the child's perspective.

Norac, Carl. *My Mommy Is Magic.* Illustrated by Ingrid Godon. 978-0-618-75766-4. New York: Clarion, 2007. Ages 3–6.

Up to a certain point in a child's life, parents are all-knowing and capable of anything. This book and its companion, *My Daddy Is a Giant* (2005), capture that belief through a series of examples. Here, for instance, a young girl relates her mother's magic in dispelling monsters, guessing secrets, and making the rest of the world disappear when she reads a book aloud. Large illustrations covering the page show Mommy as a large woman whose physical size reflects her unique abilities.

Picouly, Daniel. *Thumbelina of Toulaba.* Illustrated by Olivier Tallec. 978-1-59270-069-1. New York: Enchanted Lion, 2007. Ages 4–8.

Picouly, a French writer whose ancestors came from Martinique, retells H. C. Andersen's tale, giving it a Caribbean setting and a lovely dark-skinned heroine who is able to choose her own destiny. Thumbelina—abducted by a fish, coveted by the animals, befriended by a bird—gains a pair of dragonfly wings that allow her to come and go as she pleases. Tallec's illustrations for this oversized book vibrate with lush tropical color.

Rodriguez, Béatrice. *The Chicken Thief.* 978-0-59270-092-9. New York: Enchanted Lion, 2010. Ages 4–8.

When a fox snatches a chicken from the front yard of a cottage, they are chased by a bear, hare, and rooster for two days through forests, over mountains, and across rough waters. Through cutaways of the dens where the fox and chicken rest overnight, readers begin to suspect more than the trio of chasers knows, and when the bedraggled trio finally reaches the fox's den to save the chicken, they encounter instead a happy couple. Throughout this revelation, the rooster's body language and facial expressions are priceless. This is the first volume of a trilogy and is followed by *Fox and Hen Together* (2011) and *Rooster's Revenge* (2011).

Rosenstiehl, Agnès. *Silly Lilly in What Will I Be Today?* 978-1-935-17908-5. New York: Toon, 2011. Ages 3–6.

Lilly is a curious, imaginative, and resolute young girl who, in this book, states that she can be anything and then proceeds to try out a different occupation every day of the week. One day she's a cook, the next a city planner, and so forth. Each sequence is loosely connected to the next, and each, without being formulaic, ends in a subtle realization on Lilly's part. In France Silly Lilly is known as Mimi Cracra; for the past three decades Mimi has starred in a popular newspaper cartoon strip and animated television series as well as being the main character in over forty picture books. This is one of two Silly Lilly books that are available in English to date.

Serres, Alain. *I Have the Right to Be a Child.* Illustrated by Aurélia Fronty. 978-1-55498-149-6. Translated by Helen Mixter. Toronto: Groundwood, 2012. Ages 5–9.

The text of this book takes its cue from the Convention on the Rights of the Child passed by the United Nations General Assembly, which ensures the protection and welfare of all children below the age of 18. The child narrator here explains in simple terms all that is covered and supplies examples of her own, such as "I have the right never to experience the storm of war or the thunder of weapons. I am afraid of guided missiles and smart bombs." This colorfully illustrated book, representing diverse settings and ethnicities, stands in stark contrast to daily newscasts of the plight of children around the world.

Tallec, Olivier. *Waterloo and Trafalgar.* 978-0-59270-127-8. New York: Enchanted Lion, 2012. Ages 4–8.

Two eponymous characters, named after major battles lost by France, are positioned behind walls on either side of a no-man's land. Aside from color—one is blue and the other orange—and slight differences in appearance, both have much the same weaponry and supplies and carry out similar activities over the course of a year or so. An alternating point of view prevents readers from identifying with one side over the other, and subtly the two colors begin to infiltrate the no man's land. Resolution comes in the form of an unlikely negotiator, a bird that is both blue and orange. The book is wordless, with cut pages at strategic points in the narrative, enabling readers to work out their own scenarios.

Tullet, Hervé. *Press Here.* 978-0-8118-7954-5. San Francisco: Chronicle Books, 2011. Ages 2–4.

This clever "interactive" book has no moving parts and requires a suspension of disbelief to work, but admirably carries this off (and more). Throughout, it instructs the reader where to press, and the result is shown on the following spread. Dots come and go, they proliferate, they grow larger or smaller, all at the behest of the reader, who knows the truth but isn't telling.

Valckx, Catharina. *Lizette's Green Sock.* 978-0-618-45298-2. New York: Clarion, 2004. Ages 4–7.

Lizette, a young chick, finds a green sock on her walk and happily puts it on. When she meets Tim and Tom, two cat brothers, they make fun of her for not having the other sock and she returns home deflated. This is a story about friends and bullies—Tim and Tom show up with the sock's mate but then run off and throw it in the lake, while Lizette's good friend Bert demonstrates how one sock can be a really great cap. Then a surprise: her mother has knit a mate to the green sock. In a nice twist, Lizette opts to give it to Bert, and both take pleasure in their matching caps.

Greece

Rousaki, Maria. *Unique Monique.* Illustrated by Polina Papanikolaou. 978-0-929132-51-5. La Jolla, CA: Kane Miller, 2003. Ages 4–8.

When you're an unconventional girl in a school that requires uniforms, it's hard to find ways to stand out. Monique is a trendsetter, and when she comes to school wearing a hat, or crazy socks, or fingernail polish, everyone follows suit until the teachers forbid it. Finally Monique finds the one thing that few classmates can imitate and no teacher can ban: braces. Although not everyone may be as unconventional as Monique, this cheerful story turns braces from a curse into a blessing.

Iceland

Ásbjörnsdóttir, Anna Kristin, adapter. *Tales of the Elves: Icelandic Folktales for Children.* Ilustrated by Florence Helga Thibault. Translated by Victoria Cribb. 978-9979-788-80-5. Reykjavik: Bjartur Publishing, 2007. All ages. Order directly from www.bjartur.is.

These seven tales are adapted from tales collected by Jón Árnason in the nineteenth century. Folkloric characters are very much part of the Icelandic landscape and psyche despite Iceland's Parliament having declared the country Christian in the year 1000. Christian and Celtic mythology are combined in the first tale, "The Origin of the Elves," which explains how some of Adam and Eve's children came to be elves, while the balance of stories recount human interaction with elves. Colorful full-page illustrations in a folk-art style convey the magic that surrounds the presence of elves.

McMillan, Bruce. *The Problem with Chickens.* Illustrated by Gunnella. 978-0-618-58581-6. Boston: Houghton Mifflin, 2005. Ages 4–7.

This silly story highlights the ingenuity of Icelandic women, who buy chickens because they are unable to retrieve the eggs laid by the wild birds in the cliffs. The chickens, however, forget they are chickens, begin acting like ladies, and forget to lay eggs, forcing the ladies to come up with an even better plan. Paintings in a folk-art style foreground the coastline and rugged landscape of Iceland, reminding readers of why Icelandic women must be strong. The same duo has created a second book, *How the Ladies Stopped the Wind* (2007).

Italy

Fischetto, Laura. *Harlequin and the Green Dress.* Illustrated by Letizia Galli. 978-0-385-31073-4. New York: Doubleday, 1994. Ages 7–10.

Commedia dell'arte is a uniquely Italian art form whose influence is found in everything from Punch-and-Judy shows to the films of Charlie Chaplin. Americans have little exposure to commedia dell'arte, and this book offers a great introduction by depicting a performance in all its chaotic splendor, as Harlequin's scheme to win Columbine's heart creates havoc in the the household but results in a happy ending for all.

Nivola, Claire. *Orani: My Father's Village.* 978-0-374-35657-6. New York: Farrar, Straus, Giroux, 2011. Ages 4–8.

Nivola grew up spending her summers in her father's native village on the island of Sardinia, off the Italian coast. Her miniaturist portraits of the village scenes—whether a bird's-eye view of Orani tucked into the hillside or a close-up of children sitting astride the branches of a fig tree—depict a place where everyone knows one another and children have the run of the village. Nivola paints her childhood self wearing the same checkered dress so that the reader can readily spot her as she and her many cousins take part in both the mundane and special events of the village, from transactions with shopkeepers to weddings, festivals, and funerals. Nivola's homage to Orani embodies her deep emotional roots there, symbolized in one picture by the heart shape she gives the village when viewed from above.

The Netherlands

Bruna, Dick. *Miffy.* 978-1-59226-022-5. New York: Big Tent Entertainment, 2003. Ages 2–4.

The beloved rabbit Miffy (Nijntje in the Netherlands) is close to being a Dutch icon and is also known internationally. Bruna created this book almost fifty years ago, but its modernist design and clean lines have not become dated and still appeal to new generations. Many of Bruna's other books have also been published in the US over the past five decades under various imprints.

Dematons, Charlotte. *Holland.* 978-1-93595428-6. New York: Lemniscaat, 2013. All ages.

Dutch-born Dematons was raised in France and came to the Netherlands for art school, so she brought a set of fresh eyes to her native land. This monumental work consists of a series of 27 paintings, starting at the front endpapers, each a wordless spread packed with details of everyday Dutch life, landscape, culture, and history. Viewers are taken on a tour of the country, each painting set in a different city or region over the course of a year, beginning in the summer on the coastline, where the Dutch enjoy the beach and the water. Close observation reveals details from the past as well as the present, and the artist has included a set of recurring elements that will keep young children pouring over the pictures endlessly. A companion volume, *A Thousand Things about Holland*, written by the artist and Jesse Goossens, explicates the details found in the paintings.

Ten Cate, Marijke. *Where Is My Sock?* 978-1-59078-808-0. Honesdale, PA: Lemniscaat/Boyds Mills, 2010. Ages 2–4.

All sorts of socks adorn the endpapers of this hide-and-seek book, as the reader helps a small boy who has just emerged from the bath find the articles of clothing he needs to get dressed. First he must find his striped underpants (that's right, he's completely naked), then his shirt, and so on, until he is ready to go outside. A host of friends, animal and human, are in attendance, and clothes are scattered everywhere, from laundry basket to washtub to clothesline as well as already worn by some of his friends. It's not always easy to spot the item before the page turn, when the boy has succeeded in finding it; toddlers will be happy reading this again and again as they learn where each item is.

Thé, Tjong-Khing. *Where Is the Cake?* 978-0-8109-1798-9. New York: Abrams, 2007. Ages 3–8.

This wordless book is full of stories, but the main narrative thread begins on the first spread when two burglars (rats) steal a cake just set out by a canine housewife. All illustrations are drawn from a bird's-eye perspective so that readers simultaneously see many characters, all of whom are animals, on the various paths of this wooded rural setting. Two young frogs playing with a soccer ball accidentally conk an adolescent male cat on the head; a pig child becomes separated from his parents; a small rabbit cries because he has lost his stuffed bunny. Meanwhile, the housewife and her husband give chase, and each of the many other narratives progresses, sometimes intersecting with the main narrative. In the end, all is resolved, the burglars are captured, and the cake is shared with everyone. This book tests the observational powers of the viewer, and each return to the book brings forth new stories.

Tolman, Marije, and Ronald Tolman. *The Tree House.* 978-1-59078-806-6. Honesdale, PA: Lemniscaat/Boyds Mills, 2010. Ages 2–4.

A tree house, an ursine companion, and some books—what more could a polar bear need for the good life? In this oversized wordless book, panoramic spreads show the pair being inundated from land and sky by a flock of flamingos, a rhinoceros, two pandas, a peacock, and many, many more visitors, who come and go at their leisure. At the end of the season, with winter on the way, all depart again, leaving the polar bear and the brown bear to enjoy each other, the first snowfall, and the moonlit night. The tree with its tree house is an immutable fixture on the right-hand page; it looks to be created as an etching, while the visitors, the background, and the bears' activities are drawn or painted and change with each page turn.

Van Reek, Wouter. *Coppernickel: The Invention.* 978-0-59270-100-1. New York: Enchanted Lion, 2008. Ages 7–9.

Tungsten the dog wants to go outside to play, but his friend Coppernickel the bird has decided they should invent something new—so up go two sheets of drawing paper on the wall. Tungsten stares at his paper, while Coppernickel decides to make a machine to pick elderberries, and immediately Coppernickel's drawing becomes so complex that he continues onto the wall, around and above the paper, onto the floor, and onto the edge of Tungsten's paper, which by now contains a straight vertical line. When Tungsten pushes the encroaching drawing away, he sets the machine in motion, and it almost crushes Coppernickel. The book's brilliance comes from its three contrasting illustration styles: the simple thick black cartoon of the two friends filled with flat color; the more detailed backgrounds; and the complex mechanical drawings that represent both Coppernickel's thoughts and the machine's actions. The contrast underscores the book's theme that the simplest tool is often the most effective. Coppernickel and Tungsten also appear in a sequel, *Coppernickel Goes Mondrian* (Enchanted Lion, 2012), in which they follow a Dutch artist (a stand-in for Piet Mondrian) on a figurative and literal journey that culminates in a Manhattan studio where the artist lived out his final days pushing the boundaries of his art.

Velthuijs, Max. *Frog and the Stranger.* 978-1-84270-466-0. London: Andersen Books, 2005. Ages 4–6. Available new from online bookstores.

Unlike his friends Pig and Duck, who hold preconceived notions about Rat, Frog is open-minded and enjoys getting to know their new neighbor. When Rat's quick thinking helps out his neighbors, Pig and Duck change their minds, and all become fast friends. This animal fable is one of several books featuring the same cast of characters, all of which speak to the foibles of human nature. Frog (Kikker in Dutch) is a beloved character known to all children raised in the Netherlands. Velthuijs won the 2004 Hans Christian Andersen Illustrator Medal.

Norway

D'Aulaire, Edgar, and Ingri D'Aulaire. *D'Aulaires' Book of Norse Myths.* 978-1-59017-125-7. New York: New York Review Books, 2006. Age 7 and up.

This selection of Norse myths, first published in 1935 as *D'Aulaires' Norse Gods and Giants,* remains timeless both for the clear telling and the colorful pictures that show story elements for which readers have no reference—Yggdrasil, the world tree, or Odin's eight-legged steed, for example. The beautiful language makes these stories of the mortal gods Odin, Thor, Freya, Loki and others—along with trolls and Jotuns (a race of giants)—equally suitable for listening to or reading on one's own.

D'Aulaire, Edgar, and Ingri D'Aulaire. *D'Aulaires' Book of Trolls.* 978-1-59017-217-9. New York: New York Review Books, 2006. Age 7 and up.

The mountains of Norway are home to trolls far beyond the garden variety found in most books—giant trolls with twelve heads, or three heads and one eye to share among them, or troll-hags with long crooked noses useful for stirring soup. Although not labeled as separate stories, several different tales of human interaction with such trolls point up the weakness of trolls—too much bragging coupled with too few brains—and the cleverness with which humans are able to outwit them, thus making troll stories a particularly satisfying genre for young listeners.

Hole, Stian. *Garmann's Summer.* 978-0-8028-5339-4. Grand Rapids, MI: Eerdmans Books, 2008. Age 6 and up.

Hole's award-winning picture book is both typical and atypical of Swedish picture books. Typical is the way it takes childhood feelings seriously—Garmann is nervously anticipating first grade in the fall, and everything he sees is a portent of summer's end, including the annual visit of his three great-aunts. His conversations with each of them as well as his mother and father do nothing to alleviate his fear but help him to accept it as a natural feeling. What is atypical is the illustration style, a surrealistic collage of digitally manipulated photos and art that captures the world as Garmann sees it and contributes to an understanding of how Garmann is feeling. A sequel is *Garmann's Street* (2010).

Hovland, Henrik. *John Jensen Feels Different.* Illustrated by Torill Kove. Translated by Don Bartlett. 978-0-8028-5399-8. Grand Rapids. MI: Eerdmans, 2012. Ages 5–8.

Living as an anthropomorphic crocodile in a human world might make anyone feel different, but that isn't apparent to John Jensen, who feels different whether alone brushing his teeth or at work in the tax office. On the bus he feels as if everyone is looking at him (the illustrations show that they aren't). He swaps his bow tie for a regular tie in hopes of fitting in; he wonders if he was adopted because he doesn't think he looks like other family members (the reader will be hard pressed to notice any difference between all the crocodile faces in the group photo). As a last resort, he binds his tail to his stomach so it doesn't show, because after all, no one else has a tail. This act

causes him to lose his balance and go to the hospital, where a kindly doctor (an elephant, the only other animal character in the story) helps him
understand that it's best to be exactly who he is. Young readers will delight
in recognizing the obvious difference that eludes the protagonist. More
sophisticated readers may grasp that the reptilian body represents an inner
difference that John Jensen learns to accept and value. The Norwegian setting is most obvious at the end of the book, when Jensen, tail accentuated
with a bow in the colors of the Norwegian flag, joins his fellow citizens in
front of the Royal Palace to celebrate Norway's Independence Day. Never
didactic, this story addresses diversity and inclusion in a fresh way.

Lunde, Stein Erik. *My Father's Arms Are a Boat.* Illustrated by Øyvind
Torseter. 978-0-59270-124-7. New York: Enchanted Lion, 2012. Ages 3–7.

Nights can be long and difficult for anyone, adult or child, who incurs a
loss. Here the child narrator recounts one long winter night when he can't
sleep and returns to the living room where his father sits staring at the
fire. The book's woodsy setting and frequent bird's-eye views underscore a
feeling of emptiness even before the dialogue reveals that the boy's mother
is "asleep" forever. Although a nighttime walk to look at the stars provides
a chance for a wish, it is no cure for sleeplessness. In such a situation, all
the father can do is hold his son and reassure him: "Everything will be all
right." Recipient of multiple book prizes in Norway, Torseter exhibits an
innovative style that uses Photoshop to combine paper figures, traditional
drawing, and three-dimensional elements in a spare and effective way.

Lunge-Larsen, Lisa. *The Adventures of Thor the Thunder God.* Illustrated by Jim Madsen. 978-0-618-47301-4. Boston: Houghton Mifflin,
2007. Age 7 and up.

Lunge-Larsen's skill as a storyteller comes through in these stories of those
who populated the ancient Norse cosmology, especially the gods Thor and
Odin and the quick-witted Jotun Loki. This collection is more accessible
than the D'Aulaires' *Book of Norse Myths*, as Lunge-Larsen has chosen tried-
and-true stories with child appeal. The realistic illustrations are in keeping
with contemporary images of giants and heroes.

Lunge-Larsen, Lisa. *The Race of the Birkebeiners.* Illustrated by Mary Azarian. 978-0-618-91599-6 (ppb). Boston: Sandpiper, 2007 Ages 6–9.

The modern-day cross-country ski race known as the Birkebeiner has its roots in an important event in Norwegian history during the Middle Ages, the saving of young Prince Håkon from a faction of warriors who wanted to take over the country. Two brave Birkebeiners, whose name derived from the birchbark they wrapped around their legs for protection (hence "birch-leggers"), skied over mountainous terrain to bring the child to safety. Prince Håkon went on to unite the country. Each year in Norway this event is commemorated with a race over the same route, and today there are also American and Canadian Birkebeiner races. Azarian's watercolored woodcuts capture the warmth and simplicity of life indoors and the freezing cold as the small party struggles north against the blowing snow.

Lunge-Larsen, Lisa. *The Troll with No Heart in His Body and Other Troll Tales.* Illustrated by Betsy Bowen. 978-0-618-35403-0 (ppb). Boston: Sandpiper, 2003. Age 7 and up.

Bowen's stunning woodcuts printed in soft colors conjure up a land of northern lights, snow-topped mountains, and coastal waters, perfectly matched to Larsen's retelling of nine popular Norwegian tales about trolls, beginning with the one Americans are most likely to know, "The Three Billy Goats Gruff." All are tales she grew up on in Norway, and her retellings for American listeners and readers both retain the hallmarks of Norwegian storytelling and suggest the relevance of these tales to Norwegian life. In a foreword, she mounts a spirited defense of the importance of folktales in the life of the child.

Prøysen, Alf. *Mrs. Pepperpot and the Treasure.* Illustrated by Hilda Offen. 978-0-09945159-4 (ppb). London: Red Fox, distributed by Random House, 2007. Ages 4–8.

Prøysen's immortal character has the ability to shrink to the size of a pepper shaker but cannot control when or where, which lands her in some difficult situations but also proves handy at times. In *Mrs. Pepperpot and the Treasure,* her cat is trying to tell her something when suddenly Mrs. Pepperpot shrinks and is able to jump on the cat's back for a wild ride to the haystack in the barn. There she discovers the treasure, four newborn kittens. Mrs. Pepperpot is Norway's best-known children's book character, so representative of the country that a traveling exhibit put together by the Capital Children's Museum in Washington, D.C. was entitled "Trolls, Mrs. Pepperpot, and Beyond: Celebrating Norwegian Children's Books." Collections of Mrs. Pepperpot stories were first published in English in the 1960s and remain in many libraries; some individual stories, such as this one, have been abridged and reillustrated as picture books.

Salinas, Veronica. *The Voyage.* Illustrated by Camilla Engman. Translation by Jeanne Eirheim. 978-1-55498-386-5. Toronto: Groundwood, 2013. Ages 3–7.

The experience of the newcomer is deftly essentialized in this story of a duck that has been blown by the wind to a strange new forest. He tries to talk, but the other animals do not understand him and he feels isolated. One day someone appears who looks a bit like him and the duck asks, "Who am I?" The Zen-like response is, "You are who you are." Eventually, the duck comes to understand the language in this place and takes great pleasure in his new life. Then along comes another strong wind that blows his friends away and deposits new animals. The duck knows just what to do. "I am me. And you? Who are you?" This sparely told story with its simple, cheerful illustrations will resonate with young readers and listeners in many situations, from the immigrant, to the child who has changed schools, to the kid whose best friend has moved away. The takeaway for all readers, however, is the simple act of accepting all newcomers for who they are.

Russia

Spirin, Gennady. *Martha.* 978-0-399-23980-9. New York: Philomel, 2005. Ages 3–7.

This gem combines a strong first-person narrative about how the artist's family found a wounded bird and nursed it back to health, with illustrations that present a detailed view of apartment life in Moscow. Spirin's realistic paintings show his drawing table situated near a window, graced with art supplies and pieces of finished and unfinished art; himself at work on a painting; his son Ilya and wife Raya at the park during the winter when they first spot the bird. Traditional touches abound, from the artist's pointed slippers to Ilya's wooden sled with rounded runners to the Russian icon painting atop a cupboard. Despite the veterinarian's recommendation to put down the bird, which they name Martha, they bring it home, bandage its wing, and enjoy its antics as it recuperates. One spring day, it flies away. The following autumn, a crow's nest appears in the tree outside their window. Is it Martha?

Spirin, Gennady. *The Tale of the Firebird.* Translated by Tatiana Popova. 978-0-399-23584-9. New York: Philomel, 2002. Ages 5–10.

Spirin has woven together three folktales—"Ivan-Tsarevitch and Gray Wolf," "Baba Yaga," and "Koshchei the Immortal"—to produce one tale that introduces readers to several well-known Russian characters. A third son must find the Firebird for his father, but in order to procure the Firebird, he must bring its owner a particular object, which in turn requires that he bring another object for trade, and so on. With the help of the Gray Wolf he succeeds, and in the process he acquires a beautiful princess as his bride. The ornate book design draws on the style of old Russian churches, with many of the paintings framed as triptychs or icon paintings.

Tolstoy, Leo. *Philipok.* Retold by Ann Beneduce. Illustrated by Gennady Spirin. 978-0-399-23482-8. New York: Philomel, 2000. Ages 3–7.

Tolstoy's story of a small boy who wanted to learn is set in the nineteenth century, as are Spirin's illustrations, which portray a small Russian village during the winter. Not content to wait until he is old enough to attend school, the boy sneaks out of the house and trudges through the snow to school, meeting some fearsome dogs along the way. They propel him to the schoolhouse, and once inside, he proves to the teacher that he is ready by spelling his name. As with other books illustrated by Spirin, the illustrations are so detailed and realistic that the reader is drawn into the setting; Spirin is especially good at capturing the children and the schoolmaster, who are so real that one feels they might move at any second.

Usatschow, Andre. *Little Ant Big Thinker, or Where Does the Ocean End?* Illustrated by Alexandra Junge. 978-0-7358-2203-0. New York: NorthSouth, 2009. Ages 4–7.

Standing on the beach, Little Ant enlists his friend Elephant in an attempt to see where the ocean ends, but nothing they do works. Finally they come across a fish who knows the answer: "Right here." How happy they are to know the answer, until Little Ant later realizes that if the ocean ends where he is, it must begin somewhere else. Junge's loosely sketched characters and the lithograph-like backgrounds give this book a retro feel. Children's books have often been a site of subversion, as they often fly under the censor's radar; one cannot help but wonder if this book is a case in point, prompting as it does the idea that perhaps there may be a more desirable "somewhere else."

Slovenia

Prap, Lila. *Dinosaurs?!* 978-0-73582-284-9. New York: NorthSouth, 2010. Ages 5–8.

A hen relates to her fellow chickens what she has just learned: chickens are descended from dinosaurs! This case study of evolution is presented in a way that is accessible to many ages. Large graphic illustrations filled in with textured color are surrounded by text. Prap's training as an architect shows in her attention to all the elements of book design. Here she deftly coordinates four kinds of text per spread: a headline sentence, small speech balloons showing chickens commenting, and two informational sections, one about the picture and the other about dinosaurs in general. Among Prap's other books is *Why?* (Kane Miller, 2005), which answers questions about animals.

Spain

Duran, Teresa. *Benedict.* Illustrated by Elena Val. Translated by Elisa Amado. 978-1-55498-098-7. Toronto: Groundwood/House of Anansi, 2011. Ages 3–7.

Benny lives in a very hot place—so hot it is red. Seeing his horns and spear-shaped tail, readers can easily identify this red-hot place and will understand exactly why Benny wants out. But the next place he moves, the white North Pole, is too cold. The desert is very yellow and much too dry; the jungle is very green but too humid. Finally Benny lands in the blue sea and finds it refreshingly comfortable. Is any place perfect? It may just depend on who else is there.

Gusti. *Half an Elephant.* 978-1-933605-09-8. La Jolla, CA: Kane Miller, 2006. Ages 5–8.

Argentinian-born Gusti now lives in Spain, and this book was first published in Mexico. The story begins when the world inexplicably splits in two, and an elephant wakes up to find his back half missing. He goes in search of it, encountering the halves of many different animals, all of whom are searching for their missing parts. Meanwhile, on the other side of the world, the missing halves are having the same problem. Since it doesn't work to connect half an elephant to half a flamingo or any other animal, the elephant halves get used to their new forms and even see the advantages. Then, just as inexplicably, the world becomes whole again and the elephant halves find each other. Do they reunite? Yes, but head to tail, reinventing their form to keep the best of both worlds. Gusti has used digitized images of found objects to construct these collage illustrations, showing children that art can be created from anything. Gusti is also the illustrator of *Dog and Cat* by Ricardo Alcantara (Millbrook, 1999), where his large cartoon-style drawings expressively capture the transformation of feelings between two new pets from animosity to friendship.

Keselman, Gabriela. *The Gift.* Illustrated by Pep Montserrat. Translated by Laura McKenna. 978-0-916291-91-4. Brooklyn: Kane Miller, 1999. Ages 3–7.

Mr. and Mrs. Goodparents want to give their son a special gift for his birthday, but after much thought they come up blank and so they ask him for help. It must be big, strong, soft, sweet, warm, and so forth. With each description, they imagine something outlandish—an elephant! a weightlifter! All along, what he really wants is a hug. This silly story with a comforting ending combines the zaniness of James Marshall's Stupids books with the warm appeal of the Guess How Much I Love You series in a package with foldout pages and fresh art by one of Spain's most celebrated artists.

López, Susana. *The Best Family in the World.* Illustrated by Ulises Wensell. 978-0-935279-47-1. Tulsa, OK: Kane Miller, 2010. Ages 3–7.

Carlota is being adopted from the orphanage, and she wonders what her new family will be like. Will they be pastry chefs, or pirates, or animal trainers, or astronauts? None of the above, as it turns out, but they are a mother (postal worker) who brings home pastries now and then, a father (insurance agent) who likes to dig for treasures in the nearby vacant lot, a grandmother who has two well-trained cats, and a brother who decorates her room with glow-in-the-dark stars. Best of all, as the illustrations show, they are a family who love one another and her very much.

Rodríguez, Rachel. *Building on Nature: The Life of Antoni Gaudí.* Illustrated by Julie Paschkis. 978-0-8050-8745-1. New York: Holt, 2009. Age 6 and up.

Antoni Gaudí was an architect and an innovator of the late nineteenth century, and people the world over travel to Barcelona to see his masterpieces. The unfinished Sagrada Familia (Holy Family Church); the sculptures and mosaic walls and benches in Park Güell; and Casa Milà, the building that looks like a melting wedding cake, are some of the many testimonies to both his engineering and his artistic achievements. Paschkis's illustrations capture the wonder of Gaudí's work, while Rodríguez's simple text describes the influences on Gaudí beginning with his childhood.

Sweden

Ahvander, Ingmarie. *Pancake Dreams.* Illustrated by Mati Lepp. Translated by Elisabeth Kallick Dyssegaard. 978-9-12965-652-7. New York: R & S Books, 2002. Ages 4–7.

Stefan's grandma Elsa makes the best pancakes, and now that Stefan and his family are living in Jordan, far away from Sweden, Stefan can only dream about them. One day he is inspired by a box perfect for holding pancakes—what if he could send the box to Grandma and have her fill it and send it back? The box goes to Sweden with a relative who has visited, and Grandma advertises in the paper for someone planning to fly to Jordan. The plan is perfectly executed, and Stefan enjoys the lion's share of the pancakes, doling out a few to his brother and parents and saving a few for his friends. This book drives home the cultural importance of food, as the pancakes—even just their smell—connect Stefan to his homeland, his grandma, and the time they spent together. The illustrations reflecting scenes in Jordan contrast with those in Sweden and subliminally suggest a feeling of homesickness on Stefan's part.

Bergström, Gunilla. *Good Night, Alfie Atkins.* Translated by Elisabeth Kallick Dyssegaard. 978-9-12966-154-5. New York: R & S Books, 2005. Ages 3–5.

Alfie (Alfons Åberg in Sweden) first appeared in 1972 and is a Swedish childhood staple with his own website (www.alfons.se) and a twenty-five-book series. In this first of two books translated into English, 4-year-old Alfie lives with his father, whose patience knows no bounds. Alfie finds so many ways to prolong bedtime that when his exhausted father no longer answers his calls, Alfie goes into the living room to find his father asleep on the floor. Alfie covers him up, tucks him in, and goes back to bed, this time to sleep. *Very Tricky, Alfie Atkins* (2005) is also available in the US.

Eriksson, Eva. *A Crash Course for Molly.* Translated by Elisabeth Kallick Dyssegaard. 978-9-12966-156-9. New York: R & S Books, 2005. Ages 4–8.

Molly has just learned to ride her bike, but when she and Grandma go riding and Grandma warns her not to hit something, that's exactly what she does. When Molly hits the driving instructor, he diagnoses her problem: she must learn to look at where she wants to go, not at what she wants to avoid. As Grandma and the dapper driving instructor chat, Molly practices. Ironically, it's Grandma who hits the pole when she focuses more on waving good-bye to the driving instructor than on her bicycle. The characters are animals—dogs for Grandma, the driving instructor, and one of the mean boys, a pig for Molly, and a sheep for the other mean boy. This just may be Eriksson's subtle way of showing the diversity of contemporary Swedish children.

Landström, Lena. *Four Hens and a Rooster.* Illustrated by Olof Landström. Translated by Joan Sandin. 978-9-12966-336-5. New York: R & S Books, 2005. Age 5 and up.

Although this story of four hens who stand up to a domineering rooster speaks of gender equity, a discussion with children could easily elicit comments about other kinds of equity issues found in a child's life. Sick of being pushed around, the hens take a course in self-esteem and return to the farmyard to demand their fair share of the food. The self-important rooster realizes when he's met his match and turns his attention to one of his many building projects instead. The Landströms' comical tale shows readers that if approached wisely, change can happen peacefully and needn't result in emnity.

Lindenbaum, Pija. *When Owen's Mom Breathed Fire.* Translated by Elisabeth Kallick Dyssegaard. 978-9-12966-548-2. New York: R & S Books, 2006. Ages 4–8.

Owen (Åke in Sweden) lives with his mom, who is usually frazzled in the morning as she tries to get ready for work and get him to day care. One morning Owen wakes up to find his mother still in bed, having turned into a dragon, and completely unable to take care of herself, let alone him. Owen gets her up and out of the house, and decides they need to go to the hospital for anti-dragon medicine. En route, his mother scares little kids, eats bugs, and generally misbehaves. The doctor is no help, but a stop by Grandma's reassures Owen that his mother's condition is only temporary. And right she is—by the next morning, his mother is back to her human self and decides to take a vacation day to spend time with Owen. This psychological allegory couched as fantasy will resonate with children and parents who often find it hard to cope with the pressures of modern life.

Mathis, Nina. *The Grandma Hunt.* Illustrated by Gunilla Kvarnström. Translated by Elisabeth Kallick Dyssegaard. 978-9-12965-656-5. New York: R & S Books, 2002. Ages 6–9.

Every summer Jacob spends a week with his Grandpa in the country, where they collect junk and repurpose it into chairs, a grill, and other handy items. On the weekend before Grandpa's birthday party, they are joined by Jacob's young cousin Linnea. Jacob decides that Grandpa will be lonely when they leave, and so he and Linnea set out to find him a grandma. Unbeknownst to Grandpa, they advertise a flea market at his house for Sunday and are flooded with potential grandmas, all of whom love the stuff that Grandpa makes from found items and one of whom takes a special liking to Grandpa himself. The cartoon illustrations offer hilarious caricatures of the various women that Jacob and Linnea encounter as well as showing details of Swedish country life, such as the daybed where Grandpa and Jacob sleep head to toe.

Switzerland

Hächler, Bruno. *Anna's Wish.* Illustrated by Friederike Rave. 978-0-7258-2207-8. New York: NorthSouth, 2008. Ages 3–7.

Anna's wish is for snow, which she has never seen; the last snowfall occurred during her mother's childhood. Passing by the bakery, Anna feels a tiny brush of cold and is inspired to retrieve the old sled from the basement. Her sleep is filled with dreams of snow, and the following morning she returns to the bakery to wish on the sparkling white horse that adorns a cake. Whether this book is a cautionary tale or a realistic one, it succeeds in conveying the magic of a first snowfall. Climate change is a growing concern in Switzerland, where the snow line in the Alps has visibly receded.

Zullo, Germano. *Little Bird.* 978-1-59270-118-6. Illustrated by Albertine. New York: Enchanted Lion, 2012. Age 3 and up.

An epigraph from a poem by E. E. Cummings, "may my heart always be open to little / birds who are the secrets of living," provides the inspiration for this almost wordless picture book open to multiple readings. Graphic, flat paintings show a truck as it appears in the distance and stops before a steep drop-off. The driver gets out and releases his cargo—dozens of colorful birds, no two the same. But one small bird remains in the truck, despite the driver's antics as he shows him how to fly. When the little bird finally does fly away to catch up with the flock, it is not to leave his human friend but to bring him the gift of a lifetime. A similar theme can be found

England's Celebrated Surrealist

Anthony Browne

When Anthony Browne was awarded the 2000 Hans Christian Andersen Illustrator Medal, the jury called him "an artist of unusual talent, exceptional technical skill and unrivaled imagination who has taken picture book illustration into new dimensions" (Glistrup, *Hans Christian Andersen Awards, 1956–2002*, 105). He came by his technical skill at Leeds College of Art and honed it as a medical illustrator in Manchester, England, and then as a artist for Gordon Fraser greeting cards. He has been writing and illustrating picture books since 1971, and while his style has become more polished and sophisticated, the motifs running through his books are in evidence from the beginning. He was Britain's sixth Children's Laureate, from 2009 to 2011.

Browne's first book as author and illustrator, *Through the Magic Mirror* (1976), includes human figures rather than his signature primates, but everything else that will become more fully developed in later works is present—the visual allusions to Magritte and other artists; the association of a particular pattern with a character; the deadpan text that is made humorous only by looking at the pictures. His settings are overtly British, and his stories comment on British society and everyday life. Browne has written and illustrated over thirty books, each multilayered and yet accessible to young readers; although only four representative books are described here, all are worthy of discussion, singly or as a body of work.

Gorilla. 978-0-7636-7222-5. Cambridge, MA: Candlewick, 2014 (30th Anniversary Edition). Ages 4–8.

Both the text and the illustrations describe a single father who has distanced himself from his only child, a daughter, by always professing to be too busy. At breakfast in the cold blue-and-white kitchen, father and daughter sit at opposite ends of the table separated by the open newspaper. She is obsessed by gorillas and has asked for one for her birthday. That night, a package appears on her bed: a small stuffed gorilla. During the night her toy turns into a real gorilla, a father substitute who dons her father's coat and hat (plaid, Browne's signature pattern for fathers), takes her to the zoo, to a movie (*King Kong*, of course), and to a restaurant. The restaurant scene contrasts markedly with the earlier breakfast scene; gorilla and girl sit across from one another with no impediment, and the colors are rich warm hues. The next morning she awakens to find her father transformed, not into a gorilla but into a parent who wants to spend the day with his daughter. Mysteriously, a banana sticks out of his back pocket.

Piggybook. 978-0-679-80837-4 (ppb). New York: Dragonfly/Knopf, 1990. Ages 6–9.

The front cover image—a woman carrying her husband and two children piggyback—is vintage Browne, a verbal and visual pun on the title that also points to the theme *and* the transformation that takes place in the story. Mr. Piggott and his two sons expect Mrs. Piggott to wait on them, do all the household work, and hold down a job while they lounge on the couch in front of the television. Throughout his body of work, Browne has linked the floral pattern, found here on the couch, with the wives and mothers in his books; here symbolically the Piggott males are oppressing Mrs. Piggott. Then comes the day she is gone, leaving a simple note: "You are pigs." The illustrations show the transformation in large and small ways, with the Piggott males shown as pigs and everything in the house, including wallpaper flowers, doorknobs, and light switches, turned into pig faces. As they try to cook for themselves, the place becomes a pigsty, and soon they are snorting and snuffling around for food. When they are totally abject, Mrs. Piggott returns and the power shifts; from that point on, all share household chores and are the happier for it.

Voices in the Park. 978-0-7894-8191-7. New York: DK Children, 2001. Ages 5–11.

Two parents plus two children (all anthropomorphic primates) equals four perspectives on the same set of events. The first voice belongs to an upper-class dowager who takes the family dog, Victoria, and her son, Charles, to the park; judging by her behavior, she cherishes the dog considerably more than the son. The second voice belongs to an unemployed trade worker, sitting on the park bench reading the classifieds. He and his daughter, Smudge, have come to the park with their dog, Albert, who immediately takes to Victoria (a nod to the British queen and her consort). The third and fourth voices belong to Charles and Smudge, who begin playing together, much to the dismay of Charles's mother, who considers Smudge, her father, and their scruffy dog "frightful types." Each first-person voice is rendered in a different typeface and art style suited to the character, and the park is portrayed in a different season for each point of view. Charles's mother's domination emerges both as a shadow cast over him and as a design motif in the shape of her hat. Issues of class, social, and economic differences are all at work here in a way that young readers can recognize and respond to.

Me and You. 978-0-374-34908-0. New York: Knopf, 2010.

The *me* of the story is the baby bear of the traditional Goldilocks story; the *you* is Goldilocks herself, in the person of a girl who, while on errands with her mother, follows a balloon and finds herself lost in an unfamiliar neighborhood. The stories are told simultaneously, the girl's on the left in realistic sepia-toned watercolors, and the bear's on the right in light-hued colored pencil drawings. The stories converge when the girl happens upon the bears' bright yellow house with its open door and ends up in baby bear's bed; she awakens to find the three bears staring at her and escapes with no thought of where she is running. There baby bear's story ends, as he wonders what happened to her, and the girl's continues, as she arrives in familiar terrain and runs into the arms of her mother. The juxtaposition of the nuclear bear family living in the perfect house with the single-parent family living in a gritty neighborhood suggests a contemporary story about haves and have-nots; the warm loving relationship of the have-nots and the somewhat distanced parent-child relationship of the haves add yet another dimension to the story.

in *Mrs. Meyer the Bird* (no longer in print), written and illustrated by Wolf Erlbruch, featured illustrator from Germany.

United Kingdom and Republic of Ireland

Archbold, Tim. *Bagpipes, Beasties and Bogles.* 978-086315-911-4. Edinburgh: Floris Books, 2012. Dist. by Steiner Books. Ages 3–6.

Steeped in Scottish culture, this lively tale is part ghost story (for bogle, think bogeyman or boggart) and part fanciful pourquoi tale, explaining how the bagpipe was created. Anyone who thinks the drone of bagpipes sounds like the wails of creatures trapped inside a bag will appreciate this story of how Charlie McCandlewick, whose job was to sweep the night clear of bogles and beasties and other scary nighttime dwellers, found a perfect use for these otherworldly creatures.

Benjamin, Floella. *My Two Grandads.* Illustrated by Margaret Chamberlain. 978-1-84780-060-2. London: Frances Lincoln, distributed by Publishers Group West, 2011. Ages 6–9.

Music is used as a focal point to compare and contrast Ashton's two granddads, who live in the same town as Ashton's family. His maternal grandfather, Grandad Harry, came from Lancashire, a county in northwestern England, and plays the trumpet in a brass band. His paternal grandfather, Grandad Roy, came from Trinidad and plays the steel drum in a steel band. Ashton is learning to play both. When the band signed to play for his school's Summer Fair pulls out, Ashton volunteers his grandads' bands and then must diplomatically get them to play together, since only one band is needed. Chamberlain's lively colorful illustrations capture the granddads' personalities and Ashton's love for both; a scene in the classroom shows the children dressed in uniforms, simple blue T-shirts and gray pants or skirts. Also by this team: *My Two Grannies* (Frances Lincoln, 2009).

Burningham, John. *John Patrick Norman McHennessy—The Boy Who Was Always Late.* 978-0-375-95220-3. New York: Knopf, 2008. Ages 6–9.

Burningham's books often explore childhood imagination and the relationship between adults and children, and none is more representative of those motifs than this parable of learning, originally published in the US in 1987. The schoolboy "John Patrick Norman McHennessy set off along the road to learn" again and again, only to be waylaid by various incidents, such as a crocodile that tries to grab his schoolbag or a lion that tears his pants. Each time he arrives late to school, the schoolmaster punishes him for lying. On the day that John Patrick Norman McHennessy is on time, he finds a big hairy gorilla up in the rafters holding the schoolmaster, who orders John Patrick to get him down. The power has shifted: "There are no such things as big hairy gorillas in the roofs around here, Sir." Burningham's mixed-media illustrations vary in nature from page to page; his adventures are rendered in spreads swathed with color, and his interactions with the schoolmaster are loose drawings with shading often scribbled in. The endpapers cleverly show the lines John Patrick is forced to write, including his misspellings.

Donaldson, Julia. *The Gruffalo.* Illustrated by Axel Scheffler. 978-0-8037-2386-3. New York: Dial, 1999. Ages 3–5.

What happens when a gruffalo—a creature conjured up by a mouse to get himself away from a fox, a snake, and an owl—turns out to be real? If you are a very clever mouse, you find a way to outwit the gruffalo as well. This story was voted England's favorite bedtime story and has been called a modern classic.

Fitzpatrick, Marie-Louise. *The Long March.* Foreword by Gary White Deer. 978-1-58246-065-9 (ppb). Berkeley: Tricycle Press, 2001. Age 7 and up.

Sometimes it takes an outsider to fill in missing gaps in America's history. Irish author-illustrator Fitzpatrick tells the story of how the Choctaw Indians participated in the Quakers' efforts to raise money to send to Ireland during the Great Famine of the mid-1800s. Her narrator is a Choctaw boy, Choono, born after his family made the long march from Mississippi to Oklahoma territory just sixteen years previously, when the government took their land. At a clan meeting, some elders speak out against helping *Nahullo*, or Europeans, while Choono's grandmother recounts the long brutal winter march that killed so many Choctaw and recommends helping the Irish because "we could not help ourselves." Choona works through

Britain's New Generation

Emily Gravett

Emily Gravett took the nontraditional approach to a career in children's books—she dropped out of high school at 16 and became a New Age traveler, joining a group of people who moved around the UK following music festivals. For most of the eight years, she lived in a bus with her partner, Mik. After their daughter was born, they rented an isolated cottage in Wales, where Emily and her daughter, who was a toddler, spent a lot of time reading picture books. Thus was born her desire to become an illustrator. She applied to Brighton University's art program and was admitted only after she created a portfolio of work that chronicled a year in her life. She earned a BFA degree in 2004, the same year that her first book, *Wolves,* was accepted for publication by Macmillan in London. Since the publication of *Wolves,* she has created an average of two books a year, each unique in its own way. Several of her books are engineered, with cut pages, tip-in cards, or pop-ups, but Gravett is just as creative and clever when working in two dimensions. The following four books are good examples of her range.

Wolves. 978-1-4169-1491-4. New York: Simon and Schuster, 2006. Ages 6–9.

Gravett's debut book, created when she was still in art school, won the Kate Greenaway Award, the UK's top picture book prize. It's full of rabbitty puns, such as on the title page, which lists Emily Grrabbit as author and is stamped by the West Bucks Public Burrowing Library. A rabbit borrows a book on wolves—identical to the one the reader is holding—and becomes so engrossed in reading facts about wolves that he fails to notice he is being followed by a wolf until he is right at the tip of its nose, at which time he is reading about the wolf's meat-eating diet. The page turn comes at midsentence, and the next spread is filled with a clawed book cover. The end? Not quite. An alternative ending is provided "for sensitive readers," but its patched-together look (a collage of torn pieces from the original book) is decidedly fake. The last spread shows the doormat at rabbit's burrow covered with unopened mail, including a postcard for an overdue book from the West Bucks Public Burrowing Library.

The Odd Egg. 978-1-4169-6872-6. New York: Simon and Schuster, 2009. Ages 6–9.

This is a familiar story: a mysterious egg is adopted by Duck, a drake, and when hatched reveals an alligator who takes the duck for its mother. What keeps this story from being trite are Gravett's witty illustrations and clever design. Duck is the only bird who hasn't laid an egg; the robin, the hen, the owl, the parrot, and the flamingo are all tending theirs, and owl is reading *The Bright Baby Book.* Duck is enamored with the gigantic spotted egg he finds that is many times his size, and to the amusement of the others he perches atop it. Then the hatching begins, from smallest egg to largest, with graduated cut pages showing each mother-child union (the owlet emerges spouting a mathematical formula). But Duck's egg takes its time, which Duck uses to knit a scarf and two web-shaped booties. Then the cracks begin. SNAP! Out comes an alligator, and bird legs fly off the page in every direction. On the final endpaper the alligator follows Duck, shouting "Mama" and wearing four green booties and a scarf. The male as maternal figure, while significant, takes a backseat to the clever illustrations.

The Rabbit Problem. 978-1-4424-1255-2. New York: Simon and Schuster, 2010. Age 6 and up.

How many pairs of rabbits will there be in one year's time if you put two rabbits in a field and allow none to leave? This is the "rabbit problem," a puzzle first posed by Italian mathematician Fibonacci in the thirteenth century to illustrate a particular sequence of numbers. Gravett ingeniously uses the form of a calendar to illustrate this puzzle. In January, a rabbit burrows into the field and is joined by a mate in February; we see his invitation to the party of two pasted into the calendar. The cold of February gives way to March and an announcement of twins, who have become adult rabbits by the end of the month. In April, both pairs have twins, as does the original pair, making five pairs, and so on through the months, until 144 pairs crowd every last inch of the field. Revolution ensues, the sign is changed to read "No Rabbits May Leave the Field," and they burrow a hole to freedom. The last spread pops up—escaping rabbits everywhere! Gravett invents all sorts of notes and artifacts to add to the calendar, including a carrot cookbook. Such jokes and witticisms make the book highly appealing to readers of all ages.

Original drawings used in *The Rabbit Problem*

Blue Chameleon. 978-1-4424-1958-2. New York: Simon and Schuster, 2011. Ages 3–6.

A lonely chameleon tries hard to make friends, changing itself again and again to match whatever and whoever it meets along the way. It sees a banana, and suddenly it's yellow and curved. A pink cockatoo, a brown boot, a swirly snail, a spotty ball—none respond to the chameleon's transformations or cheery greetings. Gravett's genius here is in the way her simple colored-pencil drawings of the chameleon mimic the object or animal not only in color but in position. The despondent chameleon finally flops down on a gray rock and is in danger of disappearing altogether into the white page when it hears a cheery hello and meets another chameleon looking for a friend. This concept book with an appealing narrative thread reminds readers that sometimes finding the right friend takes time.

Again! 978-1-4424-5231-2. New York: Simon and Schuster, 2013. Ages 3–6.

Cedric's favorite bedtime book is about someone just like him—a dragon—except that the dragon in the book is a "bright angry red" and never goes to bed. Cedric is green and cuddled up with his mother as she reads the book to him. Again, he says when she finishes, and so she reads it to him a second and third time, changing the words so that the Cedric in the book "should go to bed" and then becomes a "big sleepyhead." With each rereading, her Cedric becomes more active (and redder), while the Cedric in the book becomes sleepier and starts to turn green. When his mother falls asleep during the fourth reading, Cedric himself turns an angry red and while trying to read the book himself (it's upside down) blows smoke and fire right through the pages and the back cover. Yes, it's true. There's a hole in the book to prove it.

his anger at the *Nahullo* to reach an understanding of his family's values. The sum sent by the Choctaws is stated here as $170, although it has been stated elsewhere as $710; either is an impressive sum from a group with meager resources. Fitzpatrick's realistic black-and-white pencil illustrations are true to their subjects, authentically reproducing clothing, housing, and symbols of the Choctaw; on the last spread, as Choono fully embraces his Choctaw past and future, his shadow takes the form of a bird in flight.

Foreman, Michael. *Wonder Goal!* 978-1-84270-934-4 (ppb). London: Andersen Press, 2009. Available through online sites. Age 6 and up.

Making the game-winning goal in an important match is every soccer player's dream. A young boy, new to his team, kicks the ball into the net— and for a moment, time stops. Will the goal be good, or will the goalie deflect the ball in time? That is the point at which the book fast-forwards a dozen years or so as the boy, now grown and playing in the World Cup Finals, kicks a similar goal. The story is slight, but soccer-obsessed readers will identify with the main character's desire to be a star. The text has been edited for usage—*soccer* replaces *football*—but the thirteen sketches from Foreman's travel sketchbook, reproduced on the endpapers, are labeled using the terms interchangeably ("Fuji football"; "soccer in the Straits of Malacca"). These sketches, drawn over three decades, show children playing the game in remote places, urban spaces, mountains, deserts, and even next to the Berlin Wall.

Grey, Mini. *Traction Man.* 978-0-375-83191-1. New York: Knopf, 2005. Ages 4–8.

The new, improved Traction Man, replacing the old one who went down in a "terrible parachute accident," arrives on a boy's bed on Christmas morning and accompanies him throughout the day, from breakfast to backyard to bath to Granny's house for Christmas tea. The boy's creative play with the heroic Traction Man is portrayed on pages bordered in white, while real events in the boy's day are shown on full-page bleeds. At Granny's, Traction Man suffers the humiliation of having to wear the green romper suit and hat that Granny has knitted for him. In fact, none of the family looks pleased with Granny's knitted creations ("Oh, how nice. Socks again.") The knitted suit comes in handy when Traction Man must rescue some fallen spoons from the evil Broom; his loyal companion Scrubbing Brush, taking on canine characteristics, unravels the suit and uses it to pull up the spoons in the nick of time, leaving Traction Man wearing green knitted swim trunks. The illustrations are replete with details of British households: the breakfast table with egg cups and toast rack, the tea table in Granny's living room with its tea cozy, small sandwiches, pastries, and cake; and the book *Biggles Gets His Men* (one of a British series popular in the 1950s), seen on a cart and later used as a raft for Traction Man and Scrubbing Brush as they relax after their latest mission.

Hughes, Shirley. *The Big Alfie and Annie Rose Storybook.* 978-0-099-75030-7. London: Red Fox, 2007. Ages 3–7. Carried by online bookstores.

These stories and poems about preschooler Alfie and his little sister, set in the London neighborhood where Hughes raised her own family, are as fresh today as they were when published over two decades ago. The everyday activities of family life are pitched perfectly for the preschooler set, who find themselves in the characters and their situations. Hughes's detailed illustrations show scenes at home, in front of the nursery school, and at the park. Compare these illustrations with those in Hughes's newest book, *Don't Want to Go!* (Candlewick, 2010), about a preschooler whose dad takes her to a friend's house for the day because her mother is sick in bed. Some of the same elements are present in both books—the high chair, stroller, empty cardboard box as toy—but the scenes are vignettes against a white background, as if they have been lifted from the neighborhood and given a generic setting.

Hughes, Shirley. *The Christmas Eve Ghost.* 978-0-7636-4472-7. Cambridge, MA: Candlewick, 2010. Ages 5–8.

Hughes, who has long chronicled the everyday life of children in England, goes back to her own childhood for this story, set in Liverpool in the 1930s. Two children live in a narrow row house with their widowed mother, who does laundry for the people who live in "the better part of the city." The small family from Wales is Protestant; Mam warns the children to stay away from the Catholic O'Rileys next door, "not their kind." On Christmas Eve after dark, Mam has one more errand and leaves the children alone for a bit. When they hear an irregular plonking sound coming from the back room, they imagine a ghost trying to get into the house and run shrieking out the door—right into Mrs. O'Riley. She listens to their story, brings them into the O'Riley house (but not before making them write a note for their mother), and shows them the source of the sound, her husband and boys playing darts against the shared wall. Mam comes to get them and stays for a cup of tea; it is the adult in this story, not the children, who needs the lesson in overcoming prejudice. Hughes's period-perfect illustrations show details of household and street life, including fashions of the day.

James, Simon. *Dear Mr. Blueberry.* 978-0-689-80768-8. New York: Aladdin, 1996. Ages 3–7.

Young Emily and Mr. Blueberry correspond about whales, as Emily seeks her teacher's advice about the whale that is in her backyard pond. With each letter, Mr. Blueberry gives her facts that support why it cannot be a whale (for starters, they live in saltwater, not ponds), while Emily uses that information to help her whale (she pours salt in the pond). Illustrations accompanying Emily's letters show Emily and the whale, while those accompanying Mr. Blueberry's show Emily in family situations, sans whale. Emily's whale disappears after Mr. Blueberry writes that blue whales are migratory, but happily Emily and her whale are reunited—at the beach. This book was originally titled *Dear Greenpeace* and had a postmark of Devon, Plymouth, which was changed to Nantucket, Massachusetts, for the American edition.

McBain, Chani. *No Such Thing as Nessie!* Illustrated by Kirsteen Harris-Jones. 978-086315-953-4. Edinburgh: Floris Books, 2013. Dist. by Steiner Books. Ages 6–9.

Nessie is, of course, the controversial creature reputed to live in Scotland's Loch Ness, the deepest lake in Britain. Finlay's grandmother lives nearby and claims to have seen Nessie when she was a girl, so when the family goes on holiday at Gran's, Finlay knows it is his chance to see Nessie too. But after numerous false sightings, Finlay is ready to concede that Nessie doesn't exist. On the last day, while the rest of the family goes shopping, Finlay and Gran visit Urquhart Castle on the shores of Loch Ness and then find a secluded lakeside spot for a picnic, where they are joined, for a brief moment, by one very large, very green monster. No matter that no one will believe them—Finlay is happy.

McNaughton, Colin. *Once Upon an Ordinary School Day.* Illustrated by Satoshi Kitamura. 978-0-374-35634-7. New York: Farrar, Straus, Giroux, 2005. Ages 6–9.

An ordinary British schoolboy finds his extraordinary imagination unleashed by a teacher, whom some might consider old-fashioned. This teacher plays music to the class and asks that they close their eyes and imagine a story to go along with it. Many students conjure up imitations of their favorite books ("boys with lightning-shaped scars on their foreheads"), but the ordinary boy's story is completely original. Kitamura's cartoon illustrations are set in a city neighborhood, most likely London, and begin in muted grays, only to turn into color with the entrance of the teacher and his gramophone. The first spread is a great example of the use of continuous action, showing the boy in various states in the same set of rooms—in bed, at the sink and toilet, in the tub, dressing, at the breakfast table, and kissing his mother good-bye. The book originated at Andersen Press in England, and Kitamura pays homage to Andersen's publisher, Klaus Flugge, by putting him on the cover of one of the gramophone records.

Rosen, Michael. *We're Going on a Bear Hunt.* Illustrated by Helen Oxenbury. 978-0-689-50476-1. New York: McElderry, 1989. Ages 4–8.

Rosen's retelling of a traditional chant coupled with Oxenbury's illustrations became an instant classic, and for good reason. Children love the repetitive form of the text ("We can't go over it, we can't go under it. Oh, no! We've got to go through it!") and the onomatopoeic sounds of negotiating each impediment ("Squelch squerch!"). Oxenbury's light, airy illustrations—watercolor spreads alternating with black-and-white charcoal drawings—show a dad, four children, and a dog setting out in the English countryside next to the sea; the landscape is marked by hedgerows and far-off village spires. The moment the bear is sighted in the cave, the layout changes to panels showing how quickly they backtrack until they are finally safe indoors, under the covers. Also available in a hardcover anniversary edition, in paperback, and as a board book.

Rubbino, Salvatore. *A Walk in London.* 978-0-7636-5272-2. Cambridge, MA: Candlewick, 2011. Age 6 and up.

A young girl narrates as her mother introduces her to London's famous landmarks. They get off the red double-decker bus at Westminster and head for Buckingham Palace just in time for the changing of the guard. On this spread, as throughout, small captions here and there add tidbits of information, such as the number of rooms in Buckingham Palace. After their day of walking, the two take a ferry from the Tower of London back to Westminster, and surprise!—a gatefold opens up with a bird's-eye view of the Thames and everything to be seen on either bank, including some of the landmarks viewed in close-up. This is one of two ways Rubbino orients the reader; the other is the map of London on the front and back endpapers. Rubbino grew up in London, and his book contains lots of quirky little sidenotes that make this walk a special one.

Russell, Natalie. *Brown Rabbit in the City.* 978-0-670-01234-3. New York: Viking, 2010.

Brown Rabbit is invited to visit his friend Little Rabbit in the city and arrives on the double-decker bus. Intent on showing Brown Rabbit all the sights in one day, Little Rabbit rushes him from place to place, not even giving him a chance to finish his carrot cake. Late in the day, she realizes her mistake—he has come to see her, not the city. Author-illustrator Russell lives and works in Dundee, Scotland, and her exquisite muted prints in shades of dusty blue, green, and brown present images that could be any city, although clues point in several directions as to which city it might be. The double-decker bus points one way; the subway stop marked 57th points another. This is a perfect example of a generic setting intended to suit disparate markets.

Stevenson, Robert Louis. *My Shadow.* Illustrated by Penny Dale. Out of print. Cambridge, MA: Candlewick, 1999. Ages 3–6.

Many illustrated versions exist of this beloved poem by Scotland's best-known poet, but Dale's is particularly suitable for young ones. Her realistic illustrations demonstrate exactly how shadows work, and her source of light is always obvious. Each line of the poem is interpreted literally for easy understanding; for instance, the illustration accompanying "I rose and found the shining dew on every buttercup" shows the young boy gazing out his window at the flowers. Dale sets the poem in modern-day Britain and includes outdoor scenes at a day care that reflect Britain's cultural diversity.

Willis, Jeanne. *Susan Laughs.* Illustrated by Tony Ross. 978-0-8050-6501-5. New York: Holt, 2000. Ages 3–6.

This book is exceptional in its approach to physical disability. Each page contains an illustration of Susan in action over a two-word description, such as "Susan sings" or "Susan dances." As intended, first-time readers will be taken aback by the very last page showing Susan in a wheelchair. By focusing on the many ways that this small red-headed girl can enjoy a full, rich life, readers have perceived her as a person before they are aware of her inability to walk. Tony Ross's light-hued colored-pencil illustrations contain humorous background details, but only a couple depict a particular setting and are more like the artist's in-jokes: at school behind Susan's desk is a map of Britain on the wall, and in another illustration, Susan is on her father's shoulders as they stand in front of the Mona Lisa, where "Susan grins" (presumably, they've taken a trip to Paris).

Chapter 9

Latin America
and the Caribbean

The countries and independent territories of Central America, South America, and the Caribbean represent a diverse mix of languages, cultures, ethnicities, socioeconomic strata, and political systems. Although this part of the world is on our doorstep, Americans in general know little about it. Mass media coverage has led to stereotypes of South and Central America as sites of military coups and drug smuggling, and the Caribbean islands as tropical paradises or, as in the case of the 2010 earthquake in Haiti, disaster areas. The children's books available from or about these areas are not sufficient to build a representative picture of any of these countries or even distinguish among them.

The majority of picture books available have been written by American residents with a Latin American or Caribbean connection, immigrants to the United States, or descendents of immigrants. The books are sometimes based on the author's experiences of growing up in or emigrating from another country, or photo essays featuring a child's life in the barrio. Although these books are welcome, they are essentially American voices, if nonmainstream ones. Where are the voices from outside the United States? Where are the books set in middle-class families or urban locales?

There is no shortage of literary talent emanating from this region of the world, as demonstrated by winners of the Nobel Prize for Literature from Peru, Mexico, Trinidad, the Antilles, Chile, and Guatemala. And yet the "Little Nobel," the Hans Christian Andersen Author Medal, has been awarded just twice to writers from South America, both times to

Brazilians (Ana Maria Machado and Lygia Bojunga Nunes). No artist from Latin America or the Caribbean has ever won the Hans Christian Andersen Illustrator Medal. Only Brazil and Argentina regularly submit nominees in both the Author and Illustrator categories; occasionally there has been a nominee from Colombia, Chile, or Venezuela.

Although there are established publishing programs in many of these South American countries, as well as in Mexico and Guatemala, children's books have not traditionally been part of the literary mix. During much of the twentieth century, books published for children consisted of textbooks or other didactic material. Any trade children's books that were found on bookstore shelves were imported from Spain or Portugal and not reflective of the lives of South or Central American children. The picture has changed somewhat in the past thirty years, as institutional and government support has increased. Some large publishers have added children's books to their lists, and small independent houses are emerging in Brazil, Argentina, Colombia, and Mexico with high-quality, innovative books.

Ediciones Ekaré is a Venezuelan publisher founded in early 1978 with support from Banco del Libro, a nonprofit organization that promotes reading for children. Ekaré publishes authors and illustrators from throughout Latin America and the Caribbean, and some of their books have been translated for publication in Europe and North America. Ekaré's road has not been easy, however, as former editorial director Elena Iribarren observed in listing some of the obstacles: "vast social and economic inequalities, a high rate of illiteracy, huge and inefficient educational bureaucracies, a majority of the population under the age of 25 that has not grown up reading or being read to from children's books."[1]

Ironically, the few books that do come from Latin America arrive by way of Canada, a rather indirect route. Patsy Aldana, the publisher of Groundwood Books in Toronto, was born and raised in Guatemala and has the linguistic expertise, the knowledge, and the connections to acquire contemporary Latin American books. Moreover, she is committed to do so as part of a publishing mission to offer readers perspectives they won't find in mainstream society. The large American publishers have virtually no books from South America on their lists, although some have published Caribbean writers by way of British publishers, in the case of Jamaica, Trinidad, or Tobago. Some small independent publishers in the US have published the occasional title from Latin America.

Note

1. Iribarren, "Publishing from South to North."

Caribbean Islands

Agard, John, and Grace Nichols. *Under the Moon and Over the Sea: A Collection of Caribbean Poems.* Illustrated by Cathie Felstead, Jane Ray, Christopher Corr, Satoshi Kitamura, and Sara Fanelli. 978-0-7636-1861-6. Cambridge, MA: Candlewick, 2003. Age 8 and up.

Opening this collection of poems is being instantly transported to the sounds, sights, and smells of the Caribbean: swaying palm trees, juicy pineapples, tumbling ocean waves. The poems are divided into five sections, each illustrated by one artist, and each section includes traditional proverbs and songs, poems in standard speech and dialect, and a mixture of humorous, serious, and even scary poems. It's an exceptional collection with something for everyone by writers from Jamaica, Trinidad, Barbados, and elsewhere in the Caribbean.

Landowne, Youme. *Sélavi: That's Life.* 978-0-938317-84-9. El Paso: Cinco Puntos Press, 2004. Ages 5–9.

Predating the catastrophic 2010 earthquake in Haiti, this story reveals the conditions of poverty that existed for so many children even prior to that devastation, especially in Port-au-Prince. Sélavi (whose name is a Kréyol version of the French phrase *c'est la vie,* or "that's life") is one of Haiti's street children, whose families have been killed or otherwise lost to them. Landowne's picture book, with its folk-art pictures, is based on real events in the late 1980s to mid-1990s, when a group of Haitians including Jean-Bertrand Aristede built an orphanage for these children, who had learned to look after one another and speak up for themselves; it was called Lafanmi ("the family") Sélavi. Aristede's democratic election as president was short-lived; he was ousted by a military coup, which tried to silence the children by destroying their home. The house was rebuilt and the children took to the airwaves, creating Radyo Timoun, or the children's radio, which still exists today.

Lauture, Denize. *Running the Road to ABC.* Illustrated by Reynold Ruffins. 978-0-689-83165-2 (ppb). New York: Aladdin, 2000. Ages 5–8.

Lauture's book features six fortunate children who, unlike Sélavi, live with their families and go to school. Although public school in Haiti is free, books, uniforms, lunch, and transportation is not provided, and not all Haitian families can afford to send their children to school. The six students in this poetic text rise before dawn to make their way to school, running barefoot through dark, hilly countryside as the sky lightens, past people carrying their wares to market, through the village, and finally into the open-air building that is their school. Their eagerness to learn is underscored in the illustrations that convey swift movement across the page, gaining momentum until they reach their goal.

Central and South America

Amado, Elisa. *What Are You Doing?* Illustrated by Manuel Monroy. 978-0-55498-070-3. Toronto: Groundwood, 2011. Ages 3–5.

Guatemalan-born writer Amado teams with Mexican artist Monroy to create this tribute to the many benefits of reading. Faced with the prospect of starting school that afternoon, Chepito asks, "Why, why, why," which becomes his refrain throughout the morning. Each person he encounters is reading something—the newspaper, a comic book, a travel guide, a car manual, a magazine, and even hieroglyphics on an ancient Mayan wall—and their responses pique his interest in literacy. His teacher, too, has a book that she reads to the class, and the next thing the reader knows, Chepito has brought home that very book to "read" to his little sister. The illustrations in muted blues, browns, and greens contain specific details that point to a setting in either Guatemala or southern Mexico—Mayan ruins, religious iconography in the home, embroidered clothing, and an understated use of patterns.

Argueta, Jorge. *Zipitio.* Illustrated by Gloria Calderón. Translated by Elisa Amado. 978-0-88899-487-5. Toronto: Groundwood, 2003. Ages 6–9.

From the Pipil/Nahua people of El Salvador comes this traditional folktale of a being, the Zipitio, who waits at the river for beautiful young girls on the verge of womanhood. Rufina is just such a girl, and her mother cautions her not to be afraid if she sees the Zipitio at dawn when she goes to fetch water. Small in stature but very old, the Zipitio is lonely and wants someone to love; legend has it that robbers snatched him as a baby from a wealthy woman. When Rufina does see the Zipitio, she follows her mother's advice and asks him to fill a basket with seawater for her. Although he never appears to Rufina again, he will be there when she has a daughter who comes of age. Beautiful paintings on canvas portray El Salvador's wooded, mountainous landscape, the women's embroidered clothing, and Rufina's plain home as contrasted with the elaborate one of the wealthy woman.

Buitrago, Jairo. *Jimmy the Greatest!* Illustrated by Rafael Yockteng. Translated by Elisa Amado. 978-1-55498-178-6. Toronto: Groundwood, 2012. Ages 4–7.

In a small Colombian village at the ocean's edge—really just a smattering of one-room houses, a church, and a gym—Jimmy learns to box under the tutelage of Apolinar, who sees something special in him: "In his heart, Jimmy was already a boxer, even though there were no boxing gloves at the gym." Apolinar gives Jimmy a box of books and newspaper clippings about Muhammad Ali, which Jimmy devours; from that point in the book on, the third-person narration alternates with Jimmy's thoughts delivered as Ali-style rap lyrics. Time passes as Jimmy grows stronger, thanks to his training, and more mature, thanks to his reading. The day that Apolinar moves to the big city, Jimmy takes over the gym, which has now also become a library. He has learned that he doesn't need to leave home to be "the greatest." Yockteng's colorful cartoon illustrations portray the rudiments of village life; comparing an early spread with the final one shows a village with more homes, more animals, new electrical wires, and an overall improved quality of life.

Carling, Amelia Lau. *Mama and Papa Have a Store.* 978-0-8037-2044-2. New York: Dial, 1998. Ages 6–9.

Carling's parents owned a store in Guatemala City that sold textiles and notions imported from China. This memoir, structured around a single day at the store, never strays from that site but evokes a strong sense both of young Amelia's life in a Chinese family and of everyday life in Guatemala City. We see what happens in front of the store (a man herding goats down the street, sellers who set up wares on the sidewalk), what happens inside the store (on this day, Mayan customers choosing threads for embroidery), and what happens in the back and on the roof of the store, where the family lives and plays. The illustrations include small delights, such as the Chinese calendars on the store and dining room walls and the shrine with incense, a Chinese figurine, and a picture of the Virgin of Guadaloupe. The family closes the shop for lunch, and all the children return home from school for a family meal followed by recreational time. As portrayed here, Amelia's childhood is one to envy.

Carling, Amelia Lau. *Sawdust Carpets.* 978-0-88899-625-1. Toronto: Groundwood, 2005. Ages 6–9.

Antigua, the former colonial capital of Guatemala, is the site of an annual Easter tradition that includes elaborate sawdust tapestries on the cobblestone streets that are created only to be ruined by the Easter processions walking over them. Young Amelia, whose aunt and uncle have invited her family to Antigua for Holy Week, experiences at first dismay and then understanding as a carpet she helped to create is trampled. As a neighbor explains, "This is the custom. We make the rugs as offerings to life.... Life follows death and death follows life." Carling's soft-hued drawings portray authentic details of the processions and colonial architecture, while also conveying the emotion of a child who sees her beautiful carpet destroyed.

Garay, Luis. *The Long Road.* 978-0-88776-408-8. Toronto: Tundra, 1997. Age 7 and up.

José lives in a Nicaraguan village with his mother and extended family; his father has been put into prison during a time of political turmoil and has not been heard from since. Over the Christmas holidays, José and his mother take the bus over the mountains to visit his mother's family, and when they return, it is to an empty village. An old man explains that soldiers came and shot up the town and warns them to leave right away. Thus begins their long road to safety as they escape their own country and make their way north, eventually being admitted to Canada.

Argentinean Artist, Writer, Singer

Isol

Marisol Misenta, who writes and illustrates under the single name Isol, has received international acclaim as a winner of the 2012 Astrid Lindgren Memorial Award (ALMA) and as a Hans Christian Andersen Illustrator finalist in both 2006 and 2007. Her spare, loose style with its strong lines and judicious use of color is unmistakable, even as she varies techniques and media, trying "to find a different language for each book" ("Isol Misento [sic]," *Bookbird* 44, no. 4 [2006]: 25). Whether she is illustrating the work of others or creating her own books, her imaginative and witty pictures add layers of meaning to the text. Isol's books have been published in Argentina, Belgium, Canada, Estonia, France, Germany, Mexico, Norway, Portugal, Spain, Turkey, and the UK. Much of her work is posted on her website, where one can get an idea of her wide-ranging activities (and can read many of the books in Spanish). In addition to her work as an artist and writer, she is also an accomplished singer-songwriter whose recordings have been released internationally.

Illustrated by Isol

Luján, Jorge. *Doggy Slippers.* Translated by Elisa Amado. 978-0-88899-983-2. Toronto: Groundwood, 2010. Ages 4–8.

See page 197.

It's Useful to Have a Duck by Isol is really two books in one.

Written by Isol

Petit, the Monster. Translated by Elisa Amado. 978-0-88899-947-4. Ground-wood, 2006.

The complicated issue of ethics—what distinguishes good from bad—is boiled down to the toddler level in this book about Petit, who follows in the tradition of the good-bad boy (á la Pinocchio, who is neatly tucked into one of the illustrations). Petit doesn't know how to answer when his mother wonders how a good boy can do such bad things. He's bad when he tells a lie but good when he tells stories. He's good when he takes care of his toys but bad when he doesn't want to share them. And most confusing of all, if it's so bad that he pulls Laura's hair, why does she keep sitting next to him?

It's Useful to Have a Duck. Translated by Isol. 978-0-88899-927-6. Ground-wood, 2009.

This deceptively simple but brilliant accordion board book is two stories in one, depending on which way the book is opened. In *It's Useful to Have a Duck,* a child relates the many uses he finds for a duck (a rocking horse, a hat, and so forth), and when the book closes, the back cover becomes the front of a second book, *It's Useful to Have a Boy.* Suddenly the other point of view emerges: a boy can be good for rubbing the duck's back (as he is rocking on the duck) or for being a high perch to see the world (as the duck sits on his head). What better way to show a toddler that where there are two beings, there are two perspectives.

Beautiful Griselda. Translated by Elisa Amado. 978-1-55498-105-2. Groundwood, 2011.

A common phrase taken literally, "losing one's head," becomes the crux of this story of a princess who is so beautiful that men far and wide become headless as soon as they gaze at her. The narcissistic Griselda enjoys the attention and curries it by devoting every moment to nurturing her beauty. Eventually, people hide when she goes out so as not to lose their heads. Lonely, the princess finally finds a myopic prince to spend time with, but soon he too notices her beauty and loses his head. Nine months later she gives birth to a baby so beautiful that the princess herself loses her head. Fortunately, the baby is so charming that beauty becomes secondary and all are able to keep their heads. Details in the illustrations of this very original tale allude to traditional fairy tales, where superficial beauty is prized above all.

Nocturne: Dream Recipes. 978-1-55498-179-3. Toronto: Groundwood, 2012. Ages 10-14.

Isol continues to play with the traditional format of the book, in this case creating a spiral-bound notebook that can stand up on its own and using glow-in-the-dark technology as the special ingredient in her dream recipes. Instructions include selecting a page, exposing it to a light for five minutes, and then putting it where you can see it when you are in bed. Eleven pages offer simply drawn scenarios with descriptive titles (e.g., "The Dream of being another" or "The cozy, warm Dream") that receive extra details in the dark. Whether the book is actually useful for guiding night-time dreams can't be verified. The "what if" factor, however, is the start of any imaginative enterprise, day or night, and Isol excels in challenging young people to think beyond the ordinary. A twelfth page is blank aside from its glow-in-the-dark coating, inviting readers to draw their own dreams. This element may preclude some library or school purchases, although one could easily remove this page before circulating the book. In spirit, *Nocturne* is reminiscent of *Stormy Night* by Michèle Lemieux (see annotation on page 116), in which a young girl lies in bed at night asking unanswerable questions. Both books feel particularly suited to preadolescents and teens.

Kurusa. *The Streets Are Free.* Illustrated by Monika Doppert. Translated by Karen Englander. 978-155037-370-7 (ppb, rev. ed.). Toronto: Annick Press, 1995.

This story takes place in Venezuela, but it could just as well represent any of several large South American cities where people from the countryside have flocked to find work and have ended up living in shantytowns that blanket the outskirts of the city. In Venezuela, these are called *barrios*, in Brazil, *favelas*. Children who grow up in one of these barrios, as in this story, have nowhere to play and end up in the streets. With the help of a librarian, the enterprising children in this story organize themselves and take their request for a park to city hall. The mayor, eager for publicity in an election year, makes a big show of dedicating a plot of land for a park but then abandons the project. In a wonderful example of collective action, the people in the community end up creating the park themselves, each contributing a piece of wood here and a bit of labor there.

Luján, Jorge. *Doggy Slippers.* Illustrated by Isol. Translated by Elisa Amado. 978-0-88899-983-2. Toronto: Groundwood, 2010. Ages 4–8.

Children all across Latin America responded to Luján's question asking them about their pets with descriptions that he has shaped into free verse. These poems, which range from funny to clever to poignant, truly underscore the universality of children's feelings, as in this offering: "Life is good. / Kitty makes it better / when things go wrong." Isol's loose drawings are equally simple, rendered in pencil and flat colors that give readers room for their own interpretations.

Luján, Jorge. *Stephen and the Beetle.* Illustrated by Chiara Carrer. Translated by Elisa Amado. 978-1-55498-192-2. Toronto: Groundwood, 2012. Ages 4–7.

Spare text describes a moment in Stephen's day when he sees a beetle and his knee-jerk reaction is to kill it with his shoe. He pauses in midair, perhaps for the first time realizing that the beetle has a story too. Where is it going, and why? So Stephen lowers himself to the ground, eyes the beetle up close, and sees something resembling "a terrible triceratops" that seems about to attack before continuing on to the farthest part of the yard. Stephen's change of perspective is reflected in the composition of the mixed-media illustrations: whereas Stephen dominates the illustrations in the beginning—in fact he is so large that only part of his body can fit on some pages—he shrinks as the beetle grows in importance.

Luján, Jorge. *Tarde de invierno/Winter afternoon.* Illustrated by Mandana Sadat. Translated by Elisa Amado. 978-0-88899-718-0. Toronto: Groundwood /Tigrillo, 2006. Ages 3–6

Luján, an Argentinian-born writer who lives and works in Mexico City, has crafted a poetic text that captures perfectly the feel of a child waiting at the window for a parent to return. This child is watching through a small crescent shape she has made in the frosty window, and when her mother appears, she enlarges the shape to accommodate her ever-closer mother. Once mother and child reunite, the reader is moved outside the window to peer at their warm reunion within. The colorful illustrations, spare and geometric, evoke a cold winter's night.

Machado, Ana Maria. *Nina Bonita.* Illustrated by Rosana Faría. Translated by Elena Iribarren. 978-0-916291-63-1. La Jolla, CA: Kane Miller, 1996. Ages 4–8.

Machado is a well-known writer for children in Brazil, perhaps Brazil's counterpart to America's Lois Lowry. With over a hundred books to her credit, she has written for children of all ages, though only five of her books—three picture books and two novels—are available in English. *Nina Bonita* tells of a white rabbit who admires a neighbor girl for her lovely dark skin, beautiful eyes, and pitch-black hair and would like to have children her color. Each time he asks her the secret to this beauty, she gives him a different answer—black ink, coffee drinking, blackberry eating. He tries all three but is unsuccessful. One day Nina Bonita's mother overhears their conversation and provides the real answer: "She looks just like her black grandmother!" The white rabbit realizes that he must find a black rabbit to marry, which he does, and they have bunnies of every color and shade, including a special black one who looks just like *her* mother. Faría's illustrations of street scenes reflect a diversity of skin tones representative of the Brazilian people.

Machado, Ana Maria. *What a Party!* Illustrated by Helene Moreau. Translated by Elise Amado. 978-1-55498-168-7. Toronto: Groundwood, 2013. Ages 4–7.

Brazil's population, once consisting primarily of those of Indian, European, and African ancestry, has become even more culturally diverse, as represented by the many people who arrive to help this young narrator celebrate his birthday. Each friend brings another friend, along with some food sent by their mothers, until the house is filled with a smorgasbord of international delicacies. As the evening goes on, parents who come to pick up their children end up staying as well until the backyard is turned into a miniature United Nations. Moreau's illustrations are full of movement and color, and the reader can practically hear the boisterous shouts and music coming out of the page.

Montejo, Victor. *White Flower: A Maya Princess.* Illustrated by Rafael Yockteng. Translated by Chloe Catan. 978-0-88899-599-5. Toronto: Groundwood, 2005. Age 6 and up.

The Mayan civilization stretched from what is now Mexico's Yucatan Peninsula through Belize and into part of Guatemala and Honduras. Guatemalan-born Montejo, whose ancestors were Mayan, has been active in the movement to revive Mayan culture; this story is a Mayan version of a Spanish tale told to him by his grandmother. A young prince whose family, village, and memory have been wiped out by an epidemic sets out to make a new life and becomes united with a princess and her family, but not without enduring a series of trials first. The princess's father is the powerful Witz Ak'al, a shape-shifter who has already unsuccessfully tried to buy the prince's soul. When the prince asks him for work, Witz Ak'al gives the prince tasks that are impossible to complete but for the princess's help. The king wises up, the prince and princess run away together, and all is resolved when they return and the princess insists that her parents accept the prince as her husband.

Olmos, Gabriela. *I Dreamt: A Book about Hope.* 978-1-55498-330-8. Translated by Elise Amado. Toronto: Groundwood, 2013. Age varies according to child.

While *I Dreamt* is certainly a picture book intended for the young, its engaging title and cover image belie the stark images contained within. Each spread consists of a child's dream that controverts the child's reality: that pistols shot butterflies, that drug lords sold soap bubbles, that robbers stole nightmares. Originating in Mexico, where the past decade has seen violence from the drug wars encroaching into all walks of life, this book is intended to "give children a way to talk about their fears, a reason to hope, and the inspiration to resist falling into grief and depression" (Afterword). Violence of this nature is not restricted to Mexico but also exists in some pockets of the United States, where children live in a constant state of insecurity. Twelve of Mexico's most outstanding artists have donated their work to this fund-raising endeavor to support the IBBY Fund for Children in Crisis.

Serrano, Francisco. *Our Lady of Guadalupe.* Illustrated by Felipe Dávalos. 978-1-55498-074-1 (2nd edition). Toronto: Groundwood, 2011.

The Virgin of Guadalupe is the most popular religious and cultural image in Mexico and Central America; this pop-up book tells the story of how Mary, the mother of God, appeared to a peasant man near Mexico City in the sixteenth century and told him she wanted a church on that very spot. Six engineered spreads illustrate Diego's vision; his audience with the bishop; his return to the lady to ask for proof; the appearance of roses growing in December; the miraculous image of the Virgin on his cloak; and the finished church. The text is simply told and ideal for reading aloud.

Skármeta, Antonio. *The Composition.* Illustrated by Alfonso Ruano. Translated by Elisa Amado. 978-088899-550-6 (ppb). Toronto: Groundwood, 2003. Age 8 and up.

Skármeta, an internationally known Chilean writer, tells a story that could take place in any police state, although characters' names place the story somewhere in Latin America. Pedro witnesses his friend's father being hauled away for being against the dictatorship, which prompts his parents to acknowledge that they too oppose the government and listen to a clandestine radio station in the evening. The following day, a military officer strides into Pedro's schoolroom and announces a contest: each child must write an essay entitled "What My Family Does at Night." Readers hold their breath wondering what Pedro will reveal, and Skármeta prolongs the suspense by waiting until Pedro's composition is returned several weeks later. To his parents' relief, his essay shows that he has read the situation correctly. Ruano's realistic paintings heighten the mood of fear by foregrounding the military, emphasizing silence and watchfulness, and positioning people apart or turning away from one another.

Zink, Rui. *The Boy Who Did Not Like Television.* Illustrated by Manuel Joao Ramos. Translated by Patrick Dreher. 978-1-931561-96-9. Monterey, MA: MacAdam/Cage, 2004. Ages 2–5.

This very simple story from Brazil appears to be geared to parents rather than children—parents who spend more time watching television than relating to their children. When this little boy constantly turns off the TV, the parents (and neighbors as well) assume something is wrong with him and take him to a doctor, a teacher, and a magician, none of whom can explain the problem. Finally the parents decide to leave the TV off and sit on the couch with the boy between them; the boy's smile tells it all.

Book Distributors

Consortium Book Sales and Distribution
Enchanted Lion Books
www.cbsd.com
info@cbsd.com
Tel: 800-283-3572; 612-746-2600; fax: 612-746-2606
The Keg House, 34 Thirteenth Ave. NE, Suite 101, Minneapolis, MN 55413

Independent Publishers Group
Clavis Publishing
www.ipgbook.com
frontdesk@ ipgbook.com
Tel: 312-337-0747; fax: 312-337-5985
Address: 814 N. Franklin St., Chicago, IL 60610

Lerner Publishing Group
Gecko Press
www.lernerbooks.com
info@lernerbooks.com
Tel: 800-328-4929; fax: 800-332-1132
1251 Washington Ave. N, Minneapolis, MN 55401

Publishers Group West
Frances Lincoln Children's Books
Groundwood Books
Simply Read Books
Tara Books
pgw.com
info@pgw.com
Tel: 510-809-3700; fax: 510-809-3777
1700 Fourth St., Berkeley, CA 94710

Steiner Books, Inc.
Floris Books
www.steinerbooks.org
c/o Books International
22883 Quicksilver Dr., Dulles, VA 20166

Bibliography

Bader, Barbara. *American Picturebooks from* Noah's Ark *to* The Beast Within. New York: Macmillan, 1976.

Barthelmess, Thom. Review of *Garmann's Summer*. *Booklist* 108.14 (March 15, 2012): 64.

Bell, Anthea. "The Translator's Notebook." In *The Signal Approach to Children's Books*, edited by Nancy Chambers, 129–139. Metuchen, NJ: Scarecrow, 1981.

Bowser, Betty Ann. "How Is Gulf Coast Mentally Coping with Devastation of Two Disasters?" *PBS Newshour*. August 26, 2010. www.pbs.org/newshour/bb/health/july-dec10/nolamental_08-26.html.

Cendrowicz, Leo. "Asterix at 50: The Comic Hero Conquers the World," *Time*, November 19, 2009. www.time.com/time/arts/article/0,8599,1931169,00.html.

Chimhundu, Herbert. "Intergovernmental Conference on Language Policies in Africa." Report. Harare, Zimbabwe: UNESCO, 2002. http://publikationen.ub.uni-frankfurt.de/frontdoor/deliver/index/docId/15657/file/Language_Policies_in_Africa.pdf.

"Cover Story—Lane Smith and Molly Leach." YouTube video, 5:08. Posted by BN Studio. June 23, 2008. www.youtube.com/watch?v=_NO3x6dOFCQ.

Edwards, Gail, and Judith Saltman. *Picturing Canada: A History of Canadian Children's Illustrated Books and Publishing*. Toronto: University of Toronto Press, 2010.

"Ein fall von zensur," (A case of censorship), *Hamburger Abendblatt*, July 14, 2007.

Foster, John, and Maureen Nimon. *Australian Children's Literature: An Exploration of Genre and Theme*. Wagga Wagga, NSW: Centre for Information Studies, Charles Sturt University, 1995.

Garrett, Jeffrey. "Screams and Smiles," *Bookbird* 46, no. 4 (2008): 16–24.

Germein, Katrina, and Bronwyn Bancroft. *Big Rain Coming*. New York: Clarion Books, 1999.

Glistrup, Eva. *The Hans Christian Andersen Awards, 1956–2002.* Translated by Patricia Crampton. Basel: International Board on Books for Young People, 2002.

Graham, Bob. *How to Heal a Broken Wing.* First US edition. Cambridge, MA: Candlewick Press, 2008.

Greenwood, Mark, and Frane Lessac. *The Donkey of Gallipoli : A True Story of Courage in World War I.* First US edition. Cambridge, MA: Candlewick Press, 2008.

Haber, Karen. "Shaun Tan: Out of Context." *Locus: The Newspaper of the Science Fiction Field.* December 2001. www.locusmag.com/2001/Issue12/Tan.html.

Ikonne, Chidi, Emelia Oko, and Peter Onwudinjo, eds. *Children and Literature in Africa.* Edited by Ernest N. Emenyonu, Calabar Studies in African Literature. Ibadan, Nigeria: Heinemann Educational Books, 1992.

Iribarren, Elena. "Publishing from South to North: New Perspectives from Latin America." Paper presented at the 2nd IBBY Regional Conference. Albuquerque, New Mexico, 1997.

"Isol Misento [sic]," *Bookbird* 44, no. 4 (2006): 25.

Jackett, Lynne. "Children's Books." In *Book and Print in New Zealand : A Guide to Print Culture in Aotearoa.* Edited by Keith Maslen, Harvey Ross, and Penny Griffith. Wellington, NZ: Victoria University Press, 1997.

Johnston, Rosemary Ross. "Children's Literature Advancing Australia." *Bookbird* 37, no. 1 (1999): 13–18.

Khorana, Meena. *The Indian Subcontinent in Literature for Children and Young Adults.* Westport, CT: Greenwood, 1991.

Kobayashi, Miki. "Which US Picturebooks Get Translated into Japanese? Criteria for Choice." *Bookbird* 43, no. 2 (2005): 5–12.

Künnermann, Horst. "How Much Cruelty Can a Children's Picturebook Stand?" *Bookbird* 43, no. 1 (2005): 14–19.

Linders, Joke, and Marita de Sterck. *Behind the Story: Children's Book Authors in Flanders and the Netherlands.* Amsterdam; Antwerp: Dutch Trade Publishers Association, Flemish Book Trade Association, 1996.

Marcus, Leonard. "Outside over Where? Foreign Picture Books and the Dream of Global Awareness." *Horn Book* 86.6 (November–December 2010): 49.

Martin, Douglas. *The Telling Line: Essays on Fifteen Contemporary Book Illustrators.* New York: Delacorte Press, 1990.

Millard, Glenda, and Patrice Barton. *The Naming of Tishkin Silk*. First US edition. New York: Farrar Straus Giroux, 2009.

National Geographic Education Foundation and Roper Public Affairs. "2006 Geographic Literacy Study." May 2006. www.nationalgeographic .com/roper2006/pdf/FINALReport2006GeogLitsurvey.pdf.

Nawotka, Edward. "New Prize Urges Arabic Kid's Publishers to Compete." *Publishing Perspectives*. May 25, 2009. http://publishingperspectives .com/2009/05/new-prize-urges-arabic-kids-publishers-to-compete/.

Nimon, Maureen, and John Foster. *The Adolescent Novel: Australian Perspectives*. Edited by Ken Dillo. Volume 2 of Literature and Literacy for Young People: An Australian Series. Wagga Wagga, NSW: Centre for Information Studies, 1997.

Review of *The Watertower*, by Gary Crew, *Publisher's Weekly*, November 3, 1997, www.publishersweekly.com/978-1-56656-233-1.

Robinson, Roger, and Nelson Wattie. *The Oxford Companion to New Zealand Literature*. Melbourne ; Oxford: Oxford University Press, 1998.

Roxburgh, Stephen. "The Myopic American." *School Library Journal* 50, no. 1 (2004): 50.

Salisbury, Martin C. "No Red Buses Please: International Co-Editions and the Sense of Place in Picturebooks." *Bookbird* 44, no. 1 (2006): 6–11.

Schroeder, Binette. "Illustration beyond the Ordinary." *Bookbird* 46, no. 4 (2008): 10.

Shyam, Bhajju, Sirish Rao, and Gita Wolf. The London Jungle Book. Chennai: Tara, 2004.

Smith, Alex Duval. "The Harare Book Fair Returns." Radio France International. August 8, 2009. www.rfi.fr/actuen/articles/116/article_4609.asp.

Something about the Author. "Jude Daly (1951–)." Vol. 222. Detroit, MI: Gale, 2011, 55–59.

———. "Niki Daly (1946–)." Vol. 198. Detroit, MI: Gale, 2009, 24–30.

Stan, Susan. "Conversations: Margaret McElderry." *The Five Owls* 2 (1988): 73.

———. "A Study of International Children's Picture Books Published in the United States in 1994." Doctoral thesis. University of Minnesota, 1997.

The Swedish Institute for Children's Books. "Book Market Statistics." www .sbi.kb.se/en/Resources/Trends-and-statistics.

White, Maureen. "Children's Books from Other Languages: A Study of Successful Translations." *Journal of Youth Services in Libraries* 5 (Spring 1992): 261–275.

Whitehead, Jane. "'This Is Not What I Wrote!' The Americanization of British Children's Books, Part I." *Horn Book* 72 (1996): 687–693.

Image Credits

Page 81: Cover of *Math Games* (English edition) by Mitsumasa Anno, copyright © 1982 by Kuso-kobo. Reproduced by permission of the Mitsumasa Anno and Fukuinkan Shoten.

Page 81: Cover of *Math Games* (Japanese edition) by Mitsumasa Anno, copyright © 1982 by Kuso-kobo. Reproduced by permission of Mitsumasa Anno and Fukuinkan Shoten.

Page 85: Photo copyright © by Suzy Lee, courtesy of the artist.

Page 86: Illustration from *Zoo* by Suzy Lee. Reproduced by permission of the publisher, KaneMiller.

Page 87: Illustration copyright © by Suzy Lee.

Page 102: Photo of Shaun Tan reproduced by permission of the artist.

Page 103: Cover of *The Arrival* by Shaun Tan reproduced by permission of the publisher, Levine/Scholastic.

Page 104: Illustration copyright © by Shaun Tan.

Page 124: Photo of Cybèle Young reproduced by permission of the artist.

Page 125: Cover from *Ten Birds* written and illustrated by Cybèle Young reproduced by permission of Kids Can Press Ltd., Toronto. Illustration © 2011 by Cybèle Young.

Page 125: Cover from *A Few Blocks* reproduced by permission of Groundwood Books.

Page 152: Photo of Olivier Tallec © by Sebastien Pelon, courtesy of Olivier Tallec.

Page 152: Cover of *Big Wolf and Little Wolf* copyright © 2008 by Olivier Tallec, reproduced by permission of the publisher, Enchanted Lion Books.

Page 153: "It's raining outside." Original drawing © by Olivier Tallec reproduced by permission of the artist.

Page 178: Photo of Emily Gravett reproduced by permission of the artist.

Page 180: Original drawings, © by Emily Gravett, used in *The Rabbit Problem*, reproduced by permission of the artist.

Page 193: Photo of Isol courtesy of Groundwood Books.

Page 194: Covers of *It's Useful to Have a Duck* and *It's Useful to Have a Boy* by Isol copyright © by Fondo de Cultura Economica, Mexico, D.F. Reproduced by permission of the publisher, Groundwood Books.

Author/Illustrator/Title Index

Subject Index

CPSIA information can be obtained
at www.ICGtesting.com
Printed in the USA
LVOW04s1746010916

502834LV00019B/1596/P